URBAN ANGEL

URBAN
ANGEL

Andrew Chamberlain

Authentic

10 09 08 07 06 05 04   7 6 5 4 3 2 1

First published 2001 by Vineyard International Publishing.
This revised edition published 2004 by Authentic Media
9 Holdom Avenue, Bletchley, Milton Keynes, Bucks,
MK1 1QR, UK
and PO Box 1047, Waynesboro, GA 30830-2047, USA

British Library Cataloguing in Publication Data

A catalogue record for this book is available from the British
Library

1-86024-499-8

Cover artwork by Siobhan Smith
Print Management by Adare Carwin
Printed and bound by AIT Nørhaven A/S, Denmark

www.andrewchamberlain.net
www.urbanangel.net

Acknowledgements

That this book should be published now is a testimony to God's outrageous generosity and the timely intervention and support of a number of friends.

In its first manifestation as *The Father of Orphans* my acknowledgements didn't make it into the final book, so I would like to take the opportunity to thank those who helped along the way. My thanks go especially to Duncan Banks, Paul and Sue Butler, and Revd Stephen Peake, all of whom offered constructive criticism and encouragement.

For showing great faith in me to start with, I want to thank Stephan Vosloo and Kim Whittaker from Vineyard International Publishing; and for picking up the baton and continuing to support me thank you to Malcolm Down and the team from Authentic Media.

The book would not have appeared in its current form were it not for the help and support of some new friends. Big thanks to Pippa Gilbert, who took pity on a poor author, and to Tim Leffler and family, whose generosity and support have left me genuinely speechless at times. My thanks also go to Ruth, my keenest critic, wisest counsellor and closest friend – with my love always.

Finally, I should acknowledge the small but significant contribution of my former English teacher, Mr Ian Newman, who once told my mother that I had 'a book in me'. It seems that he was right.

Invade the cities
Invade the culture
Invade the nations
                    Roger Mitchell

One

Above all else, Alex Masters wanted to be in control of her life.

In a world of inexplicable danger and uncertainty, she wanted to create a blanket of order around herself. She practised the art with diligence, especially in her own home. She had relatively little control over her working environment, but at the end of the day, she could withdraw into the safety of the anonymous suburban flat where she lived unobserved by human eyes.

On one particular day in April, Alex was desperately glad to go back into her own ordered world; to regain the control she had temporarily lost. She was nestled into the big armchair in her lounge, pondering the afternoon's events, replaying them in her mind. Uncertainty and danger had suddenly penetrated her world and she had been found wanting as a result. Her inability to act in a crisis had nearly left a child dead or injured.

Earlier that day she had visited the garage, braving the mechanics as they mumbled to each other in their own language, calling out in an apish dialect. There was an aggressive maleness about the place, confronting Alex's senses, in sight, sounds and smell. Her first visit to the garage had been a truly intimidating experience, but she had learnt to look after herself, and now she conducted business there as an equal.

The incident had happened just after that, when she was crossing the road to get back home. She had been unaware of the young man who joined the little group of waiting pedestrians, and she had remained completely unaware of the angel who attended her, although, of course, he was intimately aware of her.

He had been standing perhaps a metre in front of her, out above the road in a space occupied by exhaust fumes, observing the situation as it began to unfold. He was, of course, unaffected by the passage of traffic; vehicles moved unhindered through the space that he occupied.

A little group gathered at the crossing and a hot and restless child pulled on his mother's hand, looking for attention. For just a moment she was distracted and let the handle of the pushchair slip, which then tipped over the incline of the kerb and moved with Titanic grace into the path of the oncoming traffic. The first impact would come from an articulated lorry, barely fifty yards away, and as the scene moved irreversibly towards disaster, air brakes hissed, jarring against the scorch of tyres.

The mother screamed, and Alex assessed the situation immediately. The pushchair was just about within reach – she could lean forward, grab it, and pull it back to the pavement. It was about two metres away; one step and a body stretched, and the baby would be safe. The thought was translating into action there within her when somehow she was restrained, as if by her own indecision.

The young man had acted. He slipped past her out onto the road and rescued the baby, just as the lorry squealed past them, shuddering to a halt. For a second, the pushchair had seemed completely weightless to him, a phenomenon he would never be able to explain.

Angel stepped back from the crossing and looked over to the baby, happy in her pram. There was a great sense of relief; the young man was a hero. Fortunately, nobody noticed Alex slipping quietly across the road and away from the scene.

* * *

Hours later, in the fading light of late afternoon, she was still picking at the details. She had decided to shower, as if the confusion could somehow be washed from her body. But even in the shower, the questions would not go away. Had she been lost in her own thoughts when action was required and missed the chance to help? Had she actually been restrained at that moment? It had felt like it – as if someone had placed their hands against her shoulders.

Hot water poured down onto her head as she pictured herself again standing at the crossing. She had been restrained; the force had been gentle but strong, like the guiding hand of a parent with a small child. The mystery of it made her feel naked, and she tasted something at her throat, the human chemistry of fear, reinforcing her vulnerability.

Abruptly she turned the shower off. The thought of something unknown influencing her was enough to bring back the old fear – fear of the unknown, of forces that could toss her life around as if she were a rag doll. She could not live with that and so she decided to believe that she had been restrained by her own doubt, that she had been dreaming again, absorbed within herself. From the safety of the armchair, she was able to gain some perspective on what had happened. She thanked God for saving a life, possibly her own, and browsed through the TV channels. This was her home and she felt secure here – this was her space.

She had bought the flat five years ago and had put her mark on it. This was the place where she defined the safe environment that she craved, a place where the world's pain could be limited and controlled: a place where she could listen, as best she could, to her God.

Not only was Alex a Christian, she also went to church. There was no cultural reason for this: she lived in an age when there was little to be gained from social attendance and there were plenty of other things for a bright girl in her twenties to do on a Sunday morning. She went to church because she believed that Jesus had indeed risen from the dead, and was her personal Saviour.

She loved her church friends but saw their weaknesses. Many of them were rather taken with the melodrama of religion. They wanted to thump the table and put on a show, but she knew that beneath the frenzy, God was at work in them all. Their discussions together were full of animation, nervous talk of End Times, descriptions that sounded like a big budget movie from the golden age of Hollywood. They prayed, longing for the desired result, hoping the Deity would deliver the goods, treating him like a precocious actor who needed to be coaxed from the dressing room. It was an intense, uneasy relationship.

The supernatural had its place in the wider scheme of things but for Alex the quest for safety coloured everything. She did join in with some of the exuberance, and all of the sincerity, and, with the help of her friends, she settled into a space somewhere between the twin stereotypes of 'religious killjoy' and 'happy clapper'.

But Alex was also separate from those around her. There was a gravity in her life and a deeper sense of purpose not satisfied by spiritual fizz. Jesus was 'in the house' with all the attendant effervescence but Alex preferred to find him in the tears of her personal history. Her Saviour understood the human condition because he had tasted it for himself, and from this unique perspective, he had the right to demand everything of her. Bringing her legacy of unresolved emotion, she had chosen to give him everything she had. It had been the only personal concession she had ever made.

Alex knew that she had faults as well but they were different from those exhibited by her friends. Sometimes she fell into an introspection so absolute that the demands of the present often yielded to it, leaving her stranded and apart from those around her. Conversations washed over her and the hopes and interests of even those close to her became part of the background environment. Her friends noticed this distraction of course. Some mistook it for indifference, whilst those who knew more of her history were inclined to forgive her, making allowance for the damage that had been inflicted on her.

Alex lived out near the rim of the great capital city, in a place that was never at ease with itself; a place always pulsing with busyness and urgency; a place full of impatient people living fast and foolish lives. In her own flat, she tried to regulate the pace of time. All of the clocks ticked slowly; all of the meals where eaten with some regard to pleasure as well as expediency. This was her space, her ordered private world. Here Alex hoped to discover who she was and what she would one day be. What she didn't realise was that she had actually shared this space for all of that time.

Even now, from the corner of the room he watched her, sensing her thoughts and emotions, sensing the will of the Lord. He was a servant of God, one who some might call a 'guardian angel'. She was not the first one he had watched over, and she would not be the last, but the mere fact that he was required here meant that she must be unusual.

He sensed her unease. He had contributed to it on this occasion. There was simply no way she was going to end up dead because she had been trying to save someone else. The other life was certainly precious, but there was an order to these things and, after all of the years of preparation, Alex's time was at hand. He had simply restrained her so that someone else could do the job. He had interacted with the physical world at that moment because he had been commanded to do so and because he had been allowed to do so, by standing in the space in front of her and pressing gently on her shoulders. It had taken just under a second to achieve the desired outcome.

He recalled now the moment in time when she had come into existence, conceived in her mother's womb. At that moment, he had joined her, and he was to be with her for the rest of her life. He had no pride to be offended, but his position was such that the Lord must surely have great plans for Alex Masters.

As he watched her relaxing in front of her TV he reflected on the fact that she was very fond of uttering the words 'Thy will be done' at the end of her prayers.

Perhaps she shouldn't be surprised to see her prayers answered.

Two

In the weeks preceding her twenty-fifth birthday, Alex resisted the temptation to call her solicitor. Mr Wicks would surely phone her, or write. He would not forget her birthday. She had a solid faith in his efficiency. They had exchanged letters and phone calls over the years, and more recently, some emails, but now their business together required them to be face to face.

Her mornings became dominated by the arrival of the post. Noises imagined and real came to sound like the drop of envelopes into the mailbox. After two weeks she gave up, tired with her own frustrated anticipation. She started going into work early to avoid the temptation of looking for the postman from her window.

A week before her birthday a note arrived. Written in his own hand, Mr Wicks invited her to the office for 'a chat'. Of course, this was more than a chat; this was about the last wishes of her dead parents. She made an appointment the same day and took some leave from work at short notice.

The appointment was booked for the day before her twenty-fifth birthday. She arrived twenty minutes early and in the reception area she spent the time fidgeting and pretending to read a newspaper.

Mr Wicks's secretary offered her some tea and smiled at her.

'It's lovely to see you again, Miss Masters! We are expecting your cousin today as well – have you seen her recently?'

Alex's mind suddenly filled with questions. Did she mean Daisy? What would she be doing here? Could it be that she was a beneficiary as well? Alex felt jealousy begin to stir within her. After all, why should Daisy get anything from *her* parents?

Miss Goldsworth just smiled, and Alex felt rather ashamed of her reaction.

'I haven't seen her for a while,' she said. 'What time is her appointment?'

Miss Goldsworth perched some reading glasses on the end of her nose.

'Well it does say here . . .' she ran her finger down the page of a very large diary on her desk. 'Alexandra and Daisy Masters: 10 a.m. I remember now, Mr Wicks was anxious to see you both at the same time.'

'I see, I imagine . . .' Alex stopped in mid-sentence. She didn't know what to imagine when it came to Daisy. 'I imagine she will be here soon.'

Ten o'clock came and went, and so Daisy was late. Miss Goldsworth did not cope very well with people who were late. It offended her view of how the world should be. A large carriage clock sat on the mantelpiece, defining the embarrassment of Daisy's absence.

The office had once been a town house, but the grate was boarded up now. Miss Goldsworth sat in a small room that must have once been a lounge or perhaps a games room. She studied the diary again, as if by an act of will she could bring Daisy up the stairs and into the office.

Just before quarter-past, a thin girl with large blue eyes peered round the panel door and into the room. This was Daisy entering alien territory; her face was pale but defiant, suggesting a lack of sleep or an unforgiven hurt, possibly both. Wisps of blonde trailed from her loosely tied hair. Immediately Alex could see that Daisy had lost weight again. She wore a pair of tight jeans and a bright pink T-shirt, and she clutched an old canvas bag as if it was a source of comfort. Her eyes scanned the room, ignoring Alex and focusing on Miss Goldsworth.

'I'm seeing Mr Wicks.'

'Of course, are you Daisy Masters?'

'I have an appointment,' said Daisy with an unnecessary defiance. She hesitated and finally perched herself on a hard chair near the door.

'Would you like some tea?' For Miss Goldsworth, tea was the way to reach the rest of mankind, even the young and confused.

'No,' said Daisy. There was no courtesy in her reply. She didn't belong here. There was too much silence in this room for her taste and she felt like the others were examining her, judging her by their own standards.

Alex looked at her cousin. Daisy was like an animal trapped in a cage, nursing an injury that would not heal. She knew why she was like this; Daisy's parents had sown the seeds of all this pain long ago.

Uncle Simon, Daisy's father, had always been the rebel in the family. Here was a man whose moral framework stretched and buckled to accommodate the available business opportunity. He was always talking about his next venture, bragging about trips to Hong Kong and places he referred to as the 'East'. A generous man in financial terms, he gave nothing of himself to anyone. It was as if he had looked at the arguments for loving other people and decided it wasn't worth the cost.

His wife was a woman who, like Alex, had developed her own defences. She had quickly recognised her husband for what he was, and had resolved to stay with him. Where he was used to taking risks and pushing the limits, she made their home her domain. The decoration was conservative, as if she longed to compensate for his lifestyle with the trappings of respectability. They did not love each other, but they had an understanding.

It had worked for them, but it had not worked for their only daughter. Daisy was a casualty of the arrangement. She had needed love like any other child, but had found herself lost in their arrangement. Now she was in her first year at university, after a chequered career at school. It had taken her three years to collect the grades for a place at college, handicapped by bulimia along the way. She had had a number of brief relationships with people who had known her only as a desperate performer of sexual acts. Those who wanted to go beyond the flesh to discover the real Daisy found themselves looking into a vast black hole. None of the relationships had lasted long.

Alex looked around the waiting room. Her previous visit to this office was as a frightened child, holding her auntie's hand. At the time, the room had seemed huge; from her perspective, every item of furniture had been grand and imposing. She thought of Mr Wicks. This was the man who had arranged all the details with her guardians when her parents had died. With Auntie Helen and Uncle Max, he had formed a team that had worked to secure her future. It was only as an adult that she had realised how much he had done during those first desperate days. Over time, she had learnt to perceive his finer qualities. He was not quite the distant and pompous grown-up that he had seemed.

She suddenly recalled an event that had occurred many years ago.

* * *

She had lost her parents a couple of years before, but the pain was particularly acute at that time. She would have been about twelve, and she remembered sitting in the lounge at the table, learning the capitals of the world. She was stuck on Peru.

Mr Wicks was sitting opposite her, putting his papers in his bag. He had been visiting her auntie and uncle as usual to talk business. Alex assumed it was about her, but she had never been party to the conversations and she resented the fact that people made decisions about her without her knowledge. She looked at this strange, distant man and his floppy moustache made her think of a walrus in a suit.

She was still stuck on capitals, and on a whim she turned to him: 'Mr Wicks, what is the capital of Peru?'

He had looked at her over his glasses.

'Alexandra,' it was so typical of him to use her full name, 'important questions need considered answers. I will leave you a note, it will tell you what you need to know.' With that, he had bid her good night and ambled into the other room to say farewell to her auntie and uncle.

His reaction had upset her. She had asked a simple question and he had responded by saying that he would write her a note! If he knew the answer, why didn't he just tell her? It was typical of grown-ups to be tricky when there was no need for it. Alex completed the rest of her homework alone and then went to bed.

The next morning she discovered a note on the dining room table addressed to 'Miss Alexandra Masters'. The note was sealed.

'Auntie, what's this?'

'Didn't Mr Wicks say he would leave you a note?'

'Yes, but what does it say?'

'I don't know dear, it's your note. Why not open it and read it?'

She had taken the note and opened it later in her room:

My Dear Alexandra,

I shall tell you two facts, both of which are true. One, the capital of Peru is Lima. Two, your parents loved you very much and you were very precious to them. I trust you will not be in any doubt as to which of these facts is the more important to you.

With much affection,

      Mr C. Wicks

She had stared at the letter, and read it perhaps three times before copying the word 'Lima' into her exercise book. As she was doing this, the import of the other things he had written suddenly hit her.

Her parents had loved her very much; she had indeed been very precious to them.

It was as if a truth she had not fully comprehended suddenly became crystal clear. Tears came to her eyes as she felt a sense of love that had until then eluded her. The note had awoken a knowledge within her; she had bridged the gap to a precious realisation that she now kept as a possession of her soul.

* * *

Back in the office, a door opened, bringing her back from the memory.

And there he was, standing in front of her, peering at her over his spectacles. She remembered the moustache, a little peppered now with age, but his demeanour was the same as ever: the walrus, the fool, the gracious man that she had learnt to respect and love. He glanced first at Alex and then at Daisy and smiled.

'Good morning ladies, do come in.'

They followed him into the room. Alex had not visited this office for fifteen years but it was just as she remembered it, although scaled down from the perceptions of her childhood. The floor still creaked underfoot, and the smell of wood polish pervaded the air. A cluster of high-backed chairs stood around the mahogany desk where he worked, and the whole of one side of the room was given over to row upon row of books: legal opinion from the last hundred and fifty years.

Mr Wicks invited them to sit on a large leather sofa spread with knitted blankets; it was a rather incongruous sight among the more formal surroundings of the office.

He lowered himself into a seat opposite them, and after a moment he sighed and said, 'Well now, how are you both?'

Daisy shifted in her seat.

'Well, thank you.' Alex nodded and smiled.

'Let's get down to business then.' Mr Wicks sensed the mood and judged that a prompt despatch of his duties was the best course.

'I have called you both here in connection with Paul Masters' will. The will included a clause which states that when you, Alex, reach the age of twenty-five, and you, Daisy, reach twenty, you should both receive a sum from the estate.'

He took a file from the table and placed two envelopes in front of them.

'These envelopes contain the amounts made out to each of you. I will be happy to arrange for you to be advised on the how to invest these sums.' He made a point of glancing at Alex over the half-moon glasses.

'Thanks.' Daisy took her envelope and thought about Uncle Paul for a moment. He had been kind to her, and not just with this gift. The envelope went into the inside pocket of her jacket and she stood up.

'Is that it, can I go now?' Her wide eyes stared at him, almost begging for release.

He had no desire to hold her here for any longer than was necessary, 'Yes Daisy, you can go now.'

'Okay, thanks.' She stumbled over to the door and affected her escape.

They could hear her running down the steps and out the front door. She must have ignored Miss Goldsworth on the way out.

Mr Wicks let out a long sigh.

'Alexandra, my only consolation is that you have received the much larger sum and will, I suspect, use it rather more wisely than your cousin. I see that you are fingering the envelope. I will tell you now that the sum is four hundred and fifty thousand pounds. I have not written you a cheque, although I can if you want me to: I intended to transfer the money to an account of your choice this afternoon.'

Alex looked at him and frowned.

'How much did you say?'

Mr Wicks looked at her as if she had become temporarily, but profoundly deaf.

'Four hundred and fifty thousand pounds, my dear. The investments your father had when he died made the fulfilment of this part of the will a formality.' He paused and leaned forward, looking at her with an intensity that she found slightly unnerving. 'Of course, the balance will be made over to you on your thirtieth birthday, but a more important consideration now is the fate of your cousin.'

'The balance? How much more is there?'

'At least the same amount again, Alex, but you need to concern yourself with the present, not five years' time. I tell you, I fear for your cousin and so should you. It is because I have a duty in law to discharge that I have given her any money at all.'

She realised, at that moment, that he was doing exactly what he had done so often in the past: challenging her and encouraging her. It wouldn't have been his style to have given her the money and sent her on her way.

'You see, Alex, I never had the understanding with dear Daisy that I had with you. I have never been able to fathom the pain inside her. My fear is that she will use this money to do herself harm.'

Alex placed the envelope in her bag and was silent. Was he inviting her to take responsibility for her cousin? Her immediate reaction was that she couldn't do it. . . . Or could she? The truth was, she chose not to do it. There were too many uncertainties: it would take too much time, and emotional effort. Her cousin was a liability. Alex might spend hours with her and still achieve nothing. She thought again about Daisy running back to college, clutching her cheque.

Then there was her own money – four hundred and fifty thousand pounds.

'I had no idea that it would be that much,' she laughed, suddenly embarrassed.

'Alex,' he leaned slightly forward, as if to emphasise what he was about to say. 'Be bigger than the money. Master it, don't let it master you, if you will excuse the pun.'

He chuckled to himself and sat back again in his chair.

'I will arrange for a transfer to your account. You will need to leave your bank details with Miss Goldsworth. In the meantime, you might consider saying a prayer for your poor cousin.'

He was about to say something else when the phone on his desk rang. He was clearly irritated by the interruption, but he reached for the phone anyway. It was his next appointment: a meeting at a client's office. He promised to be there in twenty minutes.

Replacing the phone, he made his way to the door. Alex realised that their meeting was over.

'Well, goodbye my dear, you know where I am if you need me.'

'Yes of course, thank you.'

Somehow, she felt cheated. As a child, she had spent longer with him when he visited. While walking to the door, Alex realised that he had used the shortened form of her first name and he had never done this before. On an impulse, she turned and came back to him.

'Mr Wicks, what is your first name?'

He placed the file he was holding onto the leather desktop. 'Caleb . . . Caleb Wicks.' They looked at each other, and, in a defining moment, she offered her hand to him and they shook hands for the first time.

'Thank you, Caleb, I do appreciate all that you've done for me.'

For once Caleb Wicks was unsure what to say because he was not quite sure who he was dealing with. The frightened little girl he had first encountered had grown into a fine young woman, and he knew that he needed to treat her as an adult from now on.

Alex left the office, closing the door behind her and gave her account details to Miss Goldsworth. Then she walked out into the sunshine with a figure bouncing around inside her head. . . . *Four hundred and fifty thousand pounds.*

* * *

As the door closed, Caleb Wicks placed his files into his leather bag and smiled to himself. Then he sat and thought for a couple more minutes before getting down on his knees and praying for long enough to make himself rather late for his next appointment.

* * *

Daisy curled into a seat on the train. None of the other passengers had a view of her, so she took the envelope out of her pocket and looked at the cheque inside. In this private space, she allowed herself a smile. Daisy did not often smile and it was a desperate, alien gesture that made the muscles around her jaw ache. She was not used to being given good things – Daisy was a sufferer; that was what she knew best.

When she got back to the city, she took her ten thousand pound cheque and walked in and out of branches of the two banks she used to juggle her finances. In a rare moment of prudence, she decided to pay it into the account with the larger overdraft. The cashier, who recognised her, could not disguise her surprise. Daisy liked that. She wanted her to take a good look at the cheque, to realise what it meant. . . . Then she asked for one hundred pounds – in cash.

The cashier was frowning at her, 'I'm sorry Ms Masters but that amount would take you over your limit.'

'But I've just paid in *ten thousand*!' Daisy was leaning against the counter, gripping the little black pen that she had used to fill out a credit form. Her knuckles had turned white.

'Yes, but that cheque will need to clear before you can draw funds on it.'

Daisy could feel the anger rising, the fear that she would be laughed at again, and the hate; she could feel her hands start to shake; her mouth was dry. This was so unfair, so breathlessly cruel: the one time when she should have been on top, in control, and it was all being taken away from her. Even now, she was the loser, the fool. She could feel the frustration welling up.

'You will be able to draw money against it in three days' time.' The cashier's voice grated in her ears, but the woman seemed like a distant figure. There were dark creatures in her mind, climbing into her throat.

'But I want MY MONEY.' She had hit screaming pitch and the words echoed around, an aberration in the normally staid atmosphere of the banking hall. The other customers pretended to be busy with their transactions. Daisy felt as if she had been placed in the scales by all of them and had been found wanting.

Mr Hawkes, one of the personal banking managers, glided into view. Daisy had been in front of him before to explain her finances. There was something exquisitely Dickensian about him, like one of those officious clerks in a TV period drama. She loathed him . . . or at least she loathed the power he had over her financial affairs.

'Are you unwell, Ms Masters?' He knew who she was.

'I want my money!' It was all she could do to stop herself from screaming again.

Mr Hawkes looked at Daisy, and then he reached over for the cheque she had paid in.

'A solicitor's cheque, drawn on a client's account,' he held the cheque like a rare specimen, a particularly beautiful example of its kind.

'I am sure it will be honoured, but you have reached the limit of your facilities with us.' He paused and looked at her. Mr Hawkes liked to think of himself as a guardian to all these poor students; none of them had a clue. 'I will let you have fifty pounds Ms Masters; there will be an arrangement fee.'

Daisy took her fifty pounds and ran from the branch. As she fled, she could feel the eyes of the staff and customers following her. She could imagine the cashiers laughing about her during their coffee break.

'*Damn them, damn them to hell!*' Her mind ran over the words again and again, '*Damn them, damn them!*' She made it to the public toilets and locked herself in one of the cubicles before she burst into tears.

Curled in a ball on the lavatory floor she wept for about ten minutes. Above her on the wall, someone had drawn a large letter E and then turned it into the word 'Escape'. God, didn't she want to do just that! Escape from her life, from the people who despised her or ignored her. In these moments, she saw herself with a clarity that eluded her for the rest of the time.

She leaned against the door and thought about the scattered remains of her character. The little girl pampered and accommodated by a mother who hadn't wanted her, and a father who treated her like an inconvenience. Inadequate parents who had told her that her conception was an accident and had implied that her arrival was an enormous intrusion on their lives. Her mother did love her, but resented her as well. Her father did not love her. When his wife or his conscience got the better of him, he bought her a gift to stand in for his affections.

She was fifteen when she finally admitted to herself that the presents were a substitute and that she was essentially unloved. She had locked herself in the bathroom and started to shave the hair from her head, screaming as she did it. Her parents had heard her screams. They thought she had slashed her wrists. Her father had broken down the bathroom door and stared at her. Half of her hair lay in the bath. He had let out an audible sigh of relief and then simply walked away. What was left of her relationship with him died that day. Her mother had hugged her, but that had seemed like commiseration in defeat rather than an offer of support.

She had become damaged goods, and a succession of aimless relationships had only served to remind her of the fact. Nobody else loved her, and few people wanted to know about her. The only people who had shown any real compassion for her were from the 'Holy Joe' branch of the family, and half of them were dead now. She had drifted into depression and despair. Nothing would ever be able to reach her; she thought that she was completely, irredeemably alone.

She was wrong. And if she had known who her constant companions were, she would have preferred loneliness to their 'company'.

Even now, three figures stood in the cubicle with her. They surrounded her, observing and enjoying her pain, trying to reach into her, speaking words of defeat, rejection and self-pity. They whispered directly into her soul.

'Hate them, despise them, despise yourself.' The whispers continued at a level just beyond her consciousness. 'They hate you, from your parents on, all of them. You are an inconvenience. Nobody wanted you, nobody . . . .'

She thought these things as if they were a conclusion that she had come to herself:

'All these years, and you were just in the way. Mum and dad? You have no mum and dad; they never cared, nobody cares. You are just . . .'

Suddenly it stopped.

Just when they were about to administer the spiritual poison again they found that she was shielded from them. The figures recoiled and it was their turn to feel the frustration. The most offensive thing had occurred: someone had started to pray for the girl.

They withdrew, nursing their anguish, knowing there would be other times in the future. But who had prayed for her? Up to this moment, they had believed that nobody cared about Daisy. Certainly, no Christian cared about her. But that was wrong, someone did care. In one sense, it was no comfort to Daisy as the pain would not go away and there would be more suffering for her in the future. But the spirits knew that this was a very unwelcome development; the last thing they wanted was Daisy realising that someone cared about her.

At about the same time, hunched against the side panel of the cubicle, Daisy realised a truth about herself that she had never quite touched on before. As she mouthed the words, her tears hit the floor giving her pain some substance: *'I just wanted to be loved.'*

She whispered it, conscious that others might be in earshot of her. An image of Mr Wicks flickered into her mind, she saw him looking at her with something like concern in his eyes. Why? Why him?

In her mind she heard him utter some words; she saw his mouth moving, *'I love you.'*

She was at once attracted and repelled. Wicks, of all people? Disgusting! But it wasn't like that, and she knew it; it was as if the Mr Wicks in her vision was speaking on behalf of someone else. In response, she whispered her words one more time: *'I just want to be loved.'* She found herself telling the image in her mind just how desperate she was for real, simple love. She felt as if she had been given an insight into her pain, a little piece of clarity amongst the confusion in her mind.

Then it was over. The image faded, she was herself again. Out of the corner of her eye, she could see the toilet roll, a crumpled end touching the floor. Her shoulder was starting to ache where she had leaned hard against the toilet bowl. Daisy dragged herself up off the floor and wiped her eyes and nose. When there was no noise from the other side of the door, she slid the lock back. The place was deserted and she stumbled over to the basin to wash some of the despair from her face. She could feel the notes in her pocket, and she knew that she needed a drink at the Student Union bar.

* * *

When she got to the bar, she felt as if she had reached sanctuary. The noise crowded out her pain. There was always music and voices, the pinball and fruit machines in the background. This was a place to sit and relax, a place where nobody made demands. She bought a bottle of premium lager and sat in the corner.

The alcohol warmed her and she relaxed a little. She bought another bottle, and after a while, the bar started to fill up. She kept the change from ten pounds on the table but she had tucked the rest of the money away in her pocket.

'Alright Daisy?'

A young man sauntered over to her. This was Will, a mate from the course. He sat down next to her and took a swig from her bottle. Like her, Will was slim to the point of skinny, with an unkempt shock of hair and deep blue eyes. His selection of T-shirts from the most unlikely bands was a kind of uniform. Today he wore something advertising the 'Bacon Sandwich Tour, 2001' from a band whose name had long since faded from the shirt.

'Where've you been this morning? I'd saved you a seat.'

'Nowhere,' she answered. 'So what did I miss?'

'Can't remember. I'll lend you my notes and you can spend three hours trying to read my writing. Do you want another beer?'

'Please.' Daisy always said yes to another drink.

She was pleased to see Will. He didn't even try to break in to her, although it occurred to Daisy that it would be good to turn up the heat in this relationship. He was a mate and a good one too, but she had no difficulty imagining him with her in bed. By now the incident in the bank and her tears in the cubicle had receded from her mind. She had regained her composure and the wall that she placed between herself and the world was secure. And yet, there was something – she felt it now as she watched Will getting the drinks. She remembered the image of Mr Wicks, and her own response, her need for love. It would be easy to dismiss it now in the warmth and security of the Union bar, but she could not. She knew that she wanted to sleep with Will, but somehow another hunger had been awakened in her – a deeper, more fundamental need. It was as if the love and recognition of just one other person would be enough to define her as a person with value and dignity. The concept of being valuable, even precious to someone intrigued her.

She had never known anything like this before, and whilst she pondered on the novelty of love and sipped her bottle of lager, the spirits that had camped in her soul for all this time gibbered and howled in frustration and uncertainty, shaken by the unexpected power of prayer.

Three

Alex still had a job. She had no intention of playing the lottery winner and walking away with her fortune. Besides which, it wasn't millions. The day after her appointment with Mr Wicks she came into the office very early. There was a breakfast meeting and Alex was responsible for the arrangements. It was just before seven and the morning air was crisp, but she could feel the promise of the heat that would soon come.

Her boss, Lewis Ashbury, was the Managing Director of Sound, Light and Music (SLaM), an entertainment conglomerate with interests in the pop industry, publishing and fashion. Lewis had cut his teeth in the music business, and he still retained the energy and restlessness of his early days. SLaM was his baby; he owned the company and had built it up by hiring the right people at the right time. He issued short contracts at the best rates. He only really had one long-term employee, and that was his secretary and PA, Alex. He called her his 'little saviour', partly to tease her about her faith, but also because she was reliable; there was no one else in the company that he trusted, not now.

Lewis drew a strange comfort from the fact that she was the first assistant he had employed who would not sleep with him. His initial offer of sex had almost made her leave the company; but they had sorted out that little misunderstanding quickly enough. Now, after five years, he found himself trusting her with more and more of his business affairs. Trust – that was key for him, it was a rare and precious commodity in a company full of jostling egos and selfish interests. She was the first person to be employed on a permanent basis when he started the firm, and she had worked hard for him. But more than all her ability, he valued the fact that she was loyal. Lewis was prepared to pay a big premium for her commitment to him.

He had called them all together to talk about a fresh assault on the youth market. It looked like a business meeting, but for Lewis this was more like a court, and he was the judge. One side would present their case and the other side would try to 'rubbish' it. Everyone would air their views, and then Lewis would decide. That was how he liked it: he as the judge, and the rest of them could bicker and snap at one another.

The proposal on the table had come from Martin Massey, Head of Music and Promotions. Also present that day were Dave Somerville, the Head of Media Publications, and Bridget Larson, who was not officially head of anything but seemed to hold considerable influence with Lewis. Bridget ran a small team of fashion designers within SLaM, producing clothing-based merchandise to complement SLaM's other products.

They had been talking at each other for about an hour. Martin was presenting his ideas with a series of colour-ful slides and an animated speech. He had a slightly arrogant, grating voice that was beginning to give Alex a headache.

'It doesn't matter if it's house, or garage, or dance – they can play skiffle for all we should care! We take advantage of it, and we ride with it.' He seemed to have stopped, but it was only to draw breath.

'We just have to understand what is happening out there. Alcohol is a thing of the past, now it's a bottle of water and a tab. This is big, but we have to act now if we

are going to take advantage of it. That's why SEEKA has
to happen, quickly.'

Now there was silence in the room. The meeting had
been called to discuss Martin's latest project: bigger,
more far-reaching, and potentially more lucrative than
anything else they had ever done. Martin promised significant financial returns, but there was to be some initial
investment and it would have to happen quickly.

Nobody spoke. The smell of stale coffee and the
murmur of air-conditioning held sway for just a few
moments before the case for the prosecution started up.
Of course, Dave spoke first. He would oppose the plan
on principle because he disliked Martin's perpetual
arrogance, but this at least provided the opposing views
required for Lewis's adversarial style of debate.

'It won't work, Martin: it's too obvious, and it's too
illegal, even for us. We'll look like we are pushing the
stuff ourselves. You know the line we have to tread . . .
the lawyers will have a fit.'

Alex knew a reference to lawyers was a mistake.
Lewis despised lawyers.

'This company is not run by lawyers,' retorted Martin,
unable to suppress the smile that was forming at the
corner of his mouth.

'We'll certainly need one if we go ahead with this
plan,' Dave replied. The rivalry between Martin and
Dave was a constant feature of life at SLaM. The truth
was Lewis had chosen to take on Martin and Dave with
the intention of seeing them clash with each other. He
had told Alex privately that he thought the conflict
would produce the right creative mix. It seemed to her
that most of the time it just produced argument and bad
feeling.

She glanced across the room at Bridget Larson. In the
end, Lewis would almost certainly go with Bridget's

advice. This performance was being played out for her benefit. Bridget sat silently, watching the contest. There was a glitter of moisture on her forehead – the room had become very warm.

Bridget Larson was a formidable woman. Nobody knew very much about her. Forty-something, her regime was precise and clinical. Every morning she worked out at the health club. She would then shower and dress for the office and by 7 a.m. she was hard at work. She would then keep going without a break until 7 p.m., when she would leave. She had no formal title in the company and little evidence of a life outside it. She was watching Martin with a kind of hungry, almost ravenous expression. There had to be some sort of relationship between Bridget and Martin. Alex could sense an intensity between them and if she had had more experience of these things she would have called it sexual. There was a chemical, hormonal mix, like the attraction of opposites – rivalry and desire together in a confined space. Somehow, it made the room even warmer, the atmosphere close and moist.

And yet, this was business. Bridget knew the questions to ask on Lewis's behalf.

'Where do you expect the revenue to come from, Martin?'

'Where it's always come from: the magazines, the T-shirts, the different media, the music. We can stick it all over the web, we can make the culture, it's what we've always wanted to do here, isn't it? Make the culture, change it, reform it for our purposes. If we can get it right, the music, the magazines and the clothes, then SEEKA will be worth . . . .' He moved his hands in a wide arc, implying that the number, though not incalculable, was very large.

Lewis frowned slightly, 'You see, Martin, we can't be seen to be encouraging the consumption of drugs. I'm not having our merchandise with tabs all over it. I am not taking that risk.'

Now it was Dave's turn to smirk. He wanted to see Lewis sink this idea without trace. Martin was an arrogant fool who loved himself too much and took too many risks. If he thought this was such a good idea, he should leave the company and try it with his own money. Dave knew where these things went if they got out of hand. Martin would have all of them doing some ghastly publicity stunt in Oxford Street, snorting something off the pavement.

Martin shut his eyes and breathed the stale air. His scheme was in the balance. He had hoped for more support from Bridget but yet again, she had played the role of Lewis's inquisitor. He realised that in a public forum she would never favour him over Lewis, in spite of what they had. In the back of his mind, he recorded this moment, and the decision that it birthed. He thought he had conquered Bridget, but now he knew that he was still a long way off. It was hot in this room, and he couldn't think straight. With some effort, he tried to relax and spoke again: 'Look we aren't saying, "Take the stuff kids." We're not selling it are we? It's just our merchandise, just the usual stuff at the usual margin.' He had added the last comment for effect, as he knew that money was the way to Lewis's heart.

There was silence in the room again. The air-conditioning seemed unable to shift an atmosphere that was heavy with the smell of pastries and stale coffee. Alex was writing furiously, trying to keep her mind off the queasiness she felt.

Dave leaned back in his chair and flicked through one of his titles, feigning indifference: 'I don't think we need to risk the business with this sort of deal. We can sell all the current lines without looking like we are feeding off the dealers and the pimps.'

The focus of the debate swung back to Martin. His idea was in the balance, he would emerge from this meeting either the victor or the fool and now he felt the thing begin to slip away from him. None of them had any idea how much pressure he was under. He could see the smug grin on Dave Somerville's face, and felt a fresh surge of spite for the man; he wasn't going to be able to stay within the rules of the game here and he could feel the anger rising.

'A proper little saint you turned out to be,' he spat. 'Well don't worry, I won't mess up your precious magazine operation, for what it's worth. Sometimes I think you have forgotten what SLaM is about.'

Dave put down his magazine. He looked to Alex, like a man who had been offered a duel and had accepted the challenge. The air-conditioning droned on, oblivious to the heightened tension in the room. Now there was an edge to his voice.

'Martin, I want to make money just like you; I'm just not as reckless. And don't start lecturing me about what we are trying to do here. You are the one who has forgotten our roots. I think you'd sell your own mother if you thought the money was right.'

At just this moment, Lewis glanced over at Bridget and she looked up at him, their old understanding still secure despite the fact that they were no longer lovers. She seemed to be motionless, except that Alex noticed just a slight nod of her head. And then Lewis chose this moment to intervene. It was all frightfully entertaining, but the babies were about to throw their toys out of the pram and that wasn't good for business. Besides, he had now made his mind up.

'I think we need to see a few of these ideas fleshed out. You may be on to something Martin, I mean the

symbolism, the clothing, the whole thing is very powerful. There is money in it, but we have to get it right. I
think we will give it a go. We will reconvene next week.
Alex will confirm a time with all of you. Thank you.'

'God,' thought Martin, 'he's bought it!' He wanted to
shout something, but there would be time enough to
savour this victory later.

And with that, they all left the room, walking out into
the relatively fresh air of the rest of the office, and breathing something other than an atmosphere heavy with coffee and sweat.

Left alone, Alex had to sort out the mess. The food was
left untouched and wasted on the table. As she started to
clear up, she began to wonder just why she worked for
this firm. They were all playing games, they all despised
each other, and she knew that that was just how Lewis
liked things to be.

Gradually her thoughts turned into prayer, and as she
brought it all to God, her mind filled with a picture, in some
ways very clear, in others quite hazy. She was looking into a
crowded room; it might have been a canteen or a café. The
people in the room were mostly youngsters. It was dark outside, so she assumed this was late afternoon or evening; the
place was busy. She was calling the people to attention and
then she turned to someone who was standing on a small
elevated stage. She recognised her brother, Conner, playing
his guitar. The picture faded, she could discern no more
detail. That afternoon she forgot about the conduct of her
colleagues and completed the task of transcribing the notes
of the meeting. She finished her work early and went home.

* * *

That same evening, Martin was still in his office and his
mood had brightened considerably. He was working

hard on the case for his project. He knew that it was going to happen, the moment was his; Lewis could smell the money they would make from this, and in the end, he knew Bridget would support the idea. He was so engrossed in the work that when the phone rang he almost jumped in his seat. He nearly didn't answer it because he didn't want to talk to anyone at that moment; then he realised who the caller might be and picked up the receiver

For a moment there was nothing except a faint modulation of sound, then a human voice carried through it. 'Martin! Martin is that you?' the small voice sounded as if it was coming from the other end of a long tube.

'Yes, this is Martin, who is this?' he tried not to sound too impatient.

'Martin, it's George, I'm on the mobile. I'm in Greece.' The voice was shouting, but he could only just make out the words.

Greece? Martin began to wish that he had left the phone to ring. The last time he had spoken to his younger brother George, which was about six months ago, he had been trying his luck as an itinerant salesman and, as usual, that had ended in failure. The last thing he wanted now was a dependent calling on him.

'Martin,' the voice was full of excitement, 'I've been trying to call you. I'm in Greece and I'm working on a farm here. . . . I've gone into partnership,' he mentioned the name of a friend of their father. 'Now I know you Martin, you're going to be cynical about this, but really it's a great opportunity. I mean it this time. Believe me, it beats being a salesman, I'm going to see a complete return on my investment within two years.'

'That's great, George.' Martin wondered where his brother had got the money from to invest in a business; he was usually penniless. The phone hissed in his ear again.

'Anyway, we've got this big villa on the property, so if you ever want to come over for a break just let me know. Hey, if you hit on hard times you can even come and work for me!' George was laughing at the other end of the line. Martin considered the chances of him working for his brother to be practically nil. He knew very well what would happen: the whole enterprise would either prove to be a con or fail dismally, and George would be back in this country in about three months' time sleeping in his spare room, invading his space, like some over-familiar parasite.

But George wasn't finished, 'Seriously Martin, you want to come over here; the sun, the women, I don't know why I didn't do it years ago. Anyway, look, let me give you my address and phone number.'

At the third attempt, Martin got the spelling of the address right and scribbled down the phone number on a scrap of paper. He could imagine George, trying to impress the local girls with his legendary charm and wit. Well, George was a fool, and if the women didn't see through him, they deserved everything that they got.

'Great, George, I'll be in touch, yeah, bye.' He didn't want to hear any more, and he put the phone down before George could reply. He folded the scrap of paper and slipped it into the back of his diary.

It did not occur to Martin that even three months ago the suggestion of beautiful girls would have aroused some interest in him. That desire had been choked off by his obsession with the project and the profound nature of the cynicism that now engulfed him. He was about to turn his attention back to the SEEKA project when the phone rang again. He snatched at the receiver:

'Yes, who is it?'

'Hey, take it easy, Martin.' Bridget's cool voice came in stark contrast to the distant excitement of his brother.

'Oh, Bridget, I'm sorry.'

'Forget it. Do you want to have a little break from all this hard work?'

Martin felt as if he had been reminded of an important appointment that had somehow slipped his mind; he was struggling now to switch emotional gears.

'Yes. I would like that. I'll see you up there in a few minutes.'

Across the office, Bridget replaced the receiver and looked out to the cluster of desks where her team sat. No one was there to see her open a drawer and remove a tin of furniture polish and a soft cloth.

It was about 7.30 p.m. when she went up to the meeting room again. Martin was already there. Well that was one thing at least – she had made him wait for her. She smiled across to him but it was clear that in her absence his mind had moved on to something else. It was unlike Martin to be distracted when he should be looking forward to her and Bridget did not appreciate having to compete for a lover's attention. Of course, she knew what was on his mind. This SEEKA thing had absolutely consumed him for the past couple of weeks.

She sighed, and wondered why she was in this room with a man who was ignoring her.

'Martin, it will be okay, you have won, you know that. All you need to do now is make it work.' She tried to smile, but he wasn't even looking at her; she continued anyway. 'And don't worry about Lewis, he does want this to happen.'

She dropped into one of the chairs. Martin seemed to be looking past her, at something on the wall.

'There is still a lot to do. And then there's Dave.'

Now she did laugh, 'Dave is a little boy in the equation. He has nothing more to say.' She leaned forward, her eyes at last catching his, 'Martin, you are in control of this. Now stop it, okay.'

Martin fingered the rim of the table, tapping an irregular beat onto the wood. He could not tell her what was really happening here, what the true challenge was. He had to treat their engagement here as an extension of the business meeting; if he allowed himself any kind of intimacy with her the real story would come bursting out, and he would be finished.

From Bridget's viewpoint, his attitude was cold and hard. They were not going to pledge eternal love to each other and she knew the parameters of this relationship; but this was almost cruel. It was as if he wanted her in this room just so that he could walk away, judge her and then reject her like a piece of meat at the market. Bridget felt her own resolve hardening; she would not let this pass. She had come here for a purpose: he was going to make love with her now on this table, it was a matter of personal pride. Then, *she* would choose what happened the next time. Placing her bag on one of the empty chairs, she walked over to where he had stopped. She was now so close to him that she could sense his intensity, feel the warmth coming from him. It reminded her why she wanted this to happen now.

'It will all come to you in time Martin, it will all come to *us*.' She placed a hand on the front of his shirt so that she could feel the body heat coming from him; with her eyes closed, she could concentrate enough to detect an increase in his heartbeat.

Bridget did not think of herself as particularly manipulative, no more than any ambitious woman might be. Some of her acquaintances were of course married; and they manipulated their husbands, allowing them some licence in the course of achieving their own objectives. Bridget felt no desire to criticise any of them, but she chose a different path to the same end. Without the encumbrances of a partner and children, she was able to focus on her desire to obtain the luxuries in life that she wanted, and she could devote time to another hobby of hers, the acquisition and practice of power.

Until now, she had thought of Martin as an amusement rather than a challenge. She liked him in an abstract sort of way. There was an energy about him that she found strangely alluring. Now, in the meeting room alone with him, she allowed herself another chance to look him over. He was one of the most intense men she had ever met, with a thin face and sharp features. His hair was cut short, adding to the tension that seemed to surround him.

Bridget wanted him now. She felt the need to move on to the engagement, further delay would be foolish. She went to the lighting panel used for corporate presentations and dimmed the lights so that only shapes and contours could be made out. In the silence between them, she could hear the slight hum of the air-conditioning, still processing the faint aroma of coffee from their meeting that morning. His breathing was becoming deeper and more rapid. She was winning him back, as she knew she would. It was only to be expected – after all, she was very, very good at this sort of thing.

He eased away from her slightly.

'Martin? What is it?' She frowned. He was usually in the mood by this time. It had been the slightest movement, but she had noticed.

'I wanted to look at you,' he lied. He forced himself to look at her body, to get through this procedure – the sight of her was not without some consolation for him.

She studied his shadow, the glint in his eyes heightening the expectation.

'How hungry are you tonight, Martin?' she said, speaking in no more than a whisper.

In the dimmed light, he was like a shadow, but she could still make out the moisture across his forehead. Before he could answer, she slipped away from the minimal clothing that she wore in the office and stood before him, naked. Taking his right hand, she made him feel the contours and intimacies of her body. She knew well that the fire had started within him, even if his fingers were icy cold. She eased herself onto the table and stood, feet slightly apart, looking down at him.

'I said: how hungry are you?' Her question was more of a command, an irresistible demand for attention.

'Ravenous.' For the first time that day his voice was quiet, almost hoarse, now he was interested. He moved to engage with her before the feeling passed.

A few minutes later, with the room still in darkness, Bridget listened to the breath of the air-conditioning. She was still on her back, and she was alone. The sting of his thoroughness persisted inside her. At the best of times, he was energetic, but tonight the engagement had been almost brutal. He had had no regard at all for her, she had been his subject. It occurred to her that he had been trying to release some of his own tension. She judged that he had failed.

Dressing quickly, she removed the polish and cloth from her bag and started polishing. She worked at the table, rewinding and replaying the activities of the past few minutes. A dull ache in her arm reminded her that she was rubbing at a table that was already clean and she forced herself to stop. Placing the items back in her bag, she walked out, locking the door behind her.

Tonight she knew that she would be acutely aware of her loneliness as she got into her bed. Her encounters with Martin had always been a form of combat. Their bodies worked together but their minds, their personalities, were at war. It was an issue of personal pride between the two of them. But tonight Bridget felt defeated; he had worked over her with an almost vicious energy. There had been both consent and abuse.

For the first time in a long while she felt frightened. It was a feeling she thought she had exorcised many years ago but it came back to her now. She was smart enough to understand that what he had done to her tonight had been a physical demonstration of his disregard for her. She reached for the little packet of tissues in her bag and blinked at the unfamiliar tears.

Four

The weather was oppressive. The atmosphere was a breeding ground for restlessness in the city. Tonight Alex was unusually aware of the moisture of her own sweat all over her body. She stood at the open window looking out onto the high street and then closed her eyes and listened.

There were the immediate noises: a car engine sinking into the background and voices from the high street just some fifty yards from her flat. The air was full of that familiar urban smell: car exhaust mixed with a pungent aroma – the foods of the world crammed into one city – and beneath it all was the constant, subliminal roar of the city.

Still with her eyes shut, she listened to that sound, the breath of the urban jungle, and then through it she sensed an emerging click-click on the paving stones, an arrhythmic tapping that grew to a crescendo beneath her. She opened her eyes and looked down on two figures – a couple of girls, high heels tapping, hurrying to get to an unknown venue. They must have been about fifteen or sixteen. The taller one was almost shouting in conversation with the other, although they were no more than a metre apart. To Alex's ears, they sounded loud and brash and confident in their urgency, ready for whatever the evening would bring.

Alex studied them closely: the tight black skirts, plunging necklines, generous make-up; the facade of self-assurance betraying their youth. She pitied them, but at the fringes of her conscience, there was the taste of envy. They seemed to share a secret, a form of community that excluded her. She felt isolated, like the princess locked in her ivory tower.

Loneliness had been a familiar feature of her life for a long time now. She had been alone since childhood when she had lost the two people who had meant the most to her. She looked across to the mantelpiece, where the three wooden elephants stood in procession, alongside the old black and white photograph of her parents. She treasured this picture of them; it seemed to capture the love they must have shared. Every time she looked at the photo it yielded another secret to her: the way her mother held on to her father's arm; the aspects of his character caught in the line of his lips; determination and compassion. The shot also reflected the consuming purpose of their lives. The darkened angle in the background must have been the roof of the school where they worked in Kerala, South West India. She could not look at this picture now without a breaching of her defences, the hot moisture in her eyes betraying her vulnerability.

Alex had only been ten when they had died; they had been killed in a car crash. At the time, she had felt the need to be very brave about it all. She had sealed herself in an emotional tomb and nobody could reach her. A succession of experts had tried to bring her out of herself and she had decided that she would need to be on her best behaviour with all of them. No one had been able to break through to the little girl inside.

In fact, it was one of her classmates who broke the spell. Lucy was one of Alex's friends. One particular day Lucy had been crying and, in a rare excursion to the real world and the concerns of others, Alex had talked to her. Maybe she felt a sense of community with the tears in her friend's eyes. Lucy had eventually confessed the cause of her anguish: 'I loved my hamster, and he died.'

And so, Alex gave herself permission to grieve at her own loss. Her reply had been almost inaudible in the playground: 'My mummy and daddy died three weeks ago.' There had been a moment when they had joined together, the emotion welling up and finding its expression in their tears. Alex cried again many more times after that.

Standing in the living room of her flat, Alex considered the loneliness and community again. Her sense of exclusion from the girls who had walked so confidently beneath her window contrasted sharply with the flavour of community she had felt with Lucy that day. Lucy had been a blessing to her then, but now her needs were more complex.

Her Auntie Helen and Uncle Max had adopted her, and treated her like one of their own. She had become a sister to their son, Conner, and she loved him. She was thankful to God that she hadn't ended up with her father's brother and his wife, Daisy's parents. God forbid! But still, somewhere deep inside her there was an ache, a longing unresolved. She nursed the idea that one day she would love and be loved with such a depth and commitment that the gap would at last be filled. And yet, wasn't this a longing that should be filled by God? Didn't she want him above all else? These were the real questions that Alex struggled with. She didn't share them with anyone; they existed only in her mind. Did she want a man, a husband, more than she wanted God? What if it was her destiny to remain single? What if that was what God wanted for her? Could he fill that need?

The wind blew the city into her flat again. She would have shut the window, but at that moment, a car drew up to the kerb directly beneath her. She watched the driver emerge and there was a curious pressure at the sides of her head, a taste of expectation. Here was a visitor whom she would welcome into her home.

Angel sensed her mood and moved to the window. He recognised the man as someone who had visited before, but never when Alex was alone. She tidied some newspapers away and paused in front of the hall mirror to check her appearance; she did not even realise what she was doing.

The spirit stood next to her, motionless, his instructions quite clear: 'Wait, watch – do not influence this exchange.'

There were footsteps approaching. Alex opened the front door before the visitor could ring the bell. She was like a child waiting for a welcome relative, but in her enthusiasm, she startled him.

'Sorry, John. Please, come in.' Now she was embarrassed. He hovered at the doorway, regaining his balance. He wasn't sure he should be here at all. This was John Stamford, thirty-five, fair skin, blue eyes, and married to Alex's friend Laura.

For Angel, the mood of a person said as much as anything seen in the visual world. Here was a man who had chosen to do something that was not wise. He might not have decided to come here until the last moment; and when he eventually got home, he might not tell his wife that he had been here at all.

John walked into Alex's flat with a briefcase and a sense of expectation. This was the most exciting thing he had done all week.

When Laura first started seeing him she had been anxious that he make a good impression on her closest friend. She need not have worried. John and Alex had hit it off from the start, and from Laura's point of view, they had exhibited just the right amount of friendliness. It had all been managed very well. However, it was not long before John became aware of the need to be wary. He had been courteous and had kept his distance. He had made sure that whatever he said to Alex, he said to his wife as well. He patrolled the boundary around himself with care.

Angel thought of the range of human relationships he had come across: the frustrated couples who talked but never listened; the lifelong friendships between men and between women; an unexpressed love. And then there were the short-lived, urgent liaisons, which bristled with the enemy's work: secrecy, lies and sex mixed together in the most damaging way.

So, what was happening here, now? In just that moment when the door opened Angel could see that these two people were fond of each other. It was not the love of a husband and wife, but it was also not quite the love between brother and sister. This was something else that sat on the boundary between different emotions: there was excitement and uncertainty in it, and danger. It had always seemed to him that to let people come together like this was a very high-risk strategy. But he was not God and did not expect to understand everything that happened. He knew his place. He was Angel, an angelic being, occasionally a divine emissary, always a servant of God.

Alex and John embraced and Angel sensed their emotions. There was pleasure in their meeting, and genuine affection, but there was also the undercurrent of excitement engendered in both of them, a quickening pulse, the release of adrenaline. He concluded that there would be temptation – it would come soon.

John spoke first.

'I won't stay long. I just thought I would bring the home group notes round.' He hovered just inside the doorway clutching some papers. 'I don't want to disturb you.'

Alex shook her head, 'I wasn't doing anything.' She beckoned him in, but he continued to hesitate, like a rabbit caught in the lights.

Alex feigned impatience, 'Come in so I can shut the door!'

'Sorry, yes.' He took a couple of strides and joined her. She led him into the lounge, and indicated an armchair.

'I was just going to make some coffee.'

John hesitated. How long could he spend here? Was there time for a coffee? When was he expected home? He heard himself accept the offer of a drink, and he sat down in one of Alex's armchairs.

He had gone out of his way to come to her flat. She knew that this was true. He could have given the notes to her on the following Sunday, if he had wanted to. He was out on a limb here, and now Alex wanted to reassure him, make him feel welcome. He was, after all, her friend's husband.

They made conversation for a few minutes. The kettle boiled. She wondered whether she should have offered him something cold to drink, but it was too late now. John made a point of studying the items on the mantelpiece while Alex busied herself in the kitchen. She decided to use her best filter coffee because somehow instant didn't seem good enough for the occasion. When he looked at her again, she was smiling at him. Her eyes betrayed the fact that she was starting to relax. He imagined her, for a moment, confessing her sins to him as if he were the parish priest. He would have taken pleasure in granting her absolution.

'So,' he said, 'what's happening with the youth work now?'

She turned to face him and sighed. Other passions came to her now – the passion to serve and to be relevant.

'There are just so many of them, John. They need somewhere to go, somewhere that's not a pub, and not out on the street. I think if we delivered the gospel out there with the same passion and determination as the pushers and dealers showed . . .' she left her statement unfinished. Somewhere out on the high street another car glided past. 'They need somewhere to go after school and at the weekend. If I could find somewhere for them I would run it myself.'

And he knew that she would. He was familiar with her conviction; he admired her strength of will. And there was something else there too, something else within the curious mix of feelings that he had for her. He did not want to say what it was, and they fell into silence again.

Angel pondered their relationship again. He wanted to understand the situation here and it required more thought. He had almost dropped his guard when his senses screamed at him. Something approached the room, it was moving towards them from beneath the floor. In a moment, it would emerge through the carpet and into the room. He had not sensed this one before, but he felt the familiar urge to revulsion and outrage. It emerged by the door and crept towards them like a disease. The stench manifested itself immediately. The being must have sensed Angel's presence long before it entered the room, but now the two spiritual forces faced each other, sizing each other up. The demon stopped, perhaps three yards from John and Alex who were still discussing the plight of the local teenagers.

'You have no rights here,' it ventured.

Angel spoke in an even tone (this was a typical preliminary skirmish), 'I will go where the Lord bids me, you have no authority over me.'

The thing changed tack and approached Angel, more sure of itself now. It appeared as a human, in dark clerical garb, with wild eyes and a thin moustache. The eyes betrayed the boiling lust within it. The demon surveyed the room, looking at Alex as a leering smile stretched across its face.

'If I could have her . . .' it whispered, taunting Angel, curling its bony fingers into a fist. The eyes widened slightly, teeming with the potential for hate and damage.

Standing perhaps ten feet away, Angel returned the stare. 'Understand this, demon. My Lord God has authority over your master, and I have been given charge of this one,' he pointed to Alex. 'You will not touch her.'

The demon sneered; 'Have the female, but you will look on helplessly as I soil them both yet.'

Alex was in the kitchen again. She allowed herself a glimpse of John as she handed the drink to him. She had always found him attractive, but the depth of her feelings seemed to be more apparent this evening. He took the cup from her hand.

Again, John was searching for chatter, the safety of neutral conversation.

'So how's this business with the bloke at work now?'

'I think he's got the message. I told him that if he didn't leave me alone I'd have him fired.' She leaned forward to give emphasis to the point and clipped the table with her hand. Coffee slopped over the side of the mugs. She whispered something under her breath as she got up to find a cloth.

It occurred to John that he was dealing with something very fragile. He wanted to whisper reassurances to her and hold her in his arms. Almost without realising what he was doing, he found himself studying her. She had her old jeans and a checked shirt on. She seemed to possess an energy that he found compelling. Alex had recently had her hair cut short, so that the nape of her neck was now visible. The whole act of her movement captivated him and he continued to stare at her while she hunted for the cloth. His eyes began to search her out under the shirt. He could just begin to see some firmness beneath the material, the contour of her body.

The enemy was there, whispered something into John's ear. Angel did not hear the words. John was still watching her as she returned with the dishcloth and wiped the table. She paused and looked at him, and at that moment, John felt the bearings of their relationship begin to shift. He was suddenly aware of the hum of the city from the open window, the oppression in the air, the potential in a summer evening; a sense of dislocation which seemed to marginalise his senses. He felt like he was looking into her soul. It was too much, and he glanced down at the papers on the chair beside him. His eyes caught the scripture at the head of the notes; 'But among you there must not be even a hint of sexual immorality . . .'

'Oh God . . .' there was an abrupt sensation as all of his spiritual standards snapped back into place. He thought about his wife, Laura, for a moment, and remembered who he was. 'Jesus.' He whispered the name under his breath, not as blasphemy but as a prayer. Alex turned round with the cloth and walked back to the kitchen. He lowered his eyes and felt as if a danger that had been close at hand was now passed. If anything, he felt even more love for Alex now.

. . . not even a hint of sexual immorality.

They talked for a few more minutes, safe conversations. Then John stood up, 'I should be going really.'

'Okay, thanks for the notes.'

. . . not even a hint . . .

Everything seemed all right now. They embraced in a way that made neither of them vulnerable, and he left.

Another spirit accompanied John as he made his way down the corridor to the lift. This angel had observed the skirmish but had made no attempt to intervene. Whatever happened here was Angel's responsibility. They did not share any discussion during the whole incident: there was nothing that needed to be said. What they did share, though, was the beautiful moment when John had remembered that he was a Christian and the Spirit of God had swept into the room, blowing the enemy aside like a leaf.

Five

The day after the meeting the sun dominated, and summer pervaded the urban world, the heat lingering on the pavements and in the little shops and offices unlucky enough to be without air-conditioning.

At SLaM, Martin Massey's ideas were approved and rapidly developed into plans that the different parts of the business could act on. It was probably Bridget's subtle support for the project that had swung it. Lewis would always have the final say, but when he opened his mouth, it tended to be an echo of Bridget's point of view.

Of course, Lewis knew about Bridget and Martin – they were naïve to think he would not find out. But he knew Bridget too well and he had guessed almost straight away. He could recall feeling sad at the time and almost protective of her; it was a curious emotion for him. But all that aside, he reasoned that a romp on the boardroom table would not be enough to sway her judgement. Besides, he quite liked this scheme. He was no saint, and the business was there to make money out of the current youth culture and this was a good way to do it.

Bridget had made him aware that she was in favour of Martin's ideas, and Dave Somerville had seen the way the thing would go. He agreed to work on a new magazine that would promote the SEEKA ethos. He started to get some articles together and kept his misgivings to himself. His relationship with Martin remained strained; they had both invested too much personal capital in the arguments to let the matter end there.

SLaM was to invest heavily in a new range of 'culture products': music, clothing, accessories and a magazine that would feed off the drug culture and in turn promote it. The concept would be introduced immediately with some of the material they had already produced, and a couple of Lewis's contacts on the club circuit had agreed to carry out a pilot launch before the real thing later in the year.

Alex had not been party to these discussions, but she did know what they were going to talk about because Lewis had asked her to type and circulate an agenda. From what she could see of the proposals, the premise was simple enough. Amongst teenagers that are more affluent, the drug culture, including the prevalence of alcohol, had become rooted as a dominant force. The fifteen- and sixteen-year-old market was key here, and in this group the number of drug users had tripled in the last ten years. SLaM sought to both feed off and promote that culture. A number of new fashion lines had to be introduced, together with a logo. They had settled on a single brand for the whole range, from magazines to music to fashion. The logo showed a unisex head with wide staring eyes and the word 'SEEKA' in swaying typeface underneath. Below that, the simple slogan was 'After the Truth'. The underlying philosophy behind the whole initiative was that the thing to do now was explore experiences in music, drugs, sex and vision; this was the 'truth'.

The fact that the phrase had an almost biblical ring to it made Alex deeply suspicious. It was as if evil was daring to use the very words of scripture to serve its own ends. She had no power to affect this situation directly, but she knew that she could pray.

The decision to invest in the SEEKA project was Alex's cue to give in her notice. She had been in no rush to leave

SLaM, even with her misgivings about the direction of the firm, and they did pay well, but the smell of evil was so potent around this latest initiative that she could stand it no longer.

She sat alone in her flat and reflected on the day's events. When she had told Lewis she was leaving he had immediately offered to increase her salary. The sum involved was large enough to make even Alex pause, but she was not going to change her mind, she was leaving. She had not wanted to say why she was going but he had forced her in the end. He was upset, and he didn't get upset easily. Alex was part of his defences, part of the wall he put around himself and his company. He was the only one who would care about the fact that she was leaving, and he was also the only person who really cared about SLaM. Somehow these things were related: he and his company were now vulnerable. He approved of Martin's scheme, but it had just cost him an excellent PA, and he was going to make sure that it delivered every last penny of the promised reward.

Meanwhile, Alex felt a tremendous sense of relief. She found herself in a familiar place, on her knees seeking God about the direction of her life. Angel watched her, she had not spent much time on this activity recently, and he hoped that her prayers would bring some recovery to her as she struggled with her feelings for John Stamford, the husband of her friend.

* * *

Whilst Alex prayed, John was packed into a commuter train heading home. The train carriage was warm and the open windows would not alleviate the heat, or the dilemma he was facing. His mind turned constantly back and forth between opposing views. He was reminded of the caricature of the person with the devil on one shoulder and the angel on the other.

Externally his life was functioning normally, but it felt like a lie. In his heart, he could feel the constant nagging of an unresolved issue. It was all to do with Alex and how he felt about her. He had told no one because he had not wanted to risk his position in the church; but there she was in his mind again, always waiting to catch his attention. His imagination played back moments they had had together; he could not stop himself analysing previous events in an effort to discern his motives, and hers. What did she really think? The issue continually wore away at him so that it seemed as if half his mind was focused on the day-to-day duties of his life, and the other half was wrestling with emotions he did not want to feel.

Now he was thinking about her at night, and in the morning within seconds of his waking up. The whole issue descended on him like a weight, reminding him of unfinished business. Within the last few days there had been an occasion when Laura and he had switched on the answering machine and gone up to bed early. As they made love, his mind suddenly flickered to Alex. It had been only for a moment, but he had been shocked by the intrusion: he was naked with Laura, they were together, and he wanted to share it with no one else. He felt as if he had betrayed his wife.

Yet, for all his efforts to put Alex from his mind he could not stop thinking about her. 'Just supposing I was alone, if something happened to Laura, if I was single.'

Then another voice in his mind seemed to counter the first, 'This is a useless line of thought. Laura is my wife and I am committed to her. I will not be swayed by my feelings for Alex, I will stand firm.'

He remembered his last conversation with her as they sat on the sofa in her flat. He remembered the ease with which they chatted about things, the warmth of the evening. He pictured Alex's front room, the little elephants lined up on her mantelpiece, the black and white picture of her parents, the tick of the clock and the aroma of coffee. His mind flashed to the moment he had looked at her, discerning the contours, seeking out the shape of her.

'Enough,' he snapped back to his present situation. 'I don't want to know about her any more, I don't want this any more, I want my wife.' And he meant it. But then there had been those times when he had been on his knees before God turning the problem over and over in his mind, searching for some release. He had reached the point of despair and simply cried to God, 'But I love her.' In his turmoil, he was never quite sure whether he meant Alex or Laura.

And how circumstances conspire! It was the summer, and the women on the train were dressed in their short skirts and blouses, and he didn't have to look very far to see things that only hindered him in his present state.

The train pushed against the heat, and John withdrew from the battle, buried in his paper. He was not looking forward to the evening's home group. It was his turn to go and it was at Alex's flat. The train pulled into his station and he walked home; he felt like an automaton, a life absorbed by an internal struggle.

* * *

Whilst Alex contended with her God, and John wrestled with his conscience, the offices of SLaM were the venue for another kind of battle. Bridget had, again, called and Martin had almost declined the offer this time. He smiled to himself at the thought of telling Bridget that he had a headache. What a slap in the face that would be for her! He was also tempted to leave early because he did have other matters to deal with that evening, but it wasn't yet time to distance himself from this woman. And, yes, the sex was good. Well it certainly had been at the start, but he didn't know whether it was good or not now, and he simply couldn't be bothered to work it out.

For Bridget, what had started as suspicion had now turned into certainty. Even as they were locked together that night, she realised that she had lost him. He did not utter one word to her afterwards, he just walked away. He had been rough with her again and now she was in pain, finding it difficult to get up and leave. So instead, she dressed and seated herself in one of the leather chairs in their boardroom, and brooded over her anger, allowing it to burn and develop. He had relied heavily on her support to get his proposal through, and now he was almost making his excuses on the same day. She had gone out on a limb for him, and she realised now that her feelings for him had clouded her judgement, made her soft.

She sat down at the table and began to consider her options, and to think about this man who had systematically used her in a personal and professional way. Most men did indeed behave in similar ways, and yet there was something different about Martin. He was very clever, very persuasive, and it seemed he had beaten her at her own game. There was just a hint of fear in her heart. This was more than just a game of office politics, she found that she could not properly calculate the risks involved.

What was it about him though? Too often, she had seen something else in his eyes: a hunger, a passion she had not seen in other men. She thought back on her

career. There had been clever men: some were very
ambitious, people driven by power and wealth, self-justification. She had slept with men who had attracted her,
confident men attached to quiet wives who held no
interest for them. But there was something else there
with Martin, something dark which pushed him so that
pleasure became almost meaningless. She knew what
drove most men – wealth, power, influence, sexual
pleasure – but with Martin there was something which,
if she believed in such a thing, she would call evil.

She couldn't even bring herself to go through the ritual
of polishing the table. Everything was a sham. She had
engaged in a rather public affair with Martin, pledged her
support for him that morning somewhat against her better judgement, and now this. She placed her tin of polish
down on the wood. Why was she trying to clean this table
anyway? The scene from Macbeth came to her mind.
There was the distraught Lady, restless in her sleep, trying
to wash the blood of the murders from her hands.

'Out, out damned spot.' Bridget grinned, half in
humour and half in pain at the familiar words. The rou-
tines she used to protect herself were unravelling before
her eyes. It was the most frightening thing that could
happen to her.

Over the years, she had built up an elaborate defence.
She had visited healers, counsellors, psychiatrists, and
they had all said the same thing to varying degrees. She
would have to be honest with herself and deal with the
feelings of unworthiness and anger. But she had ignored
them all because they didn't understand the fundamental nature of who she was. Without her anger she was
nothing; without the potency and motivation of her passions, to love, to hate, to conquer, she would stop and fall
away to nothingness. The threat of her own irrelevance
was the spur, driving her on.

She thought about her father, a man whose memory she pitied now more than feared. He had dreamed of having a son, and had been disappointed when Bridget turned out to be a girl. That disappointment had hardened to bitterness when he discovered that his wife would not be able to have any further children. She didn't know whether he had loved her at all, and now she didn't really care. It had always seemed to be her fault that after her birth her mother had been unable to conceive again. It was so obvious to Bridget, who had gone over the history of her life so many times. With no love at home, she had looked for attention elsewhere, in the pubs and clubs of her town, in one back seat after the other. It had taken her a long time to untangle lust from love, and the absence of one had forced her into making do with the other. It was going to be almost impossible for her to love anyone now.

When her father had discovered that she was sleeping around he had beaten her, and she didn't know who had shed more tears, Bridget herself, or her mother. She had hated him, hated him so much. He had hit her mother and her mother had accepted it as a part of life. But Bridget had resolved that she would not tolerate it. She had hit back.

Things eventually came to a head: she remembered the night very well. She had come in late smelling of drink and cigarettes. He had shouted at her, calling her every name he could think of. And he had called her 'Dirty'. So often he would say that: 'You are dirty Bridget, dirty!' The phrase was etched in her mind now.

They had been in the kitchen, he had hit her, slapping her across the face, hard. She had asked him to stop; she had tried to push him away; but he kept shouting at her, and hitting her. Then her mother had come in and tried to calm him, yet he had slapped her so hard that blood trickled from her lip. It had been that last act which had stiffened her resolve. She wanted people to think that she hadn't known what she was doing, but she had known exactly what she was doing. She had picked up the kitchen knife and slashed his face. She could remember the light, pattering noise of the blood as it had hit the floor.

Her mother had screamed, her father had screamed and called her something, but she was unmoved. He had already called her every name he could think of, so it didn't really matter if he used the same words all over again. Her mother had taken him to casualty, and she didn't know how they had explained it to the doctors – she hadn't stayed long enough to find out.

When they had gone, she'd packed a bag and left. Her only regret was that she knew he would blame her mother, making her suffer for this. She spent the night at the coach station and got the first ticket to Victoria. All she could hear in her mind the next day was her father's voice calling her 'Dirty' and the spatter of his blood on the floor.

Bridget sighed and looked around the conference room. The air-conditioning hummed quietly in the background. The strategy was falling apart. She could not lead a life where the threat of abasement was the driving factor of her success. Martin had called her bluff, delivered the abuse that she almost felt she deserved, and no amount of table polishing was going to change things. Actually, nothing was going to change; she could not be free even if she wanted to. Freedom from the mental shackles was a luxury, and she had other issues to deal with now.

First of all she had to deal with Martin Massey. He had used her and she had been taken in. He was going to pay for it now though. There was going to be a moment of reckoning and she didn't mind if it meant that his whole precious SEEKA thing fell down around his ears.

She got up from the table and put the polish away. She had made a decision. She certainly wasn't going to let Martin get away with this, but she needed to be very careful, very patient. It was important now to get the timing right, to administer the blow with the utmost care and efficiency.

She needed to draft some very specific instructions to her old friend and legal advisor, Mr Shand. Bridget considered Mr Shand to be an excellent solicitor; she had found him to be sympathetic to her very particular requirements in the past, and she was going to need his special brand of tolerance and understanding for the particular job that she had in mind for him. Then there would need to be a session with the photocopier. If it came to a battle she would need to have all the ammunition she could find. Bridget let out a long sigh and focused on the dim sheen of light reflecting off the table. She was always at her best when she was under pressure, cornered like an animal.

She would call Mr Shand first thing in the morning, but the photocopying would have to wait. She touched the mahogany with the tips of her fingers. They had made love here for the last time, and things would be different from now on.

* * *

Martin Massey had left the office some minutes before and was now on the main route out west from the city. He knew he would have to make a call at some point in the evening or else Lench would be phoning him. Even though he had good news, he still didn't want to pick up the phone. He never enjoyed talking to Lench. He was just building up his resolve when the phone rang. He cursed to himself and picked it up.

'Yes?'

'Hello Martin, how are you?' Now here was that familiar voice that spoke refinement, social privilege and contempt.

'I'm fine. The board approved the ideas.' There was a silence. He cursed himself again. What a poor way to present a great piece of news. Hadn't he wanted to savour this moment? And yet, all he had managed to do was mention it as if it were casual conversation.

'That's excellent news, Martin. We need to proceed now without delay. When will the product be available?'

Martin's brain started to kick in.

'We'll be ready pretty quickly – the artwork's already done, and we booked a couple of articles today. The other stuff – the merchandise – will take longer. The whole thing is really an ad for drugs, just like we discussed – the drugs theme was what you said you wanted, wasn't it?'

His hands were moist and his heart was pumping now. He felt confined by the smart interior of his Mercedes. He needed to relax and he needed to slow the car down.

Lench's calm voice cut into his discomfort. 'Try not to get over-excited, Martin; what I want is the fulfilment of our master's will. If drugs are a means to that end, then so be it. In so far as they may separate young people from the enemy, they have potential. But it is the master's will that is central.' There was a slight pause. 'Martin, it seems that I have to keep going back to the basics with you. It's very disappointing.'

Martin could not think of an answer. He took his foot off the accelerator and eased at the brake.

The voice continued: 'The magazine – is that Somerville's responsibility?'

'I am sure he will get on with it. He knows what's good for him.'

'I am sure he will and he is not likely to cause you any trouble. But I have to tell you that there is someone else who will.'

Martin felt a pressure growing on his skull. By an enormous exercise of will, he slowed the car right down and pulled into a lay-by. It was impossible to concentrate on a conversation with Lench and drive at the same time.

'I have felt it. One of them opposes us. Who is it Martin, who is opposing the work?'

He thought about Bridget. Surely she wouldn't pose a threat to the SEEKA project. She had supported him. He wasn't going to mention her reticence now. The whole thing was going to be a success, and he was going to make a lot of money out of it. In truth, that probably meant more to him than belonging to the Group.

'Martin, are you still there?'

'Yes.'

'You would be wise to remain candid with me, Martin. Remember you are one of us now. The time for making decisions of commitment has passed; you belong with us. Now, who spoke at the meeting, who was for this project, and who was against it?'

Martin knew he was trapped. He had made his decision and he was a part of the Group, there was nothing he could do.

Lench went on: 'One of them poses a threat to us Martin, now I have been very patient with you, suffering your little ways. Some would say I have indulged you. I will call again in one hour, and then you must tell me who stands in our way. The time for doubt has passed. We must bring this thing to its proper conclusion.'

The phone line went dead.

Martin sat in the stationary car for some minutes. He thought about Bridget. There was no doubt about what Lench could do if he wanted to. This wasn't a game any more, it wasn't about making a few quid or seriously trying to have a good time. As a group, they had a strong reluctance to deal with people who were outside their circle. It carried the inevitable risk of detection, the chance that they would be discovered: but, there were exceptional occasions, exceptional situations where a project dear to them could be jeopardised by someone. If it came to that, they would act with their usual clinical efficiency and discretion. Martin wanted to know as little about it as possible.

He thought about Lench: easily the most religious person Martin knew – totally dedicated to his cause. Calm, rational, calculating, he would do anything to further his master's will. He wondered what the girl who worked as Lewis's PA would make of someone like Lench, completely opposed to her beliefs. She was a Christian, and Lench, and indeed all of them, seemed to want the name of Jesus trampled into the dust.

Martin thought about little Miss Masters, the prim PA. He had laughed when he'd heard that one of his team had tried it on with her, and then he had laughed again when he heard that she'd rebuffed his advances. All these things convinced him of the poverty of man. No, the reality was, you get what you can and you look after yourself. He'd had that creed hammered into him from the earliest age. He imagined Alex cowering in Lench's presence, all her weak religion falling away.

At least Lench was a leader of sorts, and Martin had committed himself to the Group now. He was one of them. He'd forgotten how it had started, but that didn't really matter. The point was, he had to decide what to do.

After perhaps a minute of time he picked up the phone, *'There is no choice,'* he repeated to himself over and over. Still his hands trembled as he pressed the buttons; he was sentencing someone to death.

He had entered all the digits, and he looked at the 'SEND' button. He was silent. A lorry rushed past him as he sat in the lay-by, and the car swayed slightly in its wake. Under his breath, he whispered a prayer, though he didn't know why or to whom it was directed.

'I'm sorry Bridget, God help you.'

'Hello?'

He was startled to hear Lench's voice. He must have pressed the call button without realising it. Had Lench heard him? He dismissed the thought.

'The woman . . . Bridget – it must be her.'

There was a pause.

'Why do you think so, Martin?'

'She has had second thoughts, she is suspicious. She will seek to ruin me, and the way she will do it is by ruining the project.' It was the clearest and most succinct thing he had ever said to Lench.

Martin pursued his case. 'I have felt it when I have been with her in the last couple of days. Her body is beginning to say "no", so her mind is surely saying "no" as well.'

He could almost hear Lench thinking through the consequences of what he had said.

'Bear with me a moment, Martin.'

He heard Lench's voice, muffled and distant. He was talking to someone else in the room. Bridget's name was mentioned; Martin's mouth went dry. Lench spent perhaps a minute in conversation with this other person. Martin waited, resisting the urge to talk, to ask what was happening.

The phone came alive again, and the tone of Lench's voice had mellowed considerably.

'Relax, Martin. I will handle the issue of the woman Bridget now. You have done extremely well. We will be meeting next week in the usual place at the usual time. I am arranging a reward for you which will be available on that day. Now I want you to just focus on the project. Everything is going to happen as we have planned it.'

Martin had not heard the last words that Lench uttered, because when Bridget's name had been mentioned he finally realised what he had done. The gravity of it all fell on him, he panicked, and before he could open the car door, his stomach launched its contents onto the smooth leather of the passenger seat beside him.

* * *

Whilst Martin wiped the fluid from his lips, across in the centre of town Alex's home group was progressing well. Tonight's subject was 'Service in the Church', a safe area for discussion. Although the group members held disparate views they could agree on most of the issues around this subject, and a reasonably tight grip on the study kept them all in line. For John the division in his mind between the demands of the present and the deeper issues that were affecting him cast a shadow over any interest he might have had in the debate.

At the moment, he felt particularly drawn to some of his male friends, the stirrings of a call for help that he wanted to make. It was particularly good to see Aiden there, observing the people around him, taking it all in. He gave little away, but John had the impression that he was thinking all the time. Aiden rarely came to the group: in the past, he had pleaded late nights in the office. His new job seemed to give him more time in the evenings; maybe everyone in the group would have an opportunity to get to know him a bit better.

John wondered whether his friend had been able to guess at any of his turmoil. Aiden could look into his heart like nobody else and he seemed to be watching John like a hawk tonight. The Bible study was finished and people started to chatter amongst themselves.

Aiden had been sitting next to John. Now he leaned forward and whispered: 'Where are your thoughts tonight, John?'

'Sorry?' John feigned confusion.

'Is something bugging you?'

It took a considerable amount of self-will for John to plead happiness and change the subject. 'No, I'm fine. Did you enjoy this evening? I'm pleased you could come.'

Aiden smiled at an elderly lady who was handing him a cup of tea but then he leaned forward to whisper close to John's ear.

'John Stamford, you are a liar.' He smiled again as the bearer of tea offered him a large plate of cakes. Food was a big factor at the group, as it was at many of the church's meetings. 'You can fool some of these people, but you don't fool me. Your brain was here but your heart was elsewhere. You've either stopped believing in God, or you've stolen some money, or you fancy another woman.'

Before John could reply, Aiden had turned again to the old lady, engaging her in a conversation that John could not hear.

The evening drew to a close and, as Alex went to find some coats, the phone rang. She suddenly thought of Daisy, although she didn't know why. In fact, it was Laura, who wanted to borrow a resource book for the youth club work, and wondered if Alex could give it to John to bring home.

Of course, she could.

Alex said goodbye to her guests and asked John to stay so that he could take the book for his wife. Why didn't she just give him the book while everyone else was around? She felt as if she were part of a game where the end involved her spending another few minutes with John, alone. The conclusion to this game was as yet unknown. John put his papers away. Aiden was still hovering around, and now he came over to John again.

'Let's go out sometime, John, I could do with a chat.'

John forced the smile to his lips, 'So could I.' If he had been able to spend time with Aiden right now he would probably have revealed every thought in his heart.

Aiden said goodbye to Alex and left.

Now Alex and John were alone. She quickly found the book that Laura wanted and gave it to him.

'Well, I'll see you on Sunday,' he placed the book in his bag, and put it down on the sofa.

'Yes, I think things went well tonight.'

'Yes,' she moved towards him and they embraced. He caught again the slight scent of her, and as he shut his eyes, he could feel himself falling into this embrace as if it were water to a thirsty soul. She held him and there was silence in the room. That same dislocation that he had felt before, the rush of adrenaline and an inner stirring that he did not want to acknowledge.

Across from them, Angel sensed the mood and concern grew like a shadow in his mind; these two people were having a profound effect on each other. There was a physical and emotional exchange here, certainly enough to alert his enemy to another opportunity. It would happen, he knew it was coming in seconds and, sure enough, just as they seemed to be parting, Angel sensed the spiritual atmosphere in the room change as if the air itself was starting to rot. He was soon aware of the enemy watching Alex and John. It was the same one as before, more directly invited this time and therefore stronger. It was quite enjoying the spectacle, and it felt confident enough to boast in front of Angel.

'Can you not smell their lust, angel of Jesus? Have you not yet learnt what people are? Their religion is a shabby pretence! Why, in their hearts they want nothing more than to be intimate.'

Angel looked away from the creature in front of him. He dared to believe that he was the better judge of character, and that the Lord's power could extend, like his love, right to the hearts of these people. But what the demon said was in some sense true; there was something there, something in each of them that was profoundly affected. In his infinite wisdom God had placed inside humans an almost irresistible drive, so many of them had tasted ruin through its misuse, and it was often the ones who tried to deny the physical dimension of themselves, as if they were not flesh and blood and passion.

'You are wrong, demon, it is you who does not understand the true nature of mankind. I shall not be the one to enlighten you.'

But the demon was confident now, and it fixed its eyes on him. 'Naïve! We shall name you that my little one. I told you, I will soil them both, and however much you are responsible for the woman, she will be rendered powerless by the act. Look at them, how desperate they are for it, despite themselves.'

Alex and John had parted and looked at each other. John bowed his head and in the same movement put his face next to Alex's. She kissed his lips lightly and they parted. He could not even find it in himself to say goodbye as he left.

The demon turned again to Angel, and stepped closer to him. The air between them fizzed as it approached.

'Oh yes, that is enough for now. We are patient you see, when the prize is large. And the prize is large, isn't it little one? I have seen her potential, I have seen the simple-minded plans that your God has conjured up.' The demon croaked out a laugh and then gathered itself together, bowed low in mock submission and bled away into the floor.

As John left, Alex walked into the kitchen to wash up. The place seemed very quiet now, and her mind flashed to the moment when she had kissed him. It had seemed like the taste of a sweet poison. Their embrace had at least told her what she suspected: that John felt for her as she felt for him. She was glad of something to do as she rinsed the cups and plates. She thought about Laura, her friend Laura, whose husband she had kissed and embraced this evening.

The consequence of the situation began to come over her, a disturbing sense of guilt building up in her mind. There was something else there as well. It took her a few minutes to identify what it was before she guessed at the truth. The feel of another body had been like a catalyst, encouraging something within her that had already started; she felt the need clarifying itself deep within her; it was irresistible and terrifying and wonderful. At that moment, she knew that she could no longer continue to be both single and happy.

Angel could still sense the enemy not far away. He knew it would bide its time, chip away at their resolve and then present them with the temptation, hoping it would be the prelude to sin. What was more worrying was that the plans that had been made for Alex could be rendered useless if she engaged in premeditated and sustained sin. An adulterous affair would surely destroy them both, or at least spoil the Lord's plans for them. There was forgiveness, but these things always exacted a price.

Angel could see the whole purpose of his time here coming under threat. He would need to be on his guard continually now and do whatever he could. As Alex finished her work in the kitchen, he was reminded of something else – a deep sense of God's love for these people, including Laura. They were not pawns in a game, these were real lives bought and paid for. He could sense his Lord's passion for them, a passion that had allowed the scourge of the Roman whip; that had allowed the Roman nails to enter into his hands, pinning his physical body onto the cross.

The struggle had arrived, the manoeuvring was over and the battle had begun.

Six

Saturday night was party night, but Daisy stayed in her room because Will was coming over to see her. They had organised it only that day. Rather like Alex and John, they were testing out a new dimension to their relationship. They were both used to working in larger groups, but tonight was different; tonight it was going to be just the two of them, nobody else even knew about it. This place was not like Alex's flat: the sensual chemistry might not be so easily stifled; the bed was not forbidden territory.

However, things were not quite as simple as they may have seemed. Will was coming round to help Daisy with her work, and that was a genuine motive for both of them. Will was an able and conscientious student, looking towards an upper second or maybe even a first. Daisy showed some promise but something held her back; she would be lucky to complete the course.

At around seven, he turned up with a bag full of folders and books. His rather energetic use of the intercom buzzer brought her running to the door. When she opened it, he took three strides into the heart of her living space and slid the folders across an already crowded table.

'Alright Daisy, got some beers in?'

Out of habit she looked at the T-shirt he wore to see if she had ever heard of the band it advertised. All Will's T-shirts looked well worn, and this one seemed to be from a tour by a band called Extreme Unction. Daisy thought about the words, and in the back of her mind, she registered that this was a religious rite of some kind.

For the next hour and a half they sat at the table in her room and with some degree of precision he went through the notes for the last two lectures, talking to her over the heartbeat drum and bass of her favourite radio station. This was a warm-up for the real event of the evening: Daisy's request that he review her portfolio of designs.

Sometimes she found his familiarity just a little off-putting, intrusive even, but she didn't want to do this without him. She realised now that if she gave Will permission to review her work, she was also giving him permission to be as familiar with her as he wanted. The prospect stirred a curious sense of excitement within her.

Will looked at the scatter of pictures and sketches from her portfolio.

'Yeah, well there is a bit still to do here.' He looked through the designs and sketches on the table. 'Some of it is good, when you get in the mood for it, but some of it is crap.' He leaned back and drained the can he had been drinking.

His casual dismissal of her work generated the familiar sense of outrage within her and she turned to face him leaning forward so that he found himself glancing at her neckline.

'Look, I didn't ask you up here just to rubbish my stuff.' Her tone was sharp. Will sat up and they were both silent. Behind them, the radio hammered out another garage anthem, the energy of the track seeming to encourage the desire for conflict within her.

Will laughed and sat back in his chair. 'I'm sorry Daisy. Look, I'm not here to hassle you.' The look on his face suggested genuine care, and Daisy could feel the tears begin to come, but she fought them back. She didn't want to be weak in front of Will so she took the pencil from his hand and placed one of the drawings in front of her.

'Okay, so I'll get on with this.' She started to add to a rough sketch. She drew a line and then rubbed it out, she drew another and then another which she also had to rub out. As she tried to bring the picture together, Will moved around the table and stood behind her. With another pencil, he drew one single flowing line which seemed to capture her intentions. The frustration in her heart was coming to the surface.

'What did you do that for, can't you just let me get on with it.'

Will sat back and looked at her again, the words floated through his mind: 'I don't need to put up with this,' but as he looked at her anger and passion something changed in his view of her. He suddenly saw tremendous potential in her. Up to now, he had thought of her as a crazy, attractive girl – but this showed she had spirit. He decided to take a risk. Putting the pencil back on the table, he let out a long sigh.

'Why did I help you, Daisy? Why have I come here on a Saturday night when I could have been going out on the town? What is my motive?'

'I don't know what your motive is!' she snapped and her eyes met his. Her passion left her open for just a moment, and in that moment, she felt like someone who had just walked out from the shallow end of the pool. Her feet couldn't touch the floor any more, she was out of her depth. She did not know why he had helped her.

He spoke more quietly now: 'Have I come here to patronise you and laugh at you, or have I come here to help you because you are a mate, and I care about you?'

She turned round and faced him. The shock of blond hair made him look like he had been charged with static electricity. She read the words on his shirt again as if they might give her a clue about the answer to his question.

She knew what was happening. He was breaking down the wall she used to protect herself, and it scared her, but she didn't want to stop it happening, the sweet destruction.

'Why do you care?' she whispered. Even as she said the words, something in her mind, the thing that protected her screamed: 'Don't let him in, he will hurt you, he will treat you like the others did!' But this was not the whisper of the spirits that plagued her. For some reason they found that they could not influence her tonight like they had in the past. This was her own sense of preservation.

Will found himself wanting to say, 'Because I love you,' but instead he moved over to the desk and picked up the pencil again. Looking at the design as if it contained the answer to all of the important questions, he drew a couple more lines. There was a reverence about the way he did this, as if he dared not spoil some innate beauty that she had already placed in the picture. He wanted to demonstrate his respect for her work, and by association his respect for her. Of course, the thought had occurred to him that he would quite like to make love with her, but there was a curious frustration within him. He wanted to enjoy her, to watch her undress and then he wanted to take her to bed. But at the same time, he didn't want to do that at all. Rather, he wanted to provide her with a little of the dignity that she seemed to be longing for. The desire to respect her won out against his own selfish interests. Perhaps he loved her enough to consider her more valuable than the promise of a sexual encounter. He was surprised at his own high moral tone. What was he – a saint? Normally he'd be quite happy to have a girl at the earliest reasonable opportunity.

He couldn't understand what he felt; it was too complex, too unlike the simple ways that he had enjoyed before. He retreated back to the drawing and looked at the lines he had just added:

'Is this what you are trying to say?'

'Yes that's it.' She had to admit that Will had captured the theme and mood of her work with three pencil lines. He had summed her up with similar efficiency, and she realised now that they had crossed some threshold, they had both taken risks with this relationship and they had survived.

In the background, the radio had started one of her favourite club anthems and she felt herself moving slightly in response to it. Now they worked on and between them they completed a second design. She tried to express the idea with some inadequate sketches and Will seemed to be able to fill in the gaps, taking her ideas and knitting them together. She forgot about the time.

As another design lay completed on the table Daisy looked at the clock. It was now twenty minutes to ten.

'I think we have done enough.' She threw her pencil across the table and leaned back in her chair. She could not remember the last time she had worked this hard. She felt a curious sense of fulfilment, as if she had achieved more this evening than she had in a long time.

'Do you want a can?' He nodded and she went to the fridge. While she was away, he made a decision. They drank their beer and Will put his books and papers back in a bag. She was expecting to spend some time drinking with him now, but Will had other ideas.

'Only one though, I want to take you out somewhere tonight.'

'Oh . . . where are we going?'

'Get your best frock on, girl, we're going to a party.'

She was ten minutes getting changed. In that time he lit and smoked a cigarette, wished he was in the room with her, then he was glad he wasn't, and then he browsed through her CD collection. She emerged in a short blue dress with a light touch of make-up. She was gorgeous, and Will experienced that familiar tingle. He was beginning to wonder whether he should have just stayed in the flat with her. . . .

To go for a ride in Will's car was an experience in itself. He drove like a maniac but she didn't care. As soon as the engine had rumbled under the bonnet, he turned on the radio and she expected to hear some of the rave or house stuff that he liked, but all she got was static. She leaned forward to try to tune it

'Leave it, Daisy, just listen.'

Will had a typical student car: tatty seats from a variety of sources. The sound system was probably worth more than the car itself and the engine made a noise like a jet on take-off. As he pulled away from the kerb, an almost hypnotic resonance spread through the bodywork of the car. It spread to her brain and made her feel as if anything could happen and she wouldn't care. The truth was she didn't really want to think too much. She had been thinking all night and now she wanted to relax. Closing her eyes, she let the hum fill her brain.

A voice penetrated the hiss of the radio.

'. . . this is the Shadow Man talkin', telling you how it is, and we are at the Shanty Town tonight . . . .' The voice was suddenly lost in the angry crackle of static. '. . . joined tonight by my brother Ethan D . . . We're givin' you some of that Old Skool track so if you are seeking it, seek it here . . .'

The radio reverted again to its tuneless crackle. Will tuned it to the station they had been listening to earlier.

'That's all we need to know.'

They headed off out of the city on one of the main roads north, winding their way into the countryside.

Daisy didn't know where they were and she didn't care. The resonance of the car was beginning to make her feel drowsy.

'Hey, we'll be there soon, Daisy, don't go to sleep on me.' Will nudged her slightly and patted her knee. She smiled at him and he suddenly had to force down the desire to turn the car round and go back to her flat.

More than that, he knew that if this carried on she would really start to mean something to him. She was a bit paranoid, and she had some baggage from her past, but he had shown he could break through that. Perhaps he did love her – it was a deeply unnerving thought. At least all this reflection helped to pass the journey, as she seemed to have gone quiet on him.

Daisy imagined that Will's hand was still on her knee, it was as if she still sensed the touch. She believed that he really did care about her. If anything, the fact that he had not forced himself on her made him more attractive. She imagined the sensation of his hand on her knee and tried to magnify it. Then she imagined the same touch moving up past her knee, the sensation of pressure closing in on her. She occupied a space between waking and sleeping – it was a place where her imagination took control. The sensation moved further up her leg and she recoiled slightly. Then it was upon her and in her mind she was making love to Will, but it wasn't quite right . . . it was like she was with the brother she had never had and they should not be like this. She was irritated now, annoyed that she hadn't been able to enjoy the fantasy without a tinge of moral unease.

She jolted out of her dream as the car turned off the road and bumped down a farm track. Ahead was a large building, maybe a barn or a warehouse. Light escaped here and there from the wooden structure.

Daisy could feel a steady thud through the ground as they approached this place.

'Stay with me Daisy, I want to make sure you get home.' For some reason he was beginning to wonder whether this was a good idea. 'And another thing, I've got some drink, but if you get one of your own just keep an eye on it, or someone might put goodness knows what crap in it, okay?'

They reached the building, and the music was quite audible now. About half a dozen men stood at the door.

'It's ten pounds each.'

As Will dug around for some money, Daisy got out a noticeably thick wad of notes from her jacket pocket and handed one of the security people twenty pounds, and they were in.

The music hit them like a wave. It seemed to push at them and then, like the tide on the seashore, it drew them into itself. Will was still staring at Daisy in disbelief – he had about fifty pounds in his pocket and he thought he was the boss in this situation. He whispered next to her ear, 'Where did you get that cash from, Daisy?'

But the sound and light was too much and he never heard the reply. The degree of unease in Will's heart increased. It was difficult enough to keep an eye on a woman in a place like this; it was even worse when that woman had about two hundred pounds to spend.

Inside the building Daisy felt the force of the music and saw that the place was full of people of about her age. The noise hit her like an ocean wave, invading her hearing first and then spreading to the rest of her body. The flickering lights disorientated her. She held on to Will's arm, as he mouthed the word 'DANCE', but she heard everything and nothing. So she gave herself up and danced, and bathed in the atmosphere. Daisy loved the way the power of the music made her feel good – it gave her purpose and self-assurance. The dark shades of red and orange, made her feel safe and anonymous amongst all the people there. She danced and moved and released herself to the music. This was the closest she ever felt to true safety: there was all the anonymous pleasure and none of the need for self-justification; she was with the company she craved, but no one expected anything of her. She was free.

Will got a large bottle of water from somewhere and she drank from it. On a screen to her left, she could just make out a human face with words written round it. Something about seeking after the truth . . . the words seemed familiar . . . she vaguely remembered the radio, something about seeking . . . the face appeared to her right . . . above it she could see the word SEEKA . . . the spelling was wrong but that didn't seem to matter. Surely that was her . . . surely she was seeking the truth . . . perhaps she would find it here.

Will put something like a little headache pill in her hand and she swallowed it. As she did, a small voice inside her head whispered above the anthems: *'You have just taken drugs.'*

Daisy argued with the voice and told it she hadn't, it didn't matter. And to reassure herself she looked at Will. She moved forward to hold on to him because she wanted to do nothing but dance with him. The face appeared again, and a man's voice . . . was it the DJ? Some of the music was familiar, there was some House and Jungle, but her attention was fixed on Will.

It was about half an hour after she'd had the pill that it began to hit her: she belonged here, she belonged with these people – they were all one together. She moved closer to Will and put her arms around his waist. She had taken him rather by surprise and he nearly stumbled. He took a long swig from the bottle he was holding and passed it to her. She drank quickly, breathless by the end of it and he pulled her to himself. The place was bodies and moisture and heat, and as Will drew her to himself she was ready to kiss him, and she thought she would be ready for more later, despite the fact that the drugs in her system would militate against the sexual experience she thought she wanted.

The DJ played one of her favourite tracks and they continued to dance. In the heat, she could feel moisture forming on her face. It began to trickle down to the neck-line of her dress. She thought again about the sensation of kissing Will, the sensation of his hand on her knee. By now she had lost the meaning of time; the minutes and hours moved about randomly, and though she glanced at her watch, the position of the hands meant nothing to her.

Eventually she sat down with Will and he gave her another bottle to drink. She offered it to him but he pushed it away. He gave her another little pill and she took it without really registering what she was doing. He said something about 'Disco Biscuits', but it meant nothing to her and she just grinned and hugged him.

Then they went back to the music and she felt herself joining the group again, and poor deluded Daisy thought that amongst the drugs and the sweat and the aimless volume of noise she had found a place to belong. The reality was that everything was about to fall apart. But for now, the music played and Daisy danced and lost herself in it all.

Later – she didn't know when – Daisy noticed that the bottle of water had suddenly become empty, and she wasn't sure why, but it didn't seem to matter. Then her foot hit something and she looked down and saw that Will was on the floor. It seemed to Daisy that he shouldn't be on the floor . . . surely that wasn't what was supposed to be happening.

She forced herself to stop dancing and shouted at Will,

but he didn't respond. Something about this didn't fit with the feelings inside her. They all belonged together, they were all dancing, Will shouldn't be on the floor, it was not time to go to bed yet. She giggled at the thought of going to bed. Then two men she had not seen before came over to where Will was lying. They said something to each other which she did not hear and then they picked him up. Daisy suddenly felt protective of Will and shouted at the men, 'Where are you taking him, what are you doing?'

They started to drag him away from her.

She feared that they would not let her go with them but as she followed, they made no attempt to stop her. They carried him across the rough boarded flooring to the corner of the room, Daisy bit her lip as she saw his head bumping around. Daisy picked up her bottle and followed them, trying not to be scared, trying to keep herself under control.

'Surely,' she thought, 'it should not be like this. Perhaps these men will leave Will in a quiet corner and then when he has rested we can go back to the others.' The men passed through a door and she followed.

'Who are you?' they both faced her, and she didn't answer. One of the men shut the door and the music became a dull thud. It was cooler here as well, and there were no flashing lights.

'I said, who the . . .' one spat at her, but the other one, perhaps the more intelligent of the two, closed in face to face with her. She tried to concentrate but she couldn't grasp what he was saying.

'Are you with him? What's he had?'

She was sure that this was not supposed to be happening. The situation was demanding too much of her. It was like a nightmare she'd once had where she was surrounded by angry people, and she didn't recognise them, and they were asking her questions that had no answers. Without quite realising what she was saying she whispered, 'Disco Biscuits'.

The words sounded pathetic to her ears. Suddenly she felt cold, as the sweat that had been absorbed into her dress made her shiver. She felt small and frightened, and at the margin of her conscience, the demons stirred. The second man had been looking at Will. He spoke into a walkie-talkie, and he sounded worried. Daisy tried to say something else to the man who had questioned her.

'We were seekers . . . the truth . . . we . . .'

'Shut up!' He cut her down and she was silent again. A third man entered the room. He was tall and lean with sharp blue eyes. He wore a dark suit with a collar and cuffs. His suit looked expensive.

'What's happened?'

'This one's really gone. The girl says he's been on "E", I don't know how many. There are some Doves going out there.'

The second man chipped in. 'There's a lot of gear out there tonight.'

The suited man cursed. He looked at Will, prostrate on the floor and then he checked Will's pulse. He looked over at Daisy. A frown started to spread across his forehead; he spoke with a kind of biting assurance.

'Put them in the van and dump them up at A and E, and tell Spider to get out there and find out what's changing hands.' He looked at Daisy.

'How did you get here?'

'What?' she was beginning to lose her grip on the situation. The man in the suit frightened her. She looked at Will lying motionless on the floor.

He took one stride over to her and bent down slightly so that he could look her directly in the eye. Then he slapped her across the face.

'Listen to me, you silly girl, how did you get here?'

She was in shock, and she didn't know whether she was more frightened or angry.

'His car, we came in his car.'

'What car?'

'A mini, a black mini.'

'How many of you are there here?'

'Just us two.'

He turned to the other two again. 'Put them in the van and get rid of them. Find his keys and get Spider to lose his car. Go on now!'

The men pushed Daisy back through to the warehouse, but she didn't feel part of it now. One of them was gripping her by the arm, the other was digging in Will's pockets. Daisy wanted to scream and she wanted to tell them that she hated them all, and she wanted to protect Will, but there was nothing there, except shock and silence. They led her to the exit and out into the darkness of the night. The music changed again to a dull thud and the sweat on her dress cooled in the night air. She shivered again.

'Get in the back of the van!'

The man let go of her arm at last and gestured to an old Transit parked near the entrance. She could still hear the music but it seemed like an irrelevance now. They heaved Will's unconscious body into the van and pushed Daisy in after him. The door shut, and she was in complete darkness. For Daisy, the feeling of security and well-being of half an hour ago was gone. She felt exposed, naked, abused to the core. Her face was stinging where she had been hit, and her anger flared up, but she knew it was too late now. She had just started to love someone, she realised all too well now . . . she had just started to love him and now the people around her were treating him like an object.

And he was dying. For all she knew he might die here

in the back of this van with her.

In a gesture that even she did not understand, she looked at her watch. Next to her, Will's inert body lay on the metal floor. The van started up and Daisy sensed the fact that everything was going wrong for her again. She put a hand on Will's shoulder and let the tears come. In the pitch darkness, she felt she could weep openly.

The van rumbled down the track they had driven up some hours before. The floor was moulded steel and painful to sit on. She felt for Will's body and moved his head onto her lap. It was a futile gesture but she didn't care.

The journey continued on what must have been a major road. They had stopped bumping around, and it occurred to her that she didn't even know if Will was dead or alive. The men at the front said something to each other and they slowed down. She felt the van turn one corner and stop sharply. There were footsteps and then the van doors opened. Immediately in front of her were some lights. She recognised the familiar style of hospital signs. The two men pulled Will out of the van and left him on a pavement in front of the building.

'Get out.' One of the men was looking at her, huddled in the corner of the van, clutching the bottle. 'I said, get out – now.' He reached in and dragged her out onto the pavement, next to Will.

She sat next to him and watched the van speed away out of sight and then, as her eyes grew accustomed to the strip lights in the building behind her, she became aware that someone was looking at Will.

The triage nurse had heard a vehicle brake hard and by the time he had come out to the admissions area to investigate the van had gone. He could see the girl leaning forward, a body slumped against her. The time was just before 3 a.m. He looked at her and began to guess the scenario. She was drenched with sweat, and her make-up was streaked with tears. She made a pathetic sight in her little blue dress, sitting on the kerb outside the entrance doors.

As he started towards them, he saw her face more clearly, wide-eyed with worry and drugs. She was clutching an empty mineral water bottle as if it were a panacea for all ills. By the time he reached them, he had made his diagnosis.

Seven

At 3.30 a.m. Daisy was sitting in the visitors' room. The questions were coming at her: 'What had he taken?' 'How many of them?' 'Did she have any left that they could analyse?' She felt weak, exposed and frightened. She was still clutching the empty water bottle in one hand.

The hospital had admitted Will, and he was still alive. Basically, he had overheated and now he was suffering the consequences. One of the nurses had given Daisy a cup of coffee; they were trying to be kind to her but she knew that kindness could be feigned – there was nobody who could be trusted. She had had enough. She was tired and people were still asking her questions.

Images from a few hours ago sprang into her mind.

'No, he hasn't had any drugs. At least I don't think he has,' Daisy lied, hugging herself defensively.

'Are you absolutely sure about that?' the nurse sighed. The boy had been admitted dehydrated and suffering from the effects of the cocktail of poison he had swallowed in the hours before. He would probably die in the next couple of days, and this silly girl in front of her was scared, of course, scared for her friend and scared that they would call the police. She should be more scared of what the drugs could do to her if she had taken any of them.

'You are,' the nurse glanced at a clip board in front of her, 'Ms Smith. You don't want to give us your address, but you've said that the patient's name is Will Myers, and you don't know where he lives. Is that right?'

'Yes!' Daisy felt the first signs of panic, and she remembered the morning in the bank when everyone had stared at her.

'Can you tell me,' said the nurse, 'what his full first name is.'

'Will, he's just Will,' she said. 'Look, I'm not making this up!'

'It's okay, I believe you. I see no reason why you should lie. The fact is, though, if you are a friend of Will you must tell us what he might have been on this evening. It will help us to treat him properly. I don't know if you are worried about us getting the police involved, but I can tell you we aren't intending to do that; we just want to do the best for Will.'

Daisy slid down in the chair. The fact that the police would not be involved lifted the pressure off her, but she still couldn't admit anything.

'I don't know what he's been on.' It was a concession. At least this time she was implying that he had taken something.

The nurse looked her over and decided that she nearly had the answers she needed. It was time to step up a gear.

'Let me be honest with you, Ms Smith: I'm not interested in the police arresting you or Will. What's important is the fact that things aren't too good for him at the moment. Do you think because he's alive we can just patch him up and he will be fine in a couple of days? Well it's not like that.'

The nurse leaned forward. 'The fact is Will is very ill. He has been unconscious since he was admitted, and we don't yet know what's happened to him. I think he has taken Ecstasy and his body has become dehydrated, so his salt levels will be very low too. It means that his liver might have been damaged. If the damage is severe he may need a transplant, and that can only happen if we can find a donor. Then there's the possibility that what he took had some kind of impurity in it. Did you know that 'E' might be mixed with anything from glucose to talcum powder? What passes as 'E' can sometimes be no more than fish tank cleaner.' She paused. 'He may simply have been poisoned.'

The nurse waited for it all to sink in. She had used this little speech many times now, always in the most tragic circumstances. 'Of course, I don't know all this for sure, so we will just do what we can. But if we knew what he had taken we could do more for him.'

Daisy sat on the chair and stared at the wall. Had she mentioned Ecstasy to the nurse? She thought back . . . no, it had been a guess, a lucky guess. What was she going to do now? It was no wonder she felt sorry for herself so often, but nobody could pin this present crisis on her. It wasn't her fault, but she was the one who was suffering, who had to handle the situation. A great swell of self-pity began to build up inside her, as if she were constantly the victim of some vast but undefined injustice.

'SO DEAL WITH IT!' a voice seemed to shout at her from the centre of her head, like some part of her personality had just woken up and wanted to make its presence known. Either she was finally cracking up, losing it after a twenty-year struggle or she was finding the courage inside herself to tackle life.

If this had happened even a couple of weeks ago she would have simply run away and left them to pick Will up off the pavement and do what they could for him. So what was she doing – growing up or cracking up? What was driving her now? She hadn't run away, because of what she felt for Will. She loved Will. He had become more than a mate, a friend, even someone she might sleep with. It felt like she had experienced something for the first time. Was he the first person she had ever loved? She turned to face the nurse, her eyes moist with tears. She didn't realise it but this was the first time she had cried for someone other than herself.

In a quiet voice she said, 'He gave me a couple of Ecstasy tablets – I think he called them "Disco Biscuits". I expect he had some himself.'

'Thank you, Daisy.' The nurse got up and walked to the door.

* * *

Actually, Daisy was doing really well under the circumstances, and across the room, unseen by human eyes and just a short distance from Daisy, three spirits raged in frustration, desperate to reach her. Really, it was too late to do anything now – they all knew that. Each had reason to curse the situation, each could see years of work start to unravel. It was not a lost cause, but this had been a deeply frustrating development for them.

Each of them should have been able to influence her at this moment. She was exhausted and frightened – she should have been easy to manipulate, wide open for their suggestions. But again, they had hit a barrier of prayer – someone somewhere was praying for this girl. It was about half-past three in the morning and someone had interceded for her!

Amongst them, the one that encouraged self-pity raged at its lack of power. It had seen her show genuine care for someone else, and for his own sake, not with some ulterior motive. Okay, there was a streak of sexual temptation to it all, but she had previously been taken in, deep in a wallow of self-concern. And now look at her – in tears over this man. She had started to care for someone else, and to be brave on his behalf. All the years of careful delusion were being unravelled by these present circumstances.

She remained out of their reach, shielded from their manipulations by a stronger force, one that they had known since the beginning of their existence.

They did not realise that their impotence was caused by the prayers of the bumbling solicitor who had handed her the cheque. This was the first weekend after she had received her money, an ideal time for mischief. Caleb had gone to bed and made an offer to his Maker; if he needed to pray for Daisy the Lord should call him.

It was a few minutes before 3 a.m., about the time when Will and Daisy were arriving at the hospital when Caleb had woken and left his bed – with some reluctance, it has to be said, for no one is at their best at three in the morning.

In his study he had lowered himself into his chair and sat in silence for a few moments before uttering a single word, 'Daisy.'

He knew this sleeplessness was not a result of his fondness for pickled onions last thing at night, a weakness his wife had not been able to eradicate in forty years of marriage. This was his commitment to God. He stayed in his study for about an hour, praying and interceding for Daisy and then he felt he had done all that he was required to do. Forcing his aching joints into motion, he smiled and muttered into the darkness, 'Try not to keep such unsociable hours in the future, Daisy,' and then he got into his bed and went back to sleep.

* * *

In the casualty ward, Daisy got up and looked at the nurse, who had changed from authority figure to saviour. 'Heal him,' she whispered, then she walked quickly from the room before she had to reveal her grief to anyone else.

She wandered out of the casualty entrance, and then through the hospital car park and out onto a grass verge. She didn't want to stay in the building; the oppressive heat and the scent of disinfectant were beginning to make her feel sick. In the eastern sky, she could see the first suggestion of the new day, a tinge of grey-purple in the sky. She lay back on the grass and closed her eyes. She just had to sleep.

She had expected to dream something vivid and unpleasant but nothing came. When she eventually opened her eyes the sky was lighter and she felt cold, in fact she felt terrible. Her head ached, her mouth was dry, and her body didn't want to move. She blinked a couple of times and tried to look at her watch. Eventually the hands came into focus. It was ten minutes before six in the morning. Something instinctive made her reach into her pocket. Her money was still there. She remembered cashing a cheque, then she remembered where she was, and she remembered Will.

She stood up and forced her weary body back towards the hospital, avoiding the casualty department and heading for the main entrance. Fishing some change from her pocket, she bought a cup of coffee at the machine in the foyer, and then phoned for a taxi.

Even the taxi company were asking her questions! Where did she want to go? She needed to keep her anonymity. She named a railway station some miles away, but close to where she lived. Then, after a few moments and another drink of coffee, she phoned to inquire about Will. The receptionist transferred her to the casualty department and then to the intensive care unit.

'Hello, intensive care.'

'Hi, I'm phoning about Mr Will Myers – he was admitted last night.'

'Oh yes – and you are?'

'I am a friend of his – I heard he had been taken to hospital.'

'Well we normally only discuss the patient's condition with next of kin.'

Daisy could feel the old frustration rise in her. She looked around to see if anyone was watching her, but there was no one.

'I came in with him. I brought him in. He is my friend! Now how is he?' She was surprised at her own boldness.

There was a pause at the other end of the line, then the voice said, 'Who did you say you were?'

'Ms Smith. Daisy Smith.'

'Ah yes, I see your name on the admission sheet. Well I can tell you that Mr Myers is in the intensive care unit and is likely to stay here for at least a couple of days. We are running some tests to establish the seriousness of his condition. At the moment it looks like his liver may have been damaged, but it is too early to know for sure. We are trying to contact his next of kin. Do you have a contact name or address?'

'I'll try and find one for you. Thank you.' She put the phone down. She didn't know if the person at the other end of the line had expected her to give a number or an address now, but they would have to wait.

Daisy found the toilets and washed her face. It was the first time she had been able to see what she looked like, and she was horrified. A mixture of make-up and tears had turned her into something resembling a circus clown, and her hair looked like glue had been tipped over it. She suddenly longed to be back in her room, to have a shower, and sleep. She tried to push her hair into some sort of order. She was reminded of the cubicle after her visit to the bank. She would at least walk out of here with a bit more dignity.

The smell, again, got the better of her and she walked over to the entrance doors. The day was beginning: the tinge in the sky spread and lightened.

A car bearing the name of the cab company pulled up to the entrance doors. Daisy stumbled out into the cool morning and got into the taxi. It was warm and the seat was comfortable. She could feel the sleep closing in on her as she asked the driver to take her to the station. The temptation to drift off to sleep suddenly made her panic – she mustn't fall asleep, it would make her vulnerable again.

She started to reflect on the events of the past few hours and began to identify the other emotions churning inside her. She felt angry. Initially her anger was directed at Will: he had given her drugs and not even asked her if she wanted them; he had put her through all the pain of the last few hours by making himself ill. Most of all, he had found a way to break in to her, to get past her defences. She had received the deepest wound of all because, surely, she was beginning to fall in love with him. In her mind, she could see the folly of her own accusations against him.

'Offering me drugs is one thing, Will, but how dare you break down my defences! How dare you care for me, befriend me, make me care for you, even love you. Then you go and nearly kill yourself with whatever rubbish you took last night!'

Maybe she didn't love him . . . she didn't know.

Then she was angry with God. An exercise that seemed profoundly futile, but the anger was there all the same. And what about God – cousin Alex's God? How dare he let it all happen! Wasn't he God, wasn't he in charge?

But the effort of thinking like this drained her in the end. If there were a God, he would probably point out all the occasions where she had chosen to do certain things. She and Will, like so many, had made the decisions, the choices – they were the problem, not God.

Daisy heard a voice as she came back from sleep: 'That will be £32.60 please love. I expect I could have taken you home for this much. Where have you got to go to?'

She awoke to find that she was outside the station, and she needed to think for a moment to realise why she was there. She smiled weakly at the driver. She gave him £35 and walked into the booking office.

The station was deserted, but there was a train that would take her to within a mile of her house; it was due in about twenty minutes. The emotional drain on her was now almost complete. She could think of nothing more as she waited on the platform. Her eyes scanned the posters dotted along the platform and she was drawn to one almost directly opposite her. It was simply a dark rectangle across which were emblazoned the words: 'Come to me all you who are weary and burdened and I will give you rest. Matt 11:28.'

As if to underline the exhaustion she felt, she was able to read the words three or four times without thinking anything at all. She certainly wasn't able to think of an amusing and dismissive response. Usually she had little time for religion: it had no connection with her life, with the misery that seemed to characterise her existence. But the poster wouldn't go away. She could not be bothered with moving so that it wasn't in front of her. Slowly, an idea formed in her head. It was like a figure walking out of the mist, gradually becoming more distinct. These were reckless times and she, too, could be reckless if need be.

She was facing the possibility of the death of the first person she had ever been close to, and the prospect made her realise that there was one person who really knew about losing loved ones. She thought of her cousin Alex. Her parents had died when she was just a kid. She'd had to deal with that, and still she was a Christian. What kept her going?

The train came into the station, breaking into her thoughts, and she continued her weary journey home.

The steps up to the front door were steep and demanded an extravagant effort, as if the proximity of her bed made her feel all the more tired. When she got upstairs to her room, she fought the urge to just collapse. She had five minutes in the shower, ate some toast, drank some water and then fell into bed.

As her head hit the pillow, she saw something out of the corner of her eye: Will's bag was sitting in the corner of the room. She wrestled with the idea of trying to find a contact address for Will to give to the hospital. Her body didn't want to move again, but something in her said that this needed to be done.

She forced herself out of bed and found his diary. Sure enough, there was his parents' address. She still wanted to keep her anonymity, having worked this hard to preserve it. She would call from a phone box tomorrow, somewhere away from here. She collapsed back into bed.

It was nearly 9 o'clock in the morning and she relaxed at last. As she listened to the noises of a new day, she could faintly hear church bells somewhere. She imagined huddles of people dressed in their drab greys and browns shuffling into church. She always thought the same thing about Christians. What did these people know about life; when had they ever suffered? But again, she thought about her cousin Alex. She must have drawn comfort from God over the years. Her faith must have given her structure to her life. Okay . . . so maybe some of them had been through it. Daisy thought about some of the church buildings she had been inside, then she closed her eyes and whispered into thin air, 'Not for me, thanks'.

If there was a God, she wasn't going to let him in; she wasn't going to be vulnerable to him. He may well exist, but she was not going to kneel before him. As if he had any clue about what she had been through – as if he cared! As she drifted off to sleep the last thing she saw was a picture in her mind of Alex, as a little girl, clutching a teddy bear praying to God. If she had not been so tired, the image would have disturbed her. But she was exhausted, and by the time the bells had finished, she was asleep.

Eight

Daisy slept for about eight hours, resting from the exertion and the drugs. When she woke up, at a little after five in the afternoon, she was thirsty again, but she felt better. She lay in bed trying to piece together the events of the last twenty-four hours. Through the open door of her bedroom she could see the edge of the table with her work scattered over it, and the sketch papers with the bold, sweeping lines drawn across them.

'Will.' She whispered the word under her breath as the events of the previous night flooded back into her mind.

As she lay in bed, a decision formed in her mind. She was going to pay someone a visit, today. She also wanted to see Will at some point, and she needed to let the hospital know what his parents' address was. All these things had to happen before the end of the day, and it was already late afternoon.

She pulled on some clothes and with a deep sense of unease she took Will's bag and wandered up to the college Students' Union. There weren't many people around at that time on a Sunday, and it was easy for her to find an unobserved place to leave it. The feeling of unease turned to guilt, as if it was she who had given him the drugs.

Leaving the bag, she walked back to the foyer where there were a couple of payphones. Again, no one witnessed her speak to the hospital receptionist and give Will's parents' address. Then she walked back to her flat, trying to convince herself that she had done all that could be expected of her. Back in her rooms, she spent the next hour tidying up and packing a small case. There was one more decision to act on – she was not going to be staying here tonight.

* * *

Alex was getting ready to go to church. In many ways, she preferred the Sunday evening services. They were more informal and the reflective worship suited her, particularly at the moment when she had so much on her mind. She wanted to go anyway because she was going to have a chat with the pastors after the service.

Alex's church was pastored by Steve and Elaine Pascoe. They had loved her, not quite as surrogate parents, but more as big brother and sister. Steve and Elaine were both in their forties, with three grown-up children still at home. Elaine was a woman with her own career, working two days a week for a film production company in the West End. She had been with the firm for fifteen years. The fact that Elaine had managed to combine her pastoral work with a secular role in the media world was an encouragement to Alex: Elaine had become something of a role model for her.

At their home after the service, Alex talked over her plans for the café. Elaine Pascoe had been party to many of Alex's ideas. They had talked about the café a long time ago and now the pieces were beginning to fall into place. There was still some work to do, but at least the finance was secure now, and Alex was not short of volunteers to help. They had prayed through the idea themselves, and they knew Alex's heart for young people. Maybe now was God's time for this to happen.

Alex chatted for a while, happy to be in the company of people she liked, but she had to fight down the temptation to talk about John and how she felt about him. He seemed to come into everything she thought about and everything she did at the moment. Her thoughts of him, mysterious and forbidden, stayed locked deep inside her.

It hadn't seemed right to talk about a vision she'd had relating to the shop. Alex wasn't even sure whether it was a vision or just her imagination running riot. She had seen a building that she knew was the café; it was being redecorated and there was a man painting the walls and fixing some of the electrical wiring. In her vision, this man was clearly John. Was this evidence that God wanted the café to happen? And what was the significance in the fact that it was John who was working there? Was she just imagining things?

When she had finished, Steven and Elaine said good-bye to Alex and watched her drive away. As they closed the door, Steven had a rueful smile on his face: 'What do you think?'

'Oh, it's a great idea, and it may well be God, but what I'm worried about is what she is not telling us. There's something else going on, I don't know what it is . . . I don't know . . . maybe I'm wrong.'

Steven smiled and looked at his wife. 'You know you are probably right. You usually are. I would guess it's either man trouble or some unfinished business with her old job.'

Elaine nodded, 'She would have told us if it was something to do with SLaM.'

'Okay, man trouble then, but what kind?'

Elaine thought for a moment. 'For her not to say anything at all, either she's found someone who is not a Christian or she's fallen for someone who is already attached.'

'I would go for the latter,' said Steven. 'She's a good girl, she wouldn't do anything stupid. What do you think?'

Elaine thought for a moment, genuinely uncertain about what was happening here. 'I couldn't see her getting involved with someone who is not a Christian. She isn't a teenager who wants a bit of a fling. So, it's probably a struggle she's having with her feelings for someone else. A married man? Someone in the church? Someone who she gets on with, but who is very attached . . .'

'I think we're getting warmer don't you?' He smiled and shook his head, he could think of a couple of candidates straight away.

Elaine moved over to her husband and put her arms round him.

'I think,' said Steven, 'we had better keep an eye on this for a while.'

* * *

For Alex, the journey home was over in an instant. She was still thinking about the café idea, and she was thinking about John, and the confusion in her heart.

Deep in thought, she didn't notice a figure sitting on the steps to her flat until she had parked and turned off the engine. She studied the figure in the grey light of the evening, but she couldn't tell who it was. There was nobody else around.

As she got out of her car, the figure rose and Alex could see that it was a woman, a young woman. Just twenty yards away she could see that it was her cousin, Daisy. She forgot the café for a moment. What was Daisy doing here?

'Hello Daisy. Are you all right?'

Now she saw the glistening of tears, so Daisy was not all right at all. Something had gone badly wrong, but why would she come to Alex? What did Alex have to offer her?

Alex was about to say 'Hello' again when her cousin launched herself at Alex and hugged her. There was a desperation in her embrace, as if she might find the solution to her problems if she could only cling to her cousin for a while.

Alex felt at once both flattered and apprehensive. Flattered because she knew that Daisy had decided that she, Alex, was worth a request for support, but apprehensive as well because she just didn't know what was coming next. She thought about the places she might have to go to if Daisy was in trouble. There could be trips to the family planning clinic, the police station, the college. She thought about boys she didn't want to meet who might have become involved. The one place she did not think about going to was a hospital.

After about five minutes, they had managed to get into Alex's flat. It was only now that she noticed Daisy's bag and realised that this was going to be a bit more than an evening visit. Alex put the kettle on and watched as Daisy sobbed quietly. She hadn't even been able to utter one word yet. It was as if the grief she was expressing could not be articulated in language.

As Alex emerged with some strong coffee Daisy broke her silence. 'My friend is very ill.'

Alex was silent, waiting for more of the story to unfold.

'I have a friend called Will . . . he is not well . . . he's in hospital. He and I, we are on the design course together. You see he was very kind to me, he has helped me with the work, and he hasn't tried to get me into bed, and he didn't run away when I shouted at him or gave him a hard time.' She paused, 'Am I making sense?'

Alex thought, *'No, not really,'* but this didn't seem to be the right answer, so she tried another approach.

'Why is he in hospital, Daisy? Can you tell me what's wrong with him?'

But Daisy just sobbed, pouring out her hurt through the tears on Alex's shoulder, and then crying into a hastily provided tissue. She had been sitting outside Alex's house for about two hours, but now she was beginning to unwind.

'We went to a party – a rave – last night. He was on some drugs and he got ill. They took him to hospital. I was with him. You need to understand, he has been very kind to me. You know how messed up I am.'

There was an honesty and vulnerability here that Alex found quite disarming. She struggled to think back to a counselling course she had once taken. What do you say to someone in this state?

Daisy went on, 'They said that he was really ill. They said he might have damaged his liver – he might need a transplant. I don't know what's going to happen to him. He has regained consciousness but he is still critical.'

The tears started again.

'Do you want to go to the hospital and visit him?' Alex ventured.

Daisy nodded, and then Alex said something she had not read in the counselling manual: 'Do you love him?'

Daisy was motionless now. She just sat on the couch and stared at Alex, like a lost soul. It was as if Alex had spoken the magic words, and frozen her cousin in time.

Alex leaned forward and whispered: 'Daisy. Daisy . . .'

'I need to talk to you Alex. I'm sorry, I know you think I'm mad, but I just thought of you. You have known the pain of losing someone you love. I think I'm going to lose him and I don't know if I can cope with that. I thought about people I knew who had lost someone, and thought of you. You've had to deal with loss, what with your parents dying. You know what it's like.'

Alex didn't know what to say. Now she was the one feeling fragile. Even after fifteen years, it was still painful. She couldn't pretend that she had figured out that part of her life, not completely. God knew how many hours she had spent thinking about it, turning over the question, *'If he is such a good God, why?'*

She bowed her head. She had never thought of her personal struggle as an achievement. Daisy's interpretation had humbled her.

'Oh, don't be so modest, Alex! Look at yourself, you lost your mum and dad when you were ten, but you got your act together. You didn't tell God where to go! You got your flat and your job and you've got your life in order. What about me, who do you think I can go to? I've got parents who I hardly talk to, and a succession of boys who think they know how to charm their way between my legs. If I go for comfort to them I'll get the wrong sort, if you know what I mean.' She was almost shouting now.

Alex thought briefly about her neighbours, but then she stopped herself. Daisy needed to say all this, and she, Alex, needed to hear it.

'I sat there and I thought, who's been there, who has had to cope with losing someone, who knows what it's like? It was you, Alex. I reckoned you were a sweet little naïve thing, who didn't have a clue about life, but then I thought about what had happened to you when you were just a kid, and your mum and dad were a bloody mess in a car crash and you didn't give up. You got on with it. You've got some strength! I don't know how you've done it, but I could do with some of it.'

She buried her face in another clean tissue. It was all going to come out now! She couldn't stop herself, though even as she said the words they seemed to become a jumble, reflecting the confusion within her own heart. 'I want to know how you have survived. Where does your strength come from?'

'It's complicated Daisy, I don't know the answers.'

'Is it? Well you tell me how complicated it is then. You tell me how things really are.'

Alex felt her own tears coming but, in a way, that helped. When she had first seen Daisy sitting on her front step she had taken a rather patronising attitude, as if it was up to her to dust off her poor little cousin, give her a cup of tea and send her back to college. She realised things weren't going to be like that now. They sat facing each other. This was for real now; this was going to cost.

'Okay, Daisy,' she said, 'I will tell you how it is.'

From the corner of the room Angel watched them both. He had started by watching for any opposition from the enemies within Daisy, but they seemed much weaker now than when he had first encountered them, so he just watched and listened. He knew exactly what Alex was going to say; he just hoped that Daisy would receive it well. This was a critical moment for both of them.

'When Mum and Dad died, I withdrew into myself. It took someone my own age expressing grief over losing a pet to enable me to open up and be able to grieve myself. Auntie Helen and Uncle Max were very good. They gave me the room to mourn my loss, but they were always there letting me know they loved me. And so was old Mr Wicks, bless him.' She smiled at the idea of him, the 'walrus in a suit'. Daisy couldn't help a smile, too.

'I dealt with it, and I grew up. I was surrounded by love and security – enough love to let me feel accepted; enough love even to allow me to rebel.

'Yes, I know you might find that surprising, but I was out in the back garden sneaking a fag when I was fifteen;

I was drinking with my friends when I was sixteen. When we got into the sixth form, during the holidays when I was home I would stay with a mate and we would go out. I suppose there were about four or five of us. We would go to a club in town, and hitch up with some boys for the evening.'

Daisy was smiling, despite her tears. She couldn't quite believe what she was hearing. This was her cousin Alex, little Miss Perfect. What did she know about clubs, and drinking, and fags, and boys?

'Anyway, this went on for a couple of years. Then it was coming up to my eighteenth birthday, and I knew that I needed to make some kind of decision about Jesus and what I believed. I was saying to myself, *"Do you believe it? Make your decision,"* and I realised that I had to face it. I didn't mind going to church with Auntie Helen and Uncle Max: I had some good friends there – people I was very close to – but I don't think I had ever really decided what I believed, and I hadn't made that decision because I needed to sort out in my mind whether a God who let a little child's parents die was worth believing in.

'At that time I was seeing a boy called Neil. We had been together for about six months; I think I did love him. He was gentle and kind, and sometimes when he spoke to me and held me I just wanted all of him. We would sit in my room and listen to music together. And you know how it is: sitting on the bed becomes lying on the bed. He was very good, he didn't try to push anything but we both knew that things were getting serious; the way he was with me I knew something was going to happen.'

Daisy was trying to work out in her mind whether she thought Alex had slept with this boy or not, but she really couldn't decide. Surely, Alex as she was now would never do such a thing, but what about Alex the seventeen-year-old with a boy who turns her on, and not a lot of faith? She knew what the right mood and the right boy did to her body, and she didn't think she was unusual.

The phone rang, but Alex didn't move. The answering machine clicked and she heard John's voice. He left a short message asking Alex to phone him. She half stood when she heard him, but then forced herself to sit back down. Daisy was tempted to ask her who John was, but she wanted to hear about this guy Neil.

Alex carried on: 'So anyway things came to a head,' Alex paused, 'and I asked him to sleep with me.'

Daisy looked at Alex, 'You asked *him*?'

'Yes, it was me who wanted it, but he said no. You see I knew Neil through the church, and he was a Christian. I admired him for it I suppose, but at the time, I would have slept with him without any doubt. At first I thought, *"Oh well, that's that,"* but then I started to think.

'The fact that I had asked him to sleep with me finished off our relationship and we split up, but I couldn't get the incident out of my head. What made him say no? He was male, and a bit of him wanted it as much as any other man. He could have slept with me if he wanted to, but there was something that stopped him. I was nearly eighteen, and I knew other boys who would have been quite happy to have sex with me, but I didn't know whether that was what I wanted. I felt like I was at a crossroads. There was a choice to be made about the way to live life. I suppose one way said yes to God and the other said no.

'It bugged me so much that one evening I went up to the church on my own. I took Uncle Max's keys and let myself into the building. There was nobody else there. I can remember it now: the sun was setting and there was a warmth in the place, a sense of order and peace. I stood at the front of the church and it was strange. I was so used to the church being full of people that to see it empty and quiet was really odd. There was a simple cross at one end. I had known it all my life. I stood right in front of it, as if that might help me get through to God, and I thought: *"Are you a loving God, or are you a sick, evil monster? In fact, do you really exist at all?"* I didn't believe there was no God, it was just to know whether he was the God I had been told about, or someone else – a madman or an irrelevance.

'As I stood there I tried to hear God. At first there was nothing, and I was beginning to think, *"This is a waste of time,"* then I heard a voice say to me, *"Let me in, Alex,"* and I knew no one else was there. I just thought, *"God. God is here, now!"* It was weird. What had been an empty church building suddenly became full. I mean there was nobody there, but somehow the place was full.'

Alex paused. This was the core of her story, the experience of God that changed her in ways that even now she did not understand.

'In my mind I saw a picture of Jesus on the Cross. He was hanging there with the nails in his hands and feet, the blood running from them. Then there was Mary, his mother, and one of his disciples, John. And Jesus said to Mary, "Dear Mother here is your son," and he said to John, "Here is your mother."

'Now I knew this story from John's gospel in the Bible. I had heard it several times, but now I was seeing it like a movie clip. I was shivering – shivering on this warm summer evening. I didn't know why. Then the voice said: *"Alex, I have provided for all your needs. Even as my son gave Mary and John to each other, so I have given you Uncle Max and Auntie Helen. They have looked after you well, but you will always be my child, I love you."'*

Alex felt completely exposed. Daisy could take this personal testimony of hers and accept it or rubbish it, but it was too late to worry about that now, she knew that she had to go on.

'Nobody had ever said to me that I was their child, it was as if a gap in my soul had been filled, as if suddenly I was a complete person, I was who I should be. I can't describe how it felt. I was on my knees and I don't know how I got there. I could see my tears fall onto the carpet.

'Some might say I should still be angry with God, but I realised that I had been angry for eight years, and I didn't want to be angry any more. That day I let my closest barrier down and chose God. I have never let anyone get that close to me before.'

She stopped and looked again at Daisy.

'That's how it is, Daisy. I believed and I let him in – and here I am today. I'm not perfect, and it's not easy, but I have made my decision and I don't regret it.'

There was silence in the room. The tick of the clock was like a reassurance to both of them. A car passed by at the top of the road. Alex looked away, unwilling to face Daisy and her verdict on what she had said.

In fact, Daisy had neither accepted nor rejected what Alex had told her. She was beginning to realise that what she wanted was Alex's assurance, her confidence. For Daisy all the beliefs that went with it were too much – certainly too much at that moment. She was tired, and she was still coming to terms with all that had happened in the last twenty-four hours. She longed for this kind of conviction, but it made her realise how little she really believed.

'I wish I could believe it like you do, Alex, but I just can't. I know I was right to come here though, and I'm glad you told me about yourself.' She paused, like a child asking a favour of an adult. 'Can I stay with you please: for a couple of days – please?'

'Of course you can. We will go and see Will tomorrow, if that's what you want.'

'That would be good, but please, come with me.'

'Okay, if that's what you want.'

They both relaxed and Alex flicked on the TV. There was a comedy show on, and it soon had them both giggling. Alex forgot about John's call.

Angel saw them both and smiled to himself. Alex had demonstrated a depth of courage that spoke well for the challenges that were to come.

Nine

The Lord commands his angels, and they obey. And on a warm, early summer evening, one of them was called – appointed to a specific task. He was sent from heaven, across the expanse to earth. He didn't know about the larger purpose behind his mission, but that did not trouble him as he made the journey, coming to rest in the kitchen of Bridget's flat.

He looked around in the inky darkness, seeing everything. Bridget led an uncompromising life: everything was clean, functional and expensive. The kitchen was full of symmetry and neglect. The serving spoons hung in their place on the wall and the furnishing was harsh and angular, from the square cut of the work surfaces to the steel rods of the kitchen stool. Throughout the flat, the art on the walls was directionless and aggressive, depicting an amoral environment. Compassion and vulnerability had no place in this landscape. The angel ignored the environment and focused on his purpose. Even with human eyes, he would have seen the flicker of the boiler pilot light, safe behind its glass panel. He was permitted a brief interaction with physical reality, and in that moment he reached a finger across the glass, and the flame sputtered and died.

The angel withdrew his finger and looked at the boiler. Where there had been the slim glow of a blue gas flame, there was now darkness. Sensing a fulfilment of his purpose, he moved to the edge of the kitchen and took himself away again.

* * *

Over the weekend, Bridget made plans to go into the office.

These weren't going to be extra hours for SLaM's benefit. She had given the company enough of her weekends. This time she was looking after her own interests.

The day had started badly. The shower produced nothing but a jet of cold water, and further investigation had revealed that the pilot light in her supposedly high-tech and efficient boiler had gone out. She remembered her parents' old boiler: it was hopelessly inefficient but at least you could relight it with a long piece of curled up paper. The one in her apartment would not co-operate, and after ten minutes of poking lighted matches into the thing, she stormed into the lounge and called the gas company. The receptionist promised her that an engineer would be round later, in the afternoon.

Her thoughts turned back to the job she had to do. She had prepared for this trip in advance. On the Friday, she had mentioned to the security people that she would be in at the weekend. Nobody was surprised, as it was not unusual for the head of fashion to put in some hours over the weekend and, as some of her more cynical colleagues pointed out, if you haven't got a life outside the office you tend to spend more time in it.

On Saturday morning she went to the stationery store near her apartment and bought some paper and a box of read/write CDs: all of the hardware at SLaM was CD-R compatible. She had been through this exercise before and she knew the drill. She was going to get her hands on everything she could in Martin's office, glance through it and photocopy anything interesting. That meant accounts, personal correspondence, notes relating to the SEEKA project, and anything marked confidential.

She would be reasonably careful to cover her tracks, but if he suspected something, so be it: let him fret about someone going through his files, let him challenge her if he dare.

The main thing was to find a copy of some market research that Martin had commissioned, looking at young people's attitudes to drugs, music and fashion. She also wanted to get into Martin's PC and copy anything interesting to disk. Then she was going to take it all home, open a bottle of Chianti, listen to *Carmen* and sift through the evidence on her lounge floor.

After signing in at the security desk, she went up to her office. The place was deserted, just a breath of noise coming from the air-conditioning. She knew which security guard was on duty this weekend. He was a punctilious man who liked to do his rounds at hourly intervals. She would need to take that into account.

It occurred to her again that the predictable people got the menial tasks in life; she never regretted her own volatility. Bridget would wait until he had finished his rounds. It would take a while: he had to look round every floor in the building, not just the couple of levels occupied by SLaM. This sort of job had to be done properly. It required patience.

She was going to find all the evidence she needed to show that Martin had based the SEEKA project on the burgeoning drugs culture. He was fond of saying as much to her, but that was not enough: she wanted to see the research. She had to have something tangible, something that would allow her to scare Martin if she needed to: something that would hurt him.

Still, she would wait. Revenge was a measured, disciplined art, and she concentrated on the task she had set herself. Bridget had been in this place before, and she had won in the end.

She did some of her general work while she was waiting. It suited her purposes to have something to show for her hours in the office. The guard came and went, unsurprised by her presence. She made a point of ignoring him even though she was tempted to smile and wave. Ignoring other people in the office was her usual practice and so she had to do it now. When she was sure he had disappeared, she closed her eyes and listened.

Bridget had a gift: an innate ability to sense the motives and intent of another person. She had used the gift many times in the past, for business and pleasure. It had required practise in her early years, but there had been plenty of that. She had quickly learnt to sense the fear in her mother as well as the anger and violence in her father. It would sometimes take hours before he actually got round to shouting at her, or hitting her. As she grew up and went into her early teenage years, she realised that the intentions of a person could be felt: the intentions of a friend, a lover, an enemy.

It was a valuable weapon in life, although Bridget was reconciled to the fact that this 'gift' made it impossible for her to trust anyone. Instead, she simply looked for the ulterior motive, the real agenda behind the way people were. She had long since come to terms with it – and anyway, there were so few people that you could actually trust that it was a small price to pay.

With her eyes shut, she explored the space around her. In the immediate area there was nothing, she was alone in the office and free to do what she liked. The security guard would not be around again for another hour, and she could discover a lot of secrets in that time.

She was about to open her eyes and make a start when something stabbed at her mind. At the edge of her perception she could feel the scent of an enemy. It was subtle, but real. The sensation was different to any she had felt before. Was it her nerves? She had been a bit jittery in the last few days, with the SEEKA project and worrying about Martin. If there was something, or someone, it wasn't nearby, the office was deserted – she could see that.

She sat motionless, like an animal sensing its predator. What was it?

Eventually, her desire to get on with the task won her over. She unlocked one of the drawers in her desk and took from it a sheet of paper. On the sheet was a list of the cabinets in Martin's room. She took the paper, went into his office, and opened the first cabinet. She knew, from a previous visit, that Martin was not disciplined about locking cabinets. She opened the first drawer and lifted the files from it, taking them to one of the meeting rooms.

With an efficiency born of experience, she sifted through the files and selected a few papers for photo-copying. On her own sheet, Bridget noted the number on the photocopier counter and placed some of her paper into the tray. She photocopied the sheets she wanted and replaced them where they had been in each file, then she returned all the files to Martin's office. The whole opera-tion took about seven minutes.

Happy with the process, she repeated it five times and then returned to her desk with about fifty sheets of paper. The security guard passed by and waved. She waved back and then cursed, remembering that she had decided not to acknowledge him. She thought about the man for a moment. This was Albert, harmless and forty-something. He worked weekends simply to pay the mortgage. She really believed that he would rather be with his wife and kids, pictured in the little framed pho-tograph on his desk, than working here. For a moment, Bridget was suddenly aware of the fact that there were millions of people in the world who lived like this. They got on with their work, were faithful to their partners, and loved their children. Perhaps Albert was, after all, a better man than the powerful people she had slept with. Surely he did not have to play politics every time he got between the sheets.

She had to dismiss such thoughts – they were a distraction. Sighing to herself, she carried on sifting through the papers in front of her.

She was just into her third set of papers when she found the gem she was looking for. There were two slim files, not even hidden or locked away. One held the results from the market research, the other was Martin's own work. The research dealt with youth culture, exploring the attitudes of young people to fashion, sex, drugs, work, and so on, trying to link all these things into a cultural framework. The other file contained the sales and marketing plan of the SEEKA project. The first section explained how the SEEKA ethos of trying anything to find the truth could be linked to this culture, and how SEEKA merchandise and drugs could fit together, with one encouraging the sales of the other.

She knew now that she had enough to achieve her purposes – there was no need to spend any more time on this exercise. In fact, Martin had referred to this research when they were alone together, in one of his unguarded moments. She had discovered in these times that if anything betrayed him, if he had a weakness at all, it was his pride.

She could picture him even now, the intensity in his eyes, the slightly gaunt face, like a man driven by an idea that everyone around him opposed.

'Nothing is left to chance with this project, Bridget, the research shows who our target market is – fifteen to twenty-three-year-olds. I know what they want to wear, what they

want to listen to, what they want to smoke, what colours are in, what sounds are out. The SEEKA concept will fit like a glove with them . . . thousands of them buying our merchandise, because the image is right.'

She had admired him then: his brash confidence, his arrogance. In a way her admiration had not gone, it had just changed. Now it was more like the evaluation of the capabilities of an enemy.

After another circuit by Albert, she was ready for the most difficult part of the morning's work. She wanted to look around on Martin's PC. Surely there would be more secrets hidden there, more ammunition for her campaign.

Getting in to Martin's computer was easy: IT security was something that passed Martin by. In the event that she found nothing in any of the directories that added to what she already had, the discs remained in her bag. She was about to close the machine down again when she thought about the more 'interesting' places to look for files on a PC. There would be some temporary files on Martin's computer and she really needed to look at them.

As she scanned the files, boredom set in and she started to think about the little wine bar by the river where she would go for her lunch. Her thoughts turned to food and wine, her attention blunted by reading row upon row of meaningless letters.

Because of this, she almost missed it. Buried in the text, she saw her own name.

It seemed to be the remains of something that Martin had written, addressed to her. Apparently he had been writing it and had had to turn his PC off in a hurry. The abandoned note had remained unfinished – she had certainly not seen it – but the draft was still on the PC. The pressure inside her head intensified as she read the words:

Bridget
I am not sure I will even give you this note, but if you do get
it, treat it seriously, and then destroy it – properly. If knowl-
edge of its existence is discovered then I will be dead. So I ask
you first of all to get rid of this, the only copy that will ever be
made, for your sake and mine.

   This is not about our relationship – this is about your life.
You must understand that some people are not motivated by
money or status. I belong to a group who have an interest in
seeing the SEEKA project succeed, as I do. They will let no one
stand in the way of the success of SEEKA but they have decid-
ed that someone within SLaM poses a threat to the project.
That someone is you. Because of this they . . .

It stopped there.

What the hell was this? What was he playing at? Her
anger was rising like the noise of thunder in her brain.

Her first reaction was to grab her mobile and punch
out Martin's home number. She wanted to hear an
explanation, right now. But then she remembered the
security man. She didn't want to start screaming
down the phone at Martin in front of anyone. He
could wait, and anyway, she was calming down now.
She had to think about this; she had to be smart, not
just angry.

Reaching into her handbag, she took out the CD, and
inserted it into the PC. The copying took only a moment.
She retrieved the disk, switched off the PC, and left
Martin's room exactly as she had found it, polishing the
surfaces she had touched. There would be no leisurely
drink at the wine bar now; she needed to get things done
quickly. She packed her papers into a case and headed
for the car park. Before she reached her car, the sting of
apprehension caught her senses again. Someone out
there was after her – she knew it.

As she made her way home her head was full of questions. At first she wanted to go straight round to Martin's house, and it was only with a considerable exercise of her will that she turned the car in the direction of her own flat. She could phone him from there and besides, she needed to stick to the task at hand. Bridget's head buzzed with questions as she pulled into the apartment car park. What was Martin playing at? Was this his idea of a joke? What was this crazy Group he belonged to? As she thought about the contents of the note, she got more agitated. Nobody was going to treat her like this. She was angry now, very angry.

Near the entrance to the complex she could see a gas company van. Remembering the state of her boiler she marched up to the driver's window and rapped on it. The engineer jolted from his newspaper and wound the window down.

Bridget stared down at the man. 'Have you come to mend my boiler?'

'Yes madam, you must be Ms Larson.'

'I am, please come with me.'

Bridget turned and walked briskly to the door. In her haste she nearly tripped over a bucket of soapy water perched on the steps at the front of the apartments.

'Can you move that please!' she shouted at the window cleaner who hastily removed the bucket. The gas engineer followed her in.

When she got in, she vented her aggression on the front door, swinging it shut with all her strength, so that the door virtually exploded on its hinges, the echo travelling through the whole building. The engineer busied himself with the boiler.

Bridget left him to it, pulled out the CD, and loaded the file on to her own PC. The words still held a deadly potential as she stared at the screen trying to work out what Martin would have written. Was this one of his practical jokes? What was this Group? What hold did they have on Martin? What were they intending to do to her?

Having read the note again, Bridget went over to the phone and dialled Martin's number. She got his answering machine and left a curt message asking him to call her whatever time he got in – urgently.

The anger she had felt was beginning to be overtaken by fear. What if this Group were real; what if they were watching her now? She went to the window and looked down in the road. There was nothing suspicious, the stationary cars were empty, nobody was looking at her. She could see the wavy blond hair of the window cleaner as he stared up at the windows he had just worked on: he certainly held more promise than the gas engineer. She might consider offering to entertain him in her bed if he visited regularly.

Then a sense of fear crept over her. What if he was from this Group, sent to spy on her? And what about the engineer – he was actually in the flat – what if he was one of them too?

This descent into paranoia was stupid, and she forced herself to stop. She had spent years conquering different fears that wanted to overwhelm her, and she wasn't going to give in to this one. Cursing the unease within herself, she flicked on the stereo. *Carmen* started to fill the flat while she sorted the papers into bundles. The effect of the music was rather spoilt by the repeated click of the boiler as the engineer tried to relight it.

To each bundle, she attached a note explaining what the papers said. The evidence pointed to a conspiracy within SLaM: an attempt to encourage the drugs culture, and sell related SEEKA products on the back of it. She didn't know if it would stand up in court, but the industry journals would love it. Packing all the files together, she attached a covering note to her solicitors.

Bridget took her time and set out some very clear instructions about the bundles in the envelope. After a lot of thought, she decided not to include the note from Martin. It didn't add to the case and she wanted to confront him personally about it.

She placed the bundles in a large envelope and addressed it with clear black capital letters, as if such clarity would protect the package from the wrong hands. Bridget went through to the kitchen to inspect the gas engineer's work, just as he was tidying up his tools. He had long since given up the idea of being offered a cup of tea; he just wanted to get his job done and leave.

'Have you fixed it?'

'Yes madam, it will be fine now. Good afternoon.' The man let himself out the door, and called the lift. In fact, he had not been able to detect any fault – it was quite odd really, as if the pilot had gone out on its own. He hoped that now it was relit it would stay on, as he didn't want to come back here again.

Back in the apartment, Bridget gathered all the remaining papers together and placed them in her safe. She took her keys, picked up the envelope and left the apartment. Her anger was beginning to subside now. Perhaps it was because she could feel her task for the day coming to a conclusion. At the front door to the flats, she checked the contents of the envelope once more.

Everything was in order: each little bundle was there with its attached note, and the covering letter. Her instructions were explicit and, of course, she had included a cheque to cover an initial payment for Mr Shand's trouble.

She was suddenly distracted by a noise outside the door. Already on edge, she looked up sharply. The gas man had tripped over the bucket of soapy water left by the window cleaner and the two of them were now having an argument. She didn't have the time or the inclination to watch. She was about to make an extravagant journey, but one she considered necessary under the circumstances.

She drove all the way into the centre of London, to the post office near Trafalgar Square – the only one that she knew for sure would be open. Parking illegally outside the post office, she took her package in and sent it by registered post to her solicitor.

On the way back home she took a lengthy detour and visited Martin's house. He was not in. She reasoned that she would catch up with him soon enough, and then there would be hell to pay. She even considered raising the whole thing with Lewis. The prospect of seeing Martin wriggle under Lewis's gaze made her smile. Martin was too smug by half – it would serve him right. And she wasn't going to run off either, just because Martin might belong to some nutcase group who wanted to throw their weight around.

This evening she would put on her best dress, slap on the make-up and go out hunting. She knew some places where she could be sure of having a good time, and she felt the need for one after the last few days. She checked her watch – it was 4.30.

* * *

Back at the apartment, she turned on the radio, stripped off her clothing and stepped into the shower. She usually spent about four minutes in the shower, but this afternoon she indulged herself a little and stayed in for eight. It made up for the morning's fiasco and she had time on her hands now that the job was done.

While she was in the shower the front door latch turned and the door eased open. Bridget heard nothing as the door moved inch by inch until it stood half-open. She finished her shower and stepped out. Then, as she began to dry herself, the instinct that had kept her going for so long, screamed in the middle of her brain. She froze where she was, looking, listening, sensing hostile intent. Reaching to a glass shelf in the bathroom she picked up a pair of nail scissors. Her bare feet made no sound as she left the bathroom and looked out into the living room. She immediately noticed the open door. Had it been her sixth sense? Or maybe she had just felt a slight draft. She couldn't be absolutely sure that she had closed the front door.

But her instinct, her sense of self-preservation told her something else. There was someone in her flat.

She eased her way slowly across the room and into the kitchen where she took one of the seldom-used carving knives from the wall rack. Bridget had had intruders before and her approach was always the same – confrontation. She slowly walked towards the front door. In the background, the radio was playing *Sea Symphony* by Vaughan Williams. The music seemed rather incongruous to her as she made her way across her hall carpet quite naked, knife in hand. She considered her lack of clothing to be a positive advantage in a situation like this. It wasn't the first time she had confronted an intruder naked, and yet it seemed to Bridget that there was a finality about what was happening here: this was not a political calculation, this was life or death.

To the right of her front door there was an alcove. It could probably conceal someone, and might do so now. She was walking very slowly, noiseless bare feet on the carpet. Her senses told her that there was someone there, someone with a killer's intent. She had already decided her strategy: she was going to leap at the alcove with the knife in front of her. Either her assailant would take six inches of kitchen knife, or she had deceived herself and she was going to slash one of her own coats. For some reason that she didn't understand, the package she had sent came to mind, and she felt a peculiar sense of triumph. After one more step, she was close enough. Life was full of challenges. She told herself that this was just the next one.

In the last seconds of her life, Bridget knew that her instinct had been real after all – someone was waiting in the alcove by the door. She lunged forward with the knife before her sight could confirm that anyone was there. It was her final act, a suitably dramatic end to a dramatic life. As two silenced bullets ripped into her chest, the window cleaner appeared before her. She saw the horror and pain in his eyes as her knife slashed across his face, drawing blood. The parallel with her own father was so compelling that it occupied the last seconds of her mind before the mist closed over her and she was gone.

Ten

The week started with the promise of glorious sunshine. There was already heat in the air as Alex got into the car. Daisy was collecting something from the flat, and Alex was alone for a moment.

She started to think about Daisy, her unexpected guest. It must have been God's will that she had turned up and Alex had been presented with an opportunity to talk about the deep things that drove her and made her a Christian. Had she expected Daisy to fall on her knees there and then and accept Jesus as her saviour? – no, of course not, and good for her. At least Daisy knew what that commitment would mean, so she wasn't going to make it lightly.

Then there was the café. The more Alex thought about the café, the more she wanted to go ahead with the project. She knew it was right and she was going to do it. She knew as well that it was a step closer to another vision she had carried for a long time now: something far bigger than just opening a café, although this could well be a part of it. Very few people knew about the things that really drove her; the vision that God had placed in her soul. Alex had a passion for young people. It was why she was involved in the youth club, it was why she wanted to start the café, and it was even why she had originally joined SLaM. Now, though, she wanted much more; now she wanted to influence their culture. She carried the desire to fulfil her task deep in her heart. She wanted to see revival, especially among the young people, and she felt it was her destiny to help create a culture that would encourage and nurture that revival.

To Alex it seemed that her vision was needed now more than ever. The pressure to conform was as overwhelming: the expectation amongst young people that you need to drink and smoke and sleep with someone. Then there was the prevalence of drugs: the culture of irresponsibility disguised as freedom. She thought about the way the media sensationalised stories about children hurting each other or being hurt themselves. Then, closer to home, there were the companies whose marketing policies fuelled the desire for more. For some, life was a continuum of boredom and despair, punctuated by an assortment of pleasures, none of which gave any lasting satisfaction.

Just thinking about these things stirred something in her. It was her vision, her destiny, and she was going to do whatever she could to work it out. Christians needed to be obvious in every part of the cultural landscape: music, film, TV, radio, art, literature, magazines and fashion. This was the heart of her vision – to build a Christ-centred culture, one that would contain elements of such quality that it would command a place in the minds of millions of young people across the country. This was not so much a retreat from the mainstream culture as a contribution to it. It was the antithesis of the SEEKA project.

Maybe the little café was the starting point, perhaps the first of many places where this alternative culture could be nurtured. She recalled a prayer meeting she had attended a couple of years ago, where someone had spoken some words over her. She remembered them now: *'God is calling you to be a history maker, Alex, a danger to the enemy and a light to millions. He has so much for you. Be hungry for it all.'*

And she was. Under the surface, she had an agenda burning in her soul. She would pursue it with all the strength and will that she possessed, to the very end.

* * *

Daisy had to tap on the window about half a dozen times to bring Alex back to reality.

'Alex! Hello, let me in, the door's locked.'

'Oh sorry Daisy, I was miles away.'

'On another planet by the look of it. Anyway, some guy called Lewis left a message on your answering machine as I was leaving. He said could you call him as soon as possible.'

Alex frowned. What was Lewis doing now – was this another job offer?

'I'm not doing anything about it now, Daisy. We need to go.'

Daisy's mind turned to this hospital visit. After all the effort she had gone to to conceal her identity, a visit to see Will was a huge risk. But where caution had been important to her that night, now it seemed to mean nothing. The silence in the car allowed each of them space for their own separate thoughts.

Alex had put her dreams aside for the moment. There was still life to live and problems to deal with. Principally, there was John. What was she going to do about her feelings for him? Could she ride it out? Would things die down and be as they were a few months ago? Could her involvement with him jeopardise her vision?

She thought about Laura. It would be such a betrayal if John and Alex ever succumbed. She was reminded of something the minister had said a few weeks ago about how Jesus, even though he was perfect, had known what it was to be tempted. He had spent forty days in the desert before he faced the enemy. Then she remembered that John had called her. She had not returned the call and a sudden desire to talk to him swept over her.

As they approached the hospital, Daisy was losing some of her previous optimism. What state would Will be in? Alex pulled into the car park and, switching off the engine, she turned to her cousin.

'Listen, I will do what I can, but you need to be strong now.'

Daisy nodded and said nothing. They walked into the A and E reception, and Daisy remembered the last time she had been here, just over twenty-four hours ago. She was glad that she looked very different now, in her jeans and sunflower T-shirt, with her hair tied back. At reception, Daisy gave her own name and said that she was a friend of Will. She had heard that he was unwell and had come to visit him. The receptionist disappeared for a moment and then returned with one of the duty doctors.

'Miss Masters?' Both Alex and Daisy looked at him.

'Miss Daisy Masters?'

'Yes,' said Daisy.

'Would you come with me please.'

Daisy looked at Alex, who motioned for her to follow the doctor into one of the visitors' rooms.

'Miss Masters, I am afraid I have some bad news for you. Will died early this morning, in his sleep. I am sorry.'

There was silence, and just the smell of the disinfectant filled the room. When she heard the words, Daisy felt as if she was falling in on herself, as if she had retreated into the centre of her being. She had done this before; when it was very bad she would stay locked within herself for hours, dislocated from reality.

'Why?' She could feel the moisture forming in her eyes.

'Well, as you know, Will was very ill, his liver had been damaged, and although he regained consciousness for a while he was still very unwell. During the night there were complications and I'm afraid we lost him. It may have been an allergic reaction, but we'll know more after the autopsy.'

A little voice in her mind said, *I knew this was going to happen.* It seemed to Daisy that whenever she tried to get her life together something hit her. She had just started to explore the idea that she might love someone and be loved in return, when this occurred.

The spirits that followed her around saw their chance again, but they had only a shadow of the power that they had previously enjoyed. In desperation they whispered into her soul:

'It's time for you to think about yourself, Daisy, to look after yourself. It's all very well spending time with Alex but how can she know how much pity you deserve?'

They were interrupted – this time not by prayer but by the doctor:

'Miss Masters, I need to give you this.' He handed her an envelope with her name on the front.

'During the time he was conscious Will dictated a note which he asked us to give you if he didn't make it. I am sorry Miss Masters . . .' There was a pause.

Daisy clutched the note and then got up to leave. The Doctor touched her arm as she stood.

'There is one more thing I'm afraid. Will's death has meant that the police are going to be involved now. They may want to interview his friends. You should call the police station before they call you. I have the number here.' He gave her a slip of paper.

'Thank you, I will.' The temptation to give in to fear and panic was almost too strong. What would she say to the police? She thought about Mr Wicks. Perhaps he would be able to help her. Could she tell him what had happened, or would he sit in judgement over her?

Daisy went out into the reception area, where Alex was waiting. One of the nurses had already told Alex the news. Daisy clutched the envelope that the doctor had given her – she wanted to go back to Alex's flat and read it there. They walked in silence to the car park. Daisy stopped and looked down at the pavement. Will had lain there on Saturday night, dying in front of her.

'He's dead, Alex.' Alex turned back to her cousin. Daisy stood there in the same place and held up the envelope. 'He wrote me a note before he died.' The thought of the note was the trigger for the grief, and Daisy felt the strength go from her knees. Alex caught her in her arms, supporting her for a few moments before she recovered herself.

'I loved him, Alex . . . Jesus, I loved him . . . and now . . .' She clung to Alex as if she were a point of refuge in the turbulence of her heart. Alex nodded, not speaking a word. They walked back to the car and drove home.

* * *

Daisy took herself out that afternoon for a long walk. Before she left, she told Alex that she needed to talk to Mr Wicks that afternoon about going to the police.

Once Daisy had gone, Alex listened to the messages on her answering machine. First there was the message from John, then there was a message from Lewis. He sounded pretty stressed out, and she wondered what crisis had forced him into phoning her. Then there was a third message from her brother, Conner. They had been together on Saturday when she had gone over to see them all. Conner wanted to come and visit her. It seemed that her flat, her private space, was going to be very crowded for a while.

Conner was a musician – a good one for his age. He had always loved music, and computers. His room at home had gradually filled over the years with guitars, electrical equipment, sound systems, midi systems, until it was a real mess. Currently he was in a band, although she couldn't remember what they were called. As far as she knew, Daisy and Conner had not seen each other for a long time, probably since her own eighteenth birthday party seven years ago. In other circumstances she would have expected a certain amount of 'chemistry' to fire up between the two of them, but with Daisy in the state she was in now, she didn't know what would happen. She phoned him back and left a message: she would expect him on Saturday morning.

Next, a call to Lewis at SLaM. When his secretary heard who was on the phone she was transferred to him straight away.

'Lewis, it's Alex. You called me.'

Lewis's voice sounded like a bag of gravel. 'Alex, thanks for phoning. Look, I'm afraid we've had a bit of bad news. Someone broke into Bridget's flat at the weekend and she was shot.' He wished he could think of a better way of describing what had happened, but the words wouldn't come. 'I'm afraid she is dead.'

Alex was stunned. 'Oh no, that's awful!'

Lewis continued, 'It is awful, Alex. The whole place is in chaos: we've even had the police in. I have had to give an account of my whereabouts on Saturday, and so have Dave and Martin. Some of us have had to give a blood sample.' He paused . . . there was worse to come. 'The thing is, Alex, the police want to interview anyone who's been connected with the firm in the last few months, so they want to talk to you. I expect they'll be calling you before too long, but you might want to talk to them first. I've got a number you can contact them on.' He read out a phone number and Alex scribbled it down.

'Look, I'm sorry about this Alex. I know you wanted to make a clean break of it from here, but I'm sure if you have a good alibi for Saturday they won't bother you again.'

She looked at the slip of paper with the number on it. There was an instinct within her, and it said that Martin Massey had something to do with Bridget's death. She would never be able to prove it, and she didn't really want to know any more about it. She hoped that Daisy wouldn't have to find out about this; she didn't need another complication in her life at the moment. Hopefully, it might only require a call to the police station to settle the whole thing.

From his usual corner in the room, Angel watched Alex. He knew that her involvement in the murder enquiry would be peripheral. Although Alex would be in a state of shock, it was the call to Conner and the one she was about to make to John that would matter more. Angel had not discounted Bridget's murder as insignificant. It was, at the very least, a gross act of evil, like all murders, but since the motivation for it was linked to his enemy, he had sensed the event like a ripple across his own dimension. Within the context of his own mission, things were actually going quite well: Alex was beginning to see pieces of her vision fall into place, and that was as it should be. The café was indeed the start of a whole strategy; an early move in the game. What Alex didn't yet realise was that Daisy's presence was not a complication, it was a necessity. The Lord made his plans well; there was a reason why things happened as they did. There was a reason why Daisy was here now, and there was a reason why Conner would be here next weekend. He watched as she phoned John's number at work. If there was a complication in Alex's life at the moment, surely this was it.

'Hello, can I speak to John Stamford please.' There was no mistaking the slight breathlessness in Alex, the release of adrenaline.

'Hello?' she heard John's voice and was pleased that he was available.

'John, it's Alex. I got your message.'

'Oh yes. I spoke to Steven and Elaine at the weekend and they would like you to write a summary report on the state of things in our youth work, and put in some ideas on where we should go next. I expect they want to hear more about your plans for the café, but it's also about the other things we are doing. They want you to work with Laura on it.'

'Oh . . . well, I'll give Laura a call.'

'Great, I think she's at home today. Is that okay?'

'That's fine.'

'Right, well I'll see you Sunday.'

That was the end of the conversation. She put the phone down, frustrated by her desire for a more intimate exchange with him. Why was she feeling like this? Torn in different directions by passion and reason, desire and holiness. She thought of Jesus' temptation in the desert: even after forty days of fasting he refused to turn the stones into bread. She knew that if she really was going to be a follower of Jesus she must resist the temptation to slip into an affair with John. But could she do that? Was she really in danger of doing such a thing?

She breathed out a sigh, and picked up the phone again. Someone on the enquiry team for Bridget's murder took the call and booked an interview for her. It seemed that they would want a blood sample from her as well. At least she had an alibi: she had spent Saturday with Max, Helen and Conner.

She had just finished the call when she heard Daisy come back into the flat.

'Alex, I need to get this over with, I need to talk to old Mr Wicks.'

Alex looked up at her; 'Let's do it now,' she said. It seemed to be one of those days when things got done. 'By the way, if you are around next weekend you'll get to meet Conner again.'

'Yeah, sure.' It meant nothing to her now, but Conner's arrival was destined to make an impact in its own time.

Daisy was preoccupied with the note that Will had written her. She passed it to Alex without a word.

> Daisy,
> Don't be afraid just because I've gone. Be who you are, be everything you were meant to be. I love you very much.
> Will

Neither of them spoke for a moment, and then Daisy looked at the mantelpiece. There was the picture of Alex's parents, and alongside it a picture of Uncle Max and Auntie Helen and a young man standing with them.

'That's Conner, isn't it?'

'Yes, that picture is about a year old now. It was taken when he was baptised.'

'So here was another Christian,' thought Daisy. There seemed to be quite a number of them around at the moment. She looked again at the picture of Conner, with his blue eyes and curly hair. There was something cheeky about his smile – he reminded her of Will.

'Do you want to call your parents or anything, Daisy?'

'No. I have nothing to say to them. I want to phone Mr Wicks and get myself some legal advice. There's something I haven't told you, Alex. Will and I both did some drugs on Saturday night; that's what helped to kill him.'

Eleven

In the week following Bridget's murder, Darius Lench found himself going over the details of the kill, again and again. It had been handled very badly. He was surprised that the assassin had made such a mess of it. Of course, the woman was now dead, so at least in that sense the operation had been a success, but there had been complications. Some of these were obvious and some were more subtle.

In the midst of his thoughts, Lench noticed how warm the room had become. There was a moistness across his forehead and on the palms of his hands. Confirmation – as if he needed it – that this issue was starting to hurt him.

He looked out from the window of his office. Below, a jumble of architecture spanned out in all directions. The cars and people on the roads below seemed like toys, and he imagined himself reaching down and picking them from the road, placing them wherever he wanted, having power over them.

Power. It was the thing he hungered for most. Other men craved sexual satisfaction, or money, and there was nothing wrong with these things, but within Lench there was a passion for power, a lust for control over as many people and things as possible. It was why he got so angry, so agitated when things did not go to plan; when he saw himself losing his grip on the situations around him. Lench was not a man who liked loose ends and there were plenty of them now.

Not only had the job gone wrong, but he had subsequently learnt that the woman had spent the morning in the office. He only hoped she had been doing her own harmless work. But maybe she had been up to something else, because soon after she had returned home, she had gone out again, clutching a large envelope. On top of all this, there was the fact that the assassin had dripped blood all over the place as he left. The issues churned around in his mind as he thought back to the planning stage of this particular killing.

The preparation had been thorough. The hair dye and the window cleaner disguise allowing his assassin plenty of time to inspect the building and watch the target. Lench had even taken the time to see her for himself. He understood why Martin had engaged with her, she was an impressive looking woman.

Across the room from him sat the assassin, his head now shaved. A clock ticked out the passage of time as they sat in silence. The assassin was looking down at his shoes, waiting for judgement to be passed. A fresh scar snaked across his face, stretching over his nose. The two men had been in this room for the last hour, going over the details of what had happened, trying to assess the implications.

The assassin knew that this was the first time he had not completed a job properly. The wound still gave him considerable discomfort, but what was worse was the way that it would always mark him out; he knew that the anonymity that was so vital to his trade had been compromised. As he mulled over his situation Lench's voice grabbed his attention again.

'They will have analysed your blood. They will know you if you are this stupid again. This has been badly done; I do not wish to see you for a while. You will need to go to the safe house for at least a month. Expect few comforts.'

He knew better than to respond or defend himself; excuses would only compound his leader's displeasure. Anyway, the interview seemed to be over, so he stood up, bowed to Lench and left the room. He had known this was the most likely outcome. A trip to the safe house. It was probably for the best, to be out of circulation for a while.

Lench was now alone in the room. It seemed to him that the only person left to judge and punish now was himself. He stood up and walked over to the mirror. His suit and hair were immaculate as usual, but he could feel the tension; the corner of his left eye twitched erratically and his hands sweated; he felt as if he were going to explode.

What made the situation worse was the fact that he could still feel the threat to their efforts. That was the most galling aspect of the whole episode – he was still not in control. He knew there was still someone out there who could destroy everything. It had not been this woman Bridget after all. Or if it had, there was now another.

Then, of course, there was Martin Massey. After he learned that the job had been botched he had called Martin on the mobile. He knew immediately that the threat was still there, still hanging over them. So who was it? It was only then that Martin mentioned this other woman who had now resigned from the company. Martin thought she was out of the picture, but as it turned out, she had been party to many of the discussions that had taken place. Martin had even neglected to tell him that she was a Christian, a gross piece of negligence on his part. It only confirmed Lench's suspicions that Martin was a fool, a pawn in the game. Massey had given him some scant information about where she might live, and it hadn't taken him very long to track her down.

The whole thing had almost stopped him from affording Martin his gift, but there was nothing to be gained from a harsh approach now. Lench knew that he would also have to take some of the blame himself.

Finally, he thought about the woman Alex Masters. Who was she? Did she really present a threat? Could she thwart his plans? She was probably an irrelevance, but if she belonged to the enemy, if she belonged to Jesus, that had implications and Martin wouldn't have had a clue as to what they were. He sensed the desire within himself to see this woman, to examine her for himself. He always had to take a look at his enemies.

Of course, he also knew that to confront her directly would be very rash, but sometimes desire overcame will, even for him. He could perhaps take a look at her flat. It might help him to decide on his next move. Even that was likely to be a waste of time, a diversion from the correct strategy. Perhaps the best course of action was to avoid her altogether.

He tried to return to his other work, but his mind would not focus on the papers in front of him. As the clock chimed the hour he finally gave in and decided to visit the place where this woman lived. Something within Lench pulled at him, telling him to stop, but the pressure of frustration needed to be released somehow.

He walked briskly down to the car park and settled into his Mercedes. For Lench, the expression and control of power was everything and just sitting in his recently acquired SLK 320 was the purest form of that sensation. It was such a beautiful car. Whenever he sat in it, he could feel himself regain control of his life, refocus on the things that motivated him. He sat there for perhaps two minutes trying to calm himself. Many times in the past when he had felt anger rise in him, he had just come to this car and sat until he regained his composure. Today, however, the urge to madness was too strong. He needed to see this woman. Starting the engine, he drove slowly out of the car park and glided up to the main road.

* * *

Alex and Daisy were getting ready to go out. Alex had already been to the police station to talk to someone about Bridget's murder. They hadn't even taken a blood sample from her. There had been some discussion of her alibi, which had been checked out. They had told her that she might be wanted for questioning at some future date. Mr Wicks had sat at her side and afterwards he told her that he didn't think she would hear about it again.

Things were not so clear-cut for Daisy with her involvement in Will's death. The two of them were off to another police station, via Mr Wicks's office. They were both feeling the pressure of what was to come.

In the last couple of days, Caleb Wicks had sat down with Daisy and gone through her story from start to finish, picking apart every single detail until Daisy had felt like screaming. Twice she had stormed out of his office and stood in the street sucking hard on a cigarette. Both times her return had prompted Miss Goldsworth to make some more tea, which Daisy had accepted on this occasion, and they had started the procedure again. On each return, she had taken a deep breath and strolled back into Caleb's office. He had looked up from a pile of notes and asked, 'Are you ready to continue now, my dear?' His approach to it all was beginning to get on her nerves, but at least she had her story straight. And it was better to do that with old Mr Wicks than a couple of hostile policemen in a cell. Now, though, the time had come for her to face the police to find out what they wanted from her.

Alex and Daisy took the lift down to the ground floor and walked out towards the car. Daisy had an eye for smart motors and immediately noticed the sleek Mercedes parked across from Alex's flat. The windows were tinted to make the interior of the car invisible and the driver's window had been lowered just a couple of inches.

Lench recognised Alex immediately, and not just by sight. There was a spiritual presence about her. She belonged to the enemy, he could see it in her. He cursed Martin again for the naïve fool that he was.

As he opened the door of the car a pressure in the back of his head told him to stop. This was truly a reckless action for someone in his position, but he could not resist now: nothing was going to stand in his way, especially this Jesus woman.

Daisy saw Lench walking towards them. She looked at him, and then at the car, and then at him again. He was a bit old and looked slightly 'weird', but she liked the Mercedes, it said that this guy was someone important. Daisy also noticed his shirt and suit – definitely handmade, there was something about the collar and cuffs that gave it away. She didn't like his face though, or was it his eyes? Something creepy about him, Daisy concluded.

Daisy's reaction was mild compared to Alex's. As Lench approached, she stopped and felt the blood start to pump around her. Her face had turned pale; she was paralyzed by the arrival of this man. She first noticed Lench when he got out of his car. The power of evil present in him filled her with an overwhelming urge to turn and run, just to get away from him. Now he stood there in front of the two of them and she looked into his eyes. She felt as if she was looking in through the gates of hell.

The spirits infesting Lench realised that their host was going to pursue this to the bitter end, despite their warnings. They would have to make the best of it, and deal with him later. It was enough now to guide his words.

'I will silence you, woman.' He felt his arm rise and his finger was pointing and, in a movement that made him feel like a puppet, he saw himself step forward to push her. His fingers touched her and she jumped. He could see, with some satisfaction, that she had turned very pale indeed.

But Daisy's emotions had turned from curiosity to anger. As Lench reached out at Alex, Daisy raised her hand and swung at the side of Lench's jaw. Her hand connected with his jaw producing the clear, urgent sound of a hard slap. Afterwards Daisy's fingers stung in a most satisfying way.

'Keep your hands off her. Who the hell do you think you are!' Daisy had a voice that could carry for ever when she was angry.

Lench took a step backwards, the side of his face smarting. It was for him a curiously enjoyable sensation. He was impressed in his own way; there was always a sense of combat to all these things and at least the girl had spirit. Her intense blue eyes and blond hair made her an immensely attractive morsel.

* * *

On the spiritual plane, the view that Angel got was both spectacular and horrific. He had rarely seen anything like it. Even before Alex had left the flat, there had been tension in the air, like the gathering of forces. Something told him that he was about to encounter a host of the enemy. It was an unexpected time and place but such things did happen. He sensed them almost by name, surrounding a man who was emerging from a car just a few yards away. Here was an assembly of some of the most powerful spirits he had ever seen.

This was almost unprecedented! Surely these demons didn't want their host to confront Alex in the street like this! He must be in acute turmoil to force them all out into a public place.

In the instant when Alex and Lench stood opposing each other, Angel had stepped a little ahead of her in his own dimension. From the assembly, one spirit stepped forward to oppose him. He knew this one, had known it since before it had fallen, it was even more powerful than he. They stood in their own realm, within striking distance. The demon was so powerful that a kind of peace had come over Angel. He knew, of course, that he had a profound and immediate need to rely on the Lord, and in that realisation he found comfort.

The demon looked down at Angel, trying to recall its name. It had often found that personal reference helped to unsettle the enemy.

'Angel, are you brought so low?' The voice was gentle, with just a hint of steel.

The demon had chosen to represent itself as a boy of about eighteen, fair of skin with blond hair and blue eyes. It looked beautiful and there was something in the eyes that reminded Angel of how this demon had looked before it had rebelled. A sense of sadness fell over him at the memories of times long past. In the unnatural silence of the spirit world the demon stepped closer to Angel so that in their own dimension its lips were just inches away from his ear.

'Angel,' the demon whispered, 'did we not once share a kingdom, were we not once powers before God? And look at us now. What has happened to us?'

Angel turned to his adversary, and there was more sadness than anger in his voice.

'Be gone demon; it is you who has fallen from grace, not I. You are a servant of the enemy, and you know well that the Lord is God, over me and you and your so-called 'master'. Now, may the Lord rebuke you!'

The demon laughed, although its mirth sounded forced and strained. 'Brave words indeed Angel, but the battleground is flesh and blood with all its lusts and weaknesses. Now tell me, does she really mean so much to you, this beautiful human woman?' Some of the other demons sniggered.

Angel guessed that, for all its strength, this was not a confrontation that this spirit would have wished for. He could almost feel the lips of his adversary against his ear.

The demon went on, serious now. 'You are a fool to oppose us, Angel. The woman will be tested and she will fail. And the other one . . . well, we may have her yet as a plaything for our host. She shows some character – he will like that.'

Again, some sniggering from the assembly.

The demon went on, containing its own rage, 'But, this woman, Alex Masters, will not fulfil the plans that have been made for her. Do you know why? Because at the point of testing she will prefer a man to God.' The demon looked into Angel's eyes. 'You know I speak the truth.'

As Angel's mind flashed with an image of John Stamford, the demon laughed.

'Ah, you have worked it out, at last. You know, we will have little to do, my kin and I. She will desire this man who fills her mind, they will be together, and she will be compromised. She will be separated from the strategies of God, and you, my friend, will surely have to return home in anguish and humiliation.'

'You shall not touch her!' The anger within Angel welled up, and he lashed out at his adversary.

The demon was eager to engage in the combat, knowing itself to be a greater force than its opponent. The impact resonated across the spirit world, and Angel knew in his heart that, by himself, he could not win this contest.

He could hear the half-truths of his enemy whispered in his ears. Alex might indeed fail because of John. He could feel the darkness of the demon begin to surround him and overwhelm him. What if it did happen; what if Alex did succumb to temptation? What a fool he would seem!

He could feel himself weakening and he was reminded again of his own limitations. He was weak, but in that weakness he remembered who he was, and what his purpose was; and he realised that the demon had been right – Alex did mean a lot to him. She was precious to him, because his Lord had sent him to look after her. Some words buried deep in his mind came back to him. Words spoken to him just before he'd left to fulfil this purpose.

'Love her, Angel, because I love her. Keep her because she has come freely to me desiring to be my chosen instrument.'

As he bowed his head, again he whispered the words of submission to his Lord. 'My God, I go not in my own strength, but in yours. Deal with this enemy as you see fit.' He gave himself up totally to the will of God and in doing so tapped into that familiar source of energy and strength. He sensed the irresistible will of the Lord and he knew that he was home.

Across from him, a howl of anguish erupted from his enemy and the whole assembly of demons screamed in agony and disarray. Angel pressed home his advantage by speaking out now to his enemy and the assembled company: 'Remember who the real Master is.' Then he approached the cowering figure of his enemy and under the authority of God, shouted out so that all of them could hear exactly what he said.

'Hear me, servants of the enemy. From this time, none of you shall harm this woman, for she is under my care and I am at the command of the living God.'

* * *

In the physical world, Lench seemed to be frozen, as if profoundly confused by some imaginary turn of events. He was shaken from his paralysis by the sharp tones of a traffic warden who had been inspecting his illegally-parked car.

'Is this your vehicle, sir?'

Lench was silent, transfixed by the ground in front of him. His mouth worked but there was no sound.

She spoke again, 'I said, is that your car, sir?'

'What?' He stared at the traffic warden.

'I want you, sir, to move this vehicle.'

He noticed now that his Mercedes was parked in a bus lane. The traffic warden had taken out her notebook and was writing down his registration number. Lench was finding it hard to control himself.

'Go away,' he whispered, hoarsely. The traffic warden stared at him for a moment, and then started to write out a ticket. Lench watched her for a moment, and then without saying another word he walked to his car, got in and drove off.

Daisy took Alex by the arm and guided her towards the car park.

'Do you know that bloke?'

'No I don't, but he is my adversary. He wishes to destroy me,' said Alex.

'Well he was weird, and he'd better not show up here again,' said Daisy, defiantly.

She was no nearer to understanding what had happened, but she didn't want to pursue it. They needed to get on and her thoughts were turning to her police interview. Worrying about some madman they'd met in the street would have to wait till afterwards.

Alex started the car and they headed towards Mr Wicks's office.

Travelling in the opposite direction, Lench turned the air-conditioning in his car up to maximum. His hands gripped the steering wheel but they were shaking badly. He did not seem to be able to drive in a straight line. It took him several minutes to get his breath back. This had truly been an expensive and embarrassing way to vent his frustration; he had felt the spirits within him howling; the confrontation had been a painful one for them. He assumed that he would get a ticket from the traffic warden. The fine meant nothing to him in financial terms, it just added to the humiliation, and of course it was nothing to the fiercely probing anger that might yet face him. He, the master tactician, servant of evil, a man of power, had been reduced to a sweaty wreck by these girls. He had originally wanted to return to his office, but now it was probably best to go home. The pressure of madness beat against his chest and his brain, and the ferocious air-conditioning didn't stop the sweat from appearing on his brow.

* * *

Alex and Daisy went through some final points with Mr Wicks before going on to the police station. All the preparation that Daisy had done paid off in the interview. She was precise and honest, and after so many sessions with Caleb, delivered a true and consistent story.

It helped that the investigating officer knew Caleb Wicks. Caleb beat the truth out of his clients more effectively than he did. In fact, if Caleb was representing this girl he would not need to waste his time trying to squeeze more of the story out of her. He would get the whole thing first time round. What was a big deal for Daisy was a relatively small detail for the inspector. She was quite helpful, but he knew most of it already, and he had plenty of other issues to deal with in relation to this case. He looked at the girl sitting in front of him, trying to judge her strength of will. She might, after all, turn out to be a useful witness. Her evidence had tied in with the discovery of Will's Mini and she gave a thorough description of the characters she had met that night, as well as some suggestions as to where the rave had taken place.

He told Daisy that if she co-operated she would not be charged with any offence, but she might have to stand up in court and give evidence. That wasn't a problem for Daisy. Her friend, the boy who had shown some consideration for her, was dead and now she felt she owed it to him to co-operate.

After the interview they headed back to Mr Wicks's office. Daisy would need to keep in touch with the police but she was free to get on with her life for now. She pondered her situation, while Alex and Mr Wicks discussed a couple of issues relating to Alex's purchase of the lease for the café.

The subject of the encounter with Lench did not come up again. It was something that Alex was pleased to forget, and Daisy had too many other things to worry about – she had met some odd people in her time, and this man was just another one. It was no big deal in the end.

Twelve

Conner was a free spirit. If the mood took him he would change his plans and pursue a different course without worrying too much about the consequences. He was not selfish – in fact he could be very considerate – but he trusted his impulses and followed them whenever he could. So on Friday afternoon he packed his bag, said goodbye to his parents and left for the station.

Max and Helen were not altogether surprised that he had decided to go early. When Alex had mentioned that cousin Daisy was staying, Conner had expressed an interest in seeing her.

Then there was 'King of Kings'. Someone had decided that it would be a good idea to have a big Christian event at the city's biggest stadium on the Saturday afternoon. The first of its kind, it featured musicians and worship leaders from the UK and beyond. Conner loved big events and he didn't want to miss this one. It would be much easier to travel to the event from Alex's flat than from his parents' home.

The first Alex knew about Conner's early arrival was when he turned up at about seven with his bag and guitar. When the doorbell went she thought that maybe Laura had arrived early to walk up to youth club with her, but it was Conner's cheeky grin that greeted her when she opened the door. He seemed oblivious to the rain, and his hair was crowned with little drips of water.

'Alex!' He flung himself at her and she was reminded of Daisy's hug on the doorstep a few days before; 'Big sis, how are you? And before you say anything: yes, I know I'm early, but I just felt like coming over now.' He kissed her. She felt as if a damp and enthusiastic puppy had jumped on her.

'Conner! Well, I did think you were coming tomorrow morning.' She shouldn't have been surprised; this was typical of Conner, sometimes endearing and sometimes infuriating. He strolled into the kitchen and grinned at her.

Shall I put the kettle on?'

Alex was about to reply when Daisy emerged from the spare room and saw him and they looked at each other for a moment. Their reaction was like a film, stopped for a moment on a particular frame.

They all stood motionless and then Conner said, 'Hi Daisy, I'm just making some tea, do you want some?' He smiled at her as he put the kettle on. His manner and tone of voice reminded her so much of Will that she could do little more than stare at him.

Alex tried to gauge Daisy's reaction. She hoped that they would get on together because if they didn't it was going to make for a stressful weekend. She was rather resentful of the fact that this was all going on in her flat and if there was any trouble she would not be able to get away. It would spill out into her lounge, her kitchen, her own space. Still, the least she could do was offer a belated introduction to Daisy.

'Daisy, this is Conner. I'm sure you remember him. I wasn't expecting him to come until tomorrow, but don't worry,' she cast a steely glance at her brother, 'he's sleeping on the sofa.'

'I don't mind sleeping on the sofa!' said Conner cheerfully and, as if to prove the point, he flopped onto the couch in the living room, and started to unpack some of the items from his bag.

'Conner, do you want to come down to youth club with me?' Alex watched her brother scatter half a dozen CDs onto the carpet.

'Here, Alex, I bought you a present.' He took a package from his bag and handed it to her. She opened it and inside was a little teddy bear with overalls on. On the overalls were the words 'Best Decorator in the World'.

'I thought this might encourage you with renovating the café, and all that.' He beamed at her, and she couldn't help but love him.

'It's lovely, Conner, thanks.' How could she be angry with him? This was how he was, and she had known it all her life.

'So, do you want to come to youth club?'

'Well I might come along later, but I'm going to have a drink first.' The kettle was starting to hum in the kitchen.

Daisy had still not said anything, but had walked across the room and was looking at the CDs scattered on the floor. She seemed to recognise some of the titles. Alex took it as a good sign; perhaps they wouldn't fight after all.

She was about to say something, to encourage some conversation between the two of them, but she checked herself. She wasn't here to run around after either of them. They were both adults and if they couldn't get along together then she didn't want to be around to witness it. She picked up her keys, said a brief goodbye, and left them to it.

As Alex left, she saw Daisy put on one of Conner's CDs. She could hear the dull, rhythmic beat in the hall outside. Beneath the noise, she could just hear Conner's voice, and what might have been the sound of cups. For a moment she was overcome with a sense of exclusion, as if she had been locked out of her own flat. She imagined Daisy and Conner sharing music, coffee and conversation in a world that would be alien to her. Pushing the train of thought away, she walked up the road at a brisk pace, hunched under an umbrella, trying to put some distance between herself and the faint cascade of music coming from the open window of her flat.

On the way down to church she met Laura and told her about her new 'dependents'.

'I feel responsible for them Laura; it's like I've got two children in the flat. But they are both twenty years old.'

Laura had met Conner before, so she knew what he was like. 'They will be okay Alex. You know that deep down Conner is really quite wise and sensitive. Does he know about Daisy and this lad Will?'

'He knows a little bit; I thought it was right to tell him.'

'Well anyway, perhaps his light-heartedness will do her good. She seems a bit intense from the way you have described her.'

It was true. Maybe Conner was just what Daisy needed at the moment. The five-year age gap between Alex and Daisy showed sometimes, but Conner and Daisy were both students. The thought passed through her mind that they might just get on a little too well. She dismissed it: there was enough to worry about as it was. The needs of the young people at the youth club would more than occupy her for the next two hours. At least during that time she wasn't going to feel alone.

Laura and Alex had perhaps ten minutes to get everything set up before the kids arrived. This was always like the calm before the storm, as they got the activities for the evening ready, ran over the five-minute 'God slot' that they always did, and unpacked some sweets.

As they finished their preparations, Aiden arrived. He was there to lend some muscle to the proceedings, and they liked to have a man on the premises, as most of the kids who came to this club were, in fact, boys. Aiden, with his soft accent and subtle, gentle nature had a calming influence on some of the more rowdy ones. Alex was pleased that he was there.

It was not yet the end of term and the club was busy. There was a constant barrage of noise as the young people worked their way through the different games and activities that had been laid on for them that evening. The snooker tables, chipped and marked from the years of rigorous youthful attention, were as popular as ever. Later, Aiden spoke to them. He talked about the way people in church helped each other and he used volunteers from among the youngsters to show how everyone could be both helped and a helper.

The evening finished with the tuck shop. There was the usual scraping around for small change as the kids tried to get enough money together for whatever was on offer. As a queue of sorts formed, Alex noticed that Alice, one of the quieter girls, was hanging about at the back. She usually tried to be one of the first in the queue. When it was her turn to buy something, she bought quite a few items, and paid with a fifty-pound note. There was something about this that left Alex feeling uncomfortable. Something in Alice's eyes, like a distraction, not quite sadness, more resignation, suggested that something was wrong. Alex could sense it and decided to scratch at the surface to see what she could find.

'Hello Alice, how's it going?'

'Alright.'

Alice was sitting at the back of the hall munching some of her purchases. About ten minutes of club were left, and the other kids were milling around, or playing snooker and table tennis.

'Have you got yourself a job then, Alice?'

'No, why?'

'Because I saw you had a fifty-pound note. Perhaps it was for your birthday?'

There was a pause. Alice sank back into the chair. She didn't face Alex.

'I didn't get it for my birthday.'

'Oh, so where did you get it from?'

But Alice didn't answer. Instead, she stared at the rough wooden flooring as if she were completely absorbed by some other issue or problem in her life. She ignored Alex, collected her half-eaten sweets and walked out onto the street. Alex did not see whether she was heading home or not.

* * *

Conner put two mugs down on the table by the sofa. He started to get some of his clothes out of his bag, making himself at home. Daisy continued to study the cover of a CD case.

'Do you like them?' asked Conner.

'They're okay, I've seen them live a couple of times.'

'Must have been some gig! When I saw them the lead guitarist got a wire coat hanger and started eating it halfway through the set.'

Daisy remembered a similar stunt from one of the concerts she had been to a few months ago. 'They're a bit more famous now, so I don't think he does that so much, and besides it wasn't a real coat-hanger, stupid.'

Conner laughed out loud and Daisy joined in. They sat in Alex's living room, listened to music, and talked and Daisy asked him about Alex.

'What's it like having Alex as a sister?'

'Alex is great – I mean she really is,' said Conner. 'She's worth talking to, worth listening to, if you know what I mean.'

After a moment he added, 'I think if it hadn't been for Alex I wouldn't have become a Christian. I don't know what I would be doing now . . . playing in some struggling band somewhere, out of my face on 'E' or dope or something. Jesus changed all that.' He sat back as if his last comment had capped the discussion.

'*It's always Jesus with these people,*' thought Daisy. Even though she had been very happy to stay with Alex, and meet Conner, she was beginning to find all this religion a bit stifling. She had been with Alex for a week, and it had helped her to cope with Will's death in ways that she would never have managed on her own. Now she was with Conner and he was on about Jesus as well. She consoled herself with the fact that he had good taste in music. She was intrigued by this concert he was going to. She couldn't imagine it – a whole stadium full of 'Happy Clappys'! She wanted to find out more.

'What's this thing you're going to tomorrow?'

'Oh, "King of Kings", it's a big praise and worship event. I reckon there will be about fifty to sixty thousand people there.'

Daisy was quite surprised that so many people would go to an event like this. 'Well, you had better take your coat because it's been raining all week and the forecast says it will rain tomorrow as well.'

Conner laughed, and then they both fell silent. The quiet seemed to generate an intimacy of its own, and after a moment, Conner reached out for his guitar, and he started to play some chords. As Daisy listened, familiar tunes started to take shape. He strung some Beatles together with a bit of Coldplay, and then some other music that Daisy did not recognise, but it was good to listen to. She suddenly had a desire to move closer to him as she listened to him playing, to enjoy more of the life in him, to draw some affection or support. Perhaps she wanted to kiss him: she couldn't quite understand her motivation.

She certainly felt drawn to him, but he was male, and however religious he was (she knew Alex hated that term) she didn't know him well enough to trust him. If she went to him for a hug he might expect more, and she really didn't want that at the moment.

'I tell you what, Daisy: tomorrow, why don't you come with me? We can get you a ticket on the gate.'

'I don't think it's quite me, Conner. I mean if you don't believe all that stuff then there's not much point in going.'

'Well suit yourself, but I can tell you it will be good, and it won't rain.'

'Oh yeah, and how do you know?' She was almost embarrassed for him. It had been tipping down for two days, his hair was still damp, and the forecast was the same for tomorrow.

Conner smiled at her and said, almost in a whisper, 'It's not going to rain tomorrow.'

His self-assurance was both endearing and irritating. Daisy could see why Alex was able to forgive him: he was cute. They sat at either end of the sofa, toes touching, and Conner played his guitar. The room had become dim, and Daisy sat back, letting the notes wash over her. She didn't know whether she admired or disapproved of his certainty. He would surely have been insufferable but for the fact that there was no trace of pride or arrogance in him.

Alex and Conner did not fit her view of religious people. They were complex but committed, serious about their beliefs but not like one of those fundamentalist types that she encountered occasionally. They weren't so 'holier than thou' about it that it stuck in your throat. She decided that she liked Conner; it was time to get to know him a little better.

'So isn't your girlfriend coming with you on this 'praise-up' then?'

He stopped playing for a moment and smiled; she was fishing now.

'No, because she doesn't exist.' He would give her that much. The cheeky side to him wanted to say, 'Why, are you offering?' but he did have enough common sense to realise that that wouldn't have been a good idea at the moment, for a number of reasons.

As he continued to play, Daisy stroked his foot with hers, playing a game for which there were no rules. He continued playing for a few more bars and then he stopped. Outside, clouds had hastened in the transition to dusk, and they could hear rain against the windows of the flat. The atmosphere in the room seemed to change. Conner could feel Daisy's presence as well as see her; and he thought he could detect the faintest odour of cigarette smoke from her. He wanted to tell her to stop smoking, but he knew that he didn't have the right to do that yet, and he wasn't completely sure he knew why he wanted her to stop.

She looked down at him and he raised his eyes.

'Give me a hug, please Conner,' she said, then added, 'but that's all. I just want a hug.' Something in the back of his mind told him that he was about to enter an old and familiar danger zone, but still he put the instrument down, got to his feet and took her in his arms.

They stood face to face for a few moments. Daisy closed her eyes and held him tightly. He was the first man she had touched since Will had died. Deep within herself, she drank it in, the affection and the beautiful feeling of physical contact, safe and welcome and under her control. She could almost feel the healing process, as if a veil that had been torn apart was now being woven together again. If anything, Conner was more gentle than Will. His hold of her was firm but not tight. She realised now that touch could bring restoration, as well as pain.

For his part, Conner felt compassion as well as the tingle of interest that any pretty girl might engender in him. She was dealing with the loss of a person she loved, and he respected her need. He held her tightly, undeterred by the faint odour of cigarettes in her clothes and hair.

After a few moments, he gently released her and sat down again. As she turned round and walked back to her seat he started playing the guitar. It was a soulful tune, but within it there was a grace and beauty which invited her to tears. She listened to the notes as they painted a picture of serenity and reassurance. Again, she felt the fabric of her soul healing, not just from the loss of Will but from all of the pain that she had suffered as a child.

When the tune was finished, there was silence in the room. The rain continued to drum against the window. Daisy found herself wishing for dry weather tomorrow.

'That was beautiful, Conner. What was it?'

He smiled, 'I just made it up, Daisy – you could say that God gave it to me for you.'

She had no answer. She just could not connect with his view of the world, with God hovering on the fringe of everything, ready to make an appearance at any moment. But at the same time, she knew that Conner was going to make her reassess her views on Christianity. It was going to happen; she could feel it. She might not be a Christian at the end of that process – in fact, she didn't think that she would be – but when she thought about how far she had come in the last couple of weeks it shocked her. She had had to deal with so much, but there had been people there to help her every step of the way, from Alex to Mr Wicks, and now Conner.

Alex had listened. Alex had been open about herself.
Alex had given her shelter. Then there was Conner. She
had only met him this evening, and while she could
understand one of the reasons why she found him attractive, there was something else there as well. Even old Mr
Wicks had looked after her at the police station.
Whatever she had thought about him before, she had
been very glad to have had him at her side.

They were an odd bunch, that was true enough, but
between them they had just about destroyed her image
of people who go to church. Despite their differences
they did have something in common, as if they had all
stumbled on a secret of some kind. She had to spend
some time thinking about it all, alone, away from them.
She sank back into the sofa and closed her eyes. Conner
continued to play some gentle chords as she skirted the
edge of her drowsiness. She was safe and she knew it. If
she had believed in God, she would have been thanking
him now.

When Alex arrived home from the youth club the
living room floor was scattered with CDs and Conner's
guitar was resting against one of the chairs. On the sofa,
Conner and Daisy were sitting together, while some gentle music drifted out from the stereo. Alex felt like an
intruder in her own flat, but at least they weren't
arguing.

She made a drink for them all, and then suggested to
Conner that he might like to tidy up a bit. She didn't
want the living room ending up in the same state as his
room at home. He grinned at Alex, and then started to
gather up his belongings.

Daisy had announced that she would be going back to
her flat the next evening. She was grateful to Alex for all
she had done, and she hoped this would be the start of a
deeper relationship between them.

By now it was just before midnight, and so they took turns to go to the bathroom and then got off to bed. For the first time in years Alex felt as if she had too many people around her. Having one guest was acceptable, but having two meant that she had to give up too much of her own personal space. She thought of it all as an investment, because apparently something quite important had happened between Daisy and Conner. She could not work out what it was, and to an extent, it was none of her business, but there was something going on. Although she was getting fed up with the lack of privacy, she consoled herself with the fact that God was using her flat as a place to work out his purposes.

She climbed into bed and relaxed at last. She loved the moment when she could get into bed after a busy day and just rest. Some nights she wondered what it would be like to have someone next to her; someone to keep warm with, talk with in this most intimate space; someone with whom it would be right and good to make love. Her mind went over the events of the day, and her thoughts turned to Alice. Where had she got that money from? There were any number of sources: she could have just been given it by her parents, or she could have stolen it, or . . . Alex didn't want to think about the other ways a young girl might get some money. As she lay in her bed, she realised that her secret ambitions to change the culture, to create something for young people, were sharpened again and again by kids like Alice.

Now there were tears in her eyes. She sat up in the darkness of her room and looked out past the curtain at the street light. There was no such thing as real darkness in the town. There was only a kind of subliminal grey-yellow tinge to the night. You had to go out into the country to find true darkness. She did not want to think about the deeds that might be done in the city that night, not when she was worried about Alice.

She felt herself sliding into sleep as she gazed at the street light. Pulling herself out of it for a moment, she prayed for Alice, and then she remembered about four or five other kids that she cared passionately about, and she prayed for them also. When she had done this, she eased back under the covers, just aware of Conner and Daisy's voices. They were speaking to each other very quietly in her lounge. She could not make out what they were saying and she didn't want to know either. The last thing she remembered was seeing Alice's big mournful eyes and the fifty-pound note that someone had seen fit to give her.

* * *

The next day Conner went off to 'King of Kings'. He said goodbye to his sister and gave her a hug, and then he said goodbye to Daisy and held her tightly. Alex looked on trying to gauge the relationship between them, but she couldn't read their feelings. She had other things to worry about anyway. She had to go to the café: the project was going to take up a lot of her time from now on.

Daisy went out in the morning for a visit to her parents. She felt that it was right for her to make one of her monthly duty calls or her mother would start to give her a hard time. She took the train back to her home town, and as she stared out of the carriage window at the scene moving by, the rain started to fall again. She remembered Conner's confidence about the fact that it wasn't going to rain on his event. She was almost sorry to see the raindrops spoil his assertion. It was another reason why she dared not believe: she didn't want to place her faith in something and then be disappointed.

At the stadium, Conner looked up at the sky. The clouds were thick and heavy, but there was no rain. He dug around in his pocket and found his ticket for 'King of Kings'. Borrowing a pencil from one of his friends, he wrote one word: 'Daisy'.

He was going to send her a letter and he was going to remind her of his 'no rain' prediction. He could not kid himself that that was all he was going to say to her; he was always honest with himself about his feelings, and he knew in his heart that he would rather enjoy writing to his cousin. Across the crowd, by the stage entrance, he heard the roar go up and, putting the ticket in his pocket, he uttered a prayer of thanks to God. Then he joined the noise as another band came onto the stage. He forgot about the previous evening's weather forecast as the music started, and he didn't think about it again all that day.

The rain did fall on the roof of the train taking Daisy north, and to the south of the capital across Kent, Sussex, and Surrey. In fact, it rained across most of the country that day.

But the stadium remained dry.

Thirteen

After the initial flush of enthusiasm, the number of helpers at the café died down. A week had passed since Alex had obtained the key, and there had been a lot of work done clearing the shop of all the rubbish that the previous occupants had left.

Alex had been grateful, though. She understood that people would want to help a few times but then they would grow tired and make their excuses and go. She didn't blame them, and anyway she was on her own – she could work till whenever she wanted as nobody was waiting for her to come home.

And it was all hers now. Here was her café starting to take shape, the fulfilment of one of her dreams. It was an exciting time for her and she thanked God that she could see part of her destiny mapped out here. But still her heart ached. Even in this place where her own vision was being fulfilled she felt an acute sense of dissatisfaction.

Angel stood by and watched. He had experienced the desire to help her, but he knew that he could not interfere. She needed to do this herself, with the assistance of her friends.

He knew as well that Alex was beginning to struggle with her single life. Like many people, she often took a very circuitous route to find a simple conclusion. The conclusion in this case was that she wanted a partner. She was created by God to enjoy fellowship and company and she got plenty of it, but now she needed something more, a man who she could love and work with, and desire; a man to struggle with and sleep with; a man who, like her, was defined by his faith in Christ.

It took Alex a while to come to this conclusion. At first, she had viewed the need for a partner as a weakness, because she'd had to look after herself for so long. She had not understood that when two people come together they could both be stronger for it.

These issues took their place in the back of her mind, crowded out for now by more pressing matters. There was still a lot of work to be done: sanding, painting, wiring. She needed to somehow juggle the deeper questions in her life with the urgency of the café. Breathing an audible sigh, she went to work, sanding down one of the walls.

She had been working for about twenty minutes when she heard the melodic jingle of her mobile. She was glad of the excuse to stop for a moment. Instinctively she looked at her watch: it was 7 o'clock.

'Hi Alex, it's Laura. Are you still at the café?'

'Yes, and I'm likely to be here for a while yet.'

'I thought I might send John down to help you for an hour or so. He's only watching the TV here and I've got some of the mums round so I'd like him out of the way really.'

'Oh yes, that would be great,' Alex's mouth had become dry. She longed to see John, and yet she knew that his presence would be dangerous. There was an irony in the fact that it was Laura who was putting her own husband in danger. Or was this some test? Did Laura want to force the issue, establish the loyalties of her friend and her husband? Alex couldn't believe that her friend would do that. This kind of thinking was like a dance around the edge of paranoia, and she had neither the time nor the desire to consider her response.

She was trapped: she wanted to say 'Yes' and 'No' at the same time. Perhaps John was feeling the same way as she felt. They would have to talk about this thing before something really happened.

After she had said goodbye to Laura she began to think about a suitable job for John. One of the back rooms would need to be redecorated and that would involve more sanding down. The picture she had had of him working on the wiring for the café came back to her. She did need some wiring done, but she didn't like the idea of trying to make her own vision come true. It seemed to her that that would be the act of a fraud.

She turned back to her own work, but the logic of getting John to start on the wiring began to nag at her. She could do sanding and painting but she knew nothing about rewiring. It would be sensible to get him to start on the things she could not do for herself. Of course, it made sense to get John to do it for her.

There was a knock on the whitewashed glass of the shop door. She opened it to see John dressed in his overalls, an electrician's belt around his waist. She could already sense his discomfort.

'I thought you might need a hand with some of the rewiring,' he said. She stared at him as if he had spoken to her in a foreign language.

'Is that all right, Alex? I mean, if someone else is doing it that's fine, there're plenty of other jobs to do.' He hovered at the door with his toolbox, like a lover with a bunch of flowers.

'No that would be fine, John. Please come in.'

He put the toolbox down and walked in, tripping on a strip of wood that had been screwed to the floor. It may have supported a shop counter at some point in the past.

'Have you been here all day?' He approached her and they embraced, and she could feel the heat of the evening again. As they held each other, she sought to protect herself by making a study of the café windows. The glass frontage had been poorly whitewashed but she could still see people walking by, and she could still hear the traffic. The exercise absorbed her for a few seconds before she gave in and acknowledged to herself that the feel of John's arms around her satisfied a hunger that she didn't want to feel. She withdrew from him and went to put the kettle on.

He was looking in one of the back rooms, where there were pencil marks on the wall showing where Alex wanted the sockets to go. He tried to focus on the job, the lengths of duct required, the tools he would need. At the back of his mind a restlessness prowled around. It was undefined but he knew exactly what it was.

When Laura had suggested that he go and help Alex he had almost rejected it outright, but a refusal would have required an explanation. Unfortunately, Laura had already volunteered him. He knew that he would have to deal with the pressure of temptation whilst he was in this place.

She showed him where to make a start on the wiring, and where the fuse box was. It was all very business-like. He resolved simply to start on this job, maybe do a couple of hours' work, and then go home. There was plenty here to keep him absorbed for a while.

So Alex sanded and John worked on the rewiring. Time passed and they both made an effort to focus on the work at hand. For both of them, their concentration was like the postponement of a test, some trial that they both knew they would soon have to face.

At about nine, Alex came into the room where John was working. She could see that he was making good progress. He pre-empted her question. 'It's going well, Alex. I can perhaps do another half an hour tonight and then see if I can do some more tomorrow.'

'Thanks, John, I do appreciate it.' They looked at each other for just a moment, but it was too much for her, she had to turn and go back to her sanding.

Alex became aware of how tired she was. She had been working since about 9 o'clock that morning. She yawned and stretched before returning to her work and at that moment, John had looked up and seen her. His eyes ran over her body as she stood side on to him. Her head was tipped back slightly, showing the shape of her chin and neck. The T-shirt showed the curves of her body, making them into a gentle movement, while the leggings defined the rest of her all the way down to her ankles. He looked away and closed his eyes but the image was still with him. He had thought that he was beginning to master this situation, but it seemed that one image like that was enough to breach all of his defences. His concentration was waning; he was certainly tired. Phrases from scripture passed through his mind: *The devil prowls around like a lion, seeking who he may devour. . . . My power is perfected in weakness. . . .'*

Out of the corner of his eye, he saw Alex standing in the doorway. She looked tired as well. Her short brown hair looked ruffled and her eyes betrayed her tiredness.

'I think I'm going to pack up soon, John, I don't want to do any more tonight.' She moved over to the wall and looked at his work.

'I've actually been able to get a fair bit done.' In his determination to focus on the task, he had managed to put in some ducting and fit a couple of sockets.

'That's good,' she smiled at him and energy and expectation flowed through him. Again he felt that sense of dislocation, as if the room they were in had been transported to a place far away.

Alex looked around the little office and moved next to him. She seemed drawn like a magnet, and it took some effort for her to refocus on the work.

'How much more time will you need to spend on this room?'

He looked up at her, frowning slightly, 'It's about a day's work.'

'Do you think you could do it . . . I mean are you free at some time?'

She tried to sound casual, but every word seemed to contain hidden meanings, subtle nuances that she did not intend. The conversation started to feel like a prelude to the moment of crisis.

He was focused on her completely now. There was a hint of the perfume she must have put on that morning as well as that subtle scent that always seemed to characterise Alex Masters. It occurred to him that if someone were looking through the imperfect whitewash of the shop windows they would not be able to see the two of them in this room together.

Alex bowed her head, as if the call to resist were just one battle too many. Somehow, the will to fight had gone, and as she rested her head on his shoulder, he felt no desire to move it. His only problem was the fact that if she leaned any harder he would topple over from his rather awkward standing position. He was disinclined to move, as if to do so would break a spell that had been cast upon them; the mood had captured him like an insect on the spider's web.

And John was frightened. Frightened because he realised that the only other time he felt like this was when he was in bed with Laura. He would gently touch her in a way that was open only to him, and she would be in a place somewhere between acceptance and rejection of what he had to offer. In those moments, any interruption usually meant that he lost her. He wanted to give this moment that same care and attention, as if he were in bed with Alex now instead of his wife.

Across the room, Angel stood and watched. He knew there would be nothing he could do on this occasion: he had been told as much. His enemy was already in attendance. The demon had not even tried to taunt him – it seemed to be saving its strength so that it could whisper its poison in their ears. He would never know those words, and he didn't want to. His adversary stretched itself out as it stood between John and Alex, and it seemed to place an arm on each of their shoulders, as if it were giving them both some fatherly advice. Angel was repelled by the sight. What looked like a gesture of support was in fact a determination to hurt and destroy.

Angel knew that the crisis was coming. This could be the first transgression, their first descent into a forbidden place. It could destroy the plans God had for both of them. He had been here before and he always did the same thing. Uttering a simple prayer for them both in his own language, he moved away from the room so that he could not see what occurred next. They were in God's hands now, as well as their own. Standing by the heap of Alex's overalls, he closed his eyes and felt the situation with his senses.

In the office, Alex and John were almost motionless. Deep in her heart, Alex felt that hunger again. The light was beginning to dim; the evening was drawing in; the room was becoming a blur in the half light. She could see her own sense of right and wrong blending in with the dusk. There was that hunger again for John, to touch him, to feel him, to kiss him. The words that described her view of him spun around in her head.

Brother . . . friend . . . leader . . . brother . . . lover.
Lover . . .

The idea of John as a lover, attractive and forbidden, appealed to her. She was tempted, and in a strange way, she drew some comfort from it. In that moment she accepted, once more, the fact that one day she wanted to find someone. She knew her character included the desire for a partner. It was something to be embraced not fought against. In that moment, she accepted the fact that she really wanted a man.

But not this man.

Slowly she raised her head and stepped away from him. Her eyes fixed on the blank wall in front of her. She didn't know what stopped her in the end from kissing him and plunging into the abyss. It wasn't her café project, or all of the vision and purpose that God had placed inside her – these things had seemed distant and irrelevant to her at that moment. Rather, it was her acceptance of desire as a legitimate part of who she was and the need to express that desire in a God-given way. Now that the crisis had passed, she didn't want to look at him. She heard his voice, almost a whisper:

'Alex, you are right . . . I have been a fool and I'm sorry.' He put his hand on her shoulder and she looked up at him. She felt now as if they were fellow soldiers, fighting a common enemy, and she felt an affection for him that was at last good and wholesome.

As the atmosphere eased away, he thought about the lead she had taken. Everything Alex did made him admire her even more. She had shown her courage; could he have done the same? Perhaps it was better not to worry now: the battle was won.

'I never wanted this, John – I don't think either of us did. But we will win this battle; we are not destined to be casualties here.' As she spoke he realised that her mind had taken the same path as his, seeing their situation as an act of war.

There was now a long silence between them, as if they were both recovering from the attempt on their lives. Then he said, 'I'll do this room in a day, with Aiden's help. I think I'll get him to come with me from now on.'

Across the room from them, the demon arched itself in agony, boiling with the frustration of an opportunity unfulfilled. It knew that the war would go on, but an important battle was lost. This was one chance it had had to turn temptation into sin and it had failed. It knew what was to come.

John picked up some wire cutters and put them in his tool bag. It was time for him to go home to his family. He thought about Alex and closed his eyes. A prayer formed on his lips:

'Lord, who is she to me, where do you want this to go?'

The Spirit prompted him to look inwards, into his soul. He searched for Alex there, and he felt as if he were on a journey to meet the people who were most precious to him. There was Laura and Josh, some people he was close to in the church, and then there were his parents, his brother and sister, and next to his sister, he saw Alex, smiling at him. He had looked into himself and there he had found a sister, a precious sister to love and cherish, to treat with respect and dignity. It was as if he were looking on from the Lord's perspective, and moistness gathered in his eyes. The intensity of it was such that he had to break off and go back to collecting his tools.

He finished packing and walked out into the shop. They embraced as if they were family, and he said;

'I'll see you on Sunday, Alex, good luck with the work . . .'

'Bye, John, and thanks for your help. You are a good man.' He had to leave now to save himself from tears in front of her. He walked out of the café and into the night air, turning one last time to see her tidying up. There was a briskness about her actions as if she wanted to go home as well.

Without knowing where his inspiration came from, he whispered a prayer for her. Nobody would have heard it, swamped by the traffic and the urban noise, but he prayed anyway, petitioning God that he might give Alex the man she needed.

As he went back home, he felt like a soldier returning from the battle front. He had been involved in a battle, but he knew deep within himself that neither of them was going to succumb now. He believed that he was strong enough, and he thought that she was even stronger than he was. They were going to win.

It would still require some effort on his part to refocus on his wife, but that was no surprise. It was one of the great lies of the age that a couple had to be breathlessly in love all the time, either just having had, or just about to have, an intense session of lovemaking. If you didn't feel like that then there was something wrong with you and your relationship. There was no room in this new 'wisdom' for working at a relationship; it was better to have a riotous affair than invest in a relationship with your marriage partner.

John rejected that thinking. He would work at it, and because deep down the love was there, things would be okay. He loved his wife.

And Angel rejoiced, and praised God and delighted in this victory, and the fact that this hopeless and permissive age still contained heroes. He was beginning to think that Alex was one of them.

She had nearly finished tidying the place when her
mobile went off again, the insistent bleep jolting her
from her thoughts. Still holding a can of paint and a
brush, she ran into the shop to the counter where she had
left the phone. As she reached the phone, her foot hit the
same strip of wood that John had tripped on earlier. She
was unable to steady herself since her hands were full,
and her momentum carried her forwards. She had just
managed to let the can of paint go and put out her hands
so that in the end all she did was graze her knees on the
floor. The paint can bounced off the floor, knocking the
lid off and spinning it over onto its side. Paint spewed
out in a ragged arc as the tin spun around.

Alex sat down breathless, and the mobile phone
stopped. She bowed her head and felt that acute sense of
loneliness again. Her eyes moistened, she had no will to
get up.

Outside, the traffic carried on passing the shop.

It seemed so unjust! She had struggled to keep her life
holy, she worked hard for God, and then this happens.
Under her breath, she whispered a prayer, in hope and
anguish: 'When are you going to do something for me?'

Laura put the phone down, concern clouding her face.
Why hadn't Alex answered the phone? What was going
on? Her first thought was that Alex had hurt herself, but
then John was there with her so he could have answered.
So what could have happened?

'John was there with her.'

In fact, John had been gone a bit longer than she had
anticipated.

Laura was not a stupid woman, she could see the
attraction between John and Alex, but she trusted them
both. Really, she had to trust them both. But trust only
stretched so far, and she had seen a tension in John

recently. It was not something he had talked about and now she wondered if it might have had something to do with Alex.

These last few weeks had been a difficult time for her. She had wrestled with the issue of going back to work, whether it was right or not, and for how long, and what about Josh? And John had been a bit distant, a bit preoccupied with his own work and the church. Was this the reason why? Did he feel something for Alex? After all, he was with her now. But he was her husband, her man, not Alex's!

'Keep your hands off him he's mine!' She was shocked to hear her thoughts translated into words – quite involuntarily, she had blurted it out. She listened, but the house was quiet.

He was her man. She reflected on it again, like some kind of territorial dispute.

She was jolted from her thoughts by the sound of the front door opening. John came in, and she immediately noticed that there was something different about him, as if a weight had been lifted from his shoulders. It was a woman's intuition, the sensitivity of a wife who knows her man. He, of course, had no clue as to what had been going through her mind.

'Hi!' He kissed her. 'Look, I thought I would get us a little something.' He had bought a tub of double chocolate ice cream. John knew that she loved ice cream, especially this flavour, and he had not bought any for quite a while. He went into the kitchen and took two bowls out of the cupboard.

She knew that this was no prelude to a confession of adultery, this was a celebration of their love. He was rummaging around in the kitchen as if he did not have a care in the world. She sat looking at the ice cream. This was a good sign, she could feel it; the old sense of security came back to her.

'John, was Alex okay when you left her.'

He emerged from the kitchen again with two spoons. 'Yes I think so. Why do you ask?'

'Because I just tried to phone her and I got no answer.'

John was poised with the ice cream scoop, this was not a conversation he wanted to have right now.

'Well why don't you call her again, I'm sure she's okay.'

Laura picked up the phone and dialled the number. This time there was an answer.

'Alex, it's Laura, I tried to phone just now, are you alright?'

She could hear Alex's voice at the other end of the line, 'Yes, I'm okay. I had a bit of an accident with the paint just when you called so I didn't get to the phone.'

'Oh no! What happened?'

'Oh, I just tripped and dropped a can of paint on the floor. I'm okay now, just a few splashes of paint to wash off. Look, I'll give you a call tomorrow, okay?'

'Okay, I'll see you soon anyway, Alex. Bye.'

It was over; Laura didn't know why or how but if there had been a crisis it was finished and there was no harm done. She watched John scooping out the ice-cream;

'Is everything okay?' he asked, handing a bowl to her.

'Yes,' said Laura, 'everything's fine.'

They ate their ice cream and he offered her some more.

'No, John, that was enough. Take me to bed now please.' She had caught him in the middle of taking the lid off the tub; he hesitated, processing her last comment, and a liquid blob of ice cream fell onto the table.

They tidied up, and then she led him to the stairs and let him go momentarily while he unplugged the phone. Then they went up to their bedroom and she took something from the wardrobe and into the bathroom. Josh's soft snores could be heard through the door to his room.

It was only as he was waiting for her that it dawned on John that Laura might have guessed at the danger he and Alex had been in. At first, he was worried, and rather distracted from the mood of the moment. But then he thought about the relationship between Alex and Laura. Women seemed to be able to communicate with each other in all sorts of ways, and Laura was obviously happy with what she had heard, so that was enough for him. He had the wisdom to see a good thing and not spoil it with unnecessary talk. . . .

He sat back in the bed, feeling more relaxed than he had done for some time. He gave thanks to God and then gave thanks again when Laura came back into the room. She was wearing the white lace lingerie he had bought her a couple of years ago. They both loved it for different reasons, and he was struck by how good she still looked.

As she came into the bed next to him, he felt her warmth, the pressure of her against him, and he forgot all about the recent struggles. There were no distractions for either of them as they celebrated that night.

Fourteen

During the summer months of that year, the sun beat down, fulfilling the promise of a warm spring. Each evening there was sultriness in the air, encouraging a restlessness and sense of expectation. The summer nights held a sense of potential, and the people felt it.

The SEEKA ethos with its emphasis on experience as the root of truth touched a nerve amongst the young and the affluent. The T-shirts started to appear, the magazine articles – even a mineral water supplier started to produce a 'SEEKA' brand. At SLaM the royalties started to roll in.

Amongst SLaM's employees and contractors there was a mood of buoyant optimism. The big project, the one they had worked so hard on, was really taking off. The workers buzzed around the office and there was a sense of energy that matched the city heat. Sitting like the queen bee at the centre of it all was Martin Massey. The success of the project, his project, had been like a drug to him, making him feel important and powerful. The project, which he had fought for, was proving itself. Of course, he couldn't have done it without his backers, the obvious ones like Bridget, and the more silent ones in the background like Lench and the rest of the Group.

He almost wished Bridget were here to witness the triumph: whether she approved or what she thought of him would be irrelevant now. The problem with that was, of course, the fact that they had been coming to the end of their relationship and things had started to look messy. In a sense he had the best of both worlds: it had been Lench's idea to have her killed, so he'd arranged everything; but her departure from the scene had worked to Martin's advantage.

Dave Somerville had been one of the projects fiercest critics, but now he had completely changed his tune and was speaking up for SEEKA whenever he got the chance. They had all seen sales of the SEEKA magazine exceed even their most optimistic target. It meant a bigger bonus for Dave and that had been enough to shut him up: he was playing a political game now.

It was only now that the project was proving to be such a success that Martin realised how much he despised Dave. He was going to benefit from the success of SEEKA like they all would; but Martin could see the scowl on his face. After all, neither of them was that naïve; Dave harboured a grudge that no bonus, however large, would shift. If Martin had his way, he would see Dave removed from the firm before too long.

On a happier note, he felt that he could now look Lewis in the eye. The boss had made it clear that Martin succeeded or failed with SEEKA. He had been especially angry when his PA resigned, but as far as Martin was concerned, she was better off out of the way. He recalled that this was the woman that Lench had made such a fuss about. In fact, Lench was being a bit of an 'old woman' about all of this. He worried too much. If the Bridget thing was a mess, it was a mess of his own making. Martin cursed them all: his project was a winner, and they were all getting what they wanted as a result.

SEEKA was going to be a good thing for a couple of years, and in that time, he was going to make some very good money. Maybe then he could strike out on his own, and form his own company. After all, why should the benefits of his ideas go to others?

Even Lench had begun to settle down. He had got in a flap because his stupid assassin had botched the Bridget murder, but as the weeks went by and the police ran round in circles chasing each other, he had calmed down. Things were still a bit fraught when the Group met but Martin was able to report on how much poison he was helping to put into the minds and bodies of the young: it was the sort of thing they all liked to hear.

Martin sat back in his chair and looked at the sales sheet on his desk. The line progressed upwards, veering towards the top of the page. What a beautiful sight! In his mind, he surveyed his colleagues and he despised them all.

It was the end of another successful week and the evening was beginning to draw in. Tonight he was going to go out and celebrate.

Across the corridor from Martin's office, Lewis sat studying his copy of the same chart. There was no doubt about it, the project was making the company a fortune – and making him a fortune. It was all he had ever asked for, up to now. He should have been happy. In fact, he should have been able to share some of the arrogant pride that Martin so obviously felt. But somehow, the success was sour, and it wasn't just that this was Martin's project. He was surprising himself because he still felt troubled about the morality of SEEKA, and he was heartily sick of seeing Martin Massey walking around as if he owned the place.

There was more to it than that though. He had been upset by what had happened to Bridget, and he had still not been able to find a replacement for Alex. Two women, of whom he was fond for very different reasons, had now disappeared from his life and one was never going to come back. When he had called Alex to tell her about Bridget's murder he had had to suppress the desire to ask her to come back and work for him again. He knew she would never do that and it seemed that she was starting a new career by opening a café. Well, good luck to her. She had once mentioned to him that she would be getting some money when she turned twenty-five, and that would have been about now. It must have made it easier for her to leave SLaM – but he needed her now in ways that he could not quite define.

Things had become complicated recently, and his mood was not improved by the thought that Bridget's murder might have had something to do with her work. He had no evidence to back this up and the police had been unable to shed any light on the motive. They had tracked down the gas engineer who had visited her flat that after-noon, but they had not been able to trace a window cleaner who was also working there at the time. There had been a photofit picture but that had yielded nothing.

He looked up at the clock. Again, time had rushed away from him, and he was no further along. The prob-lems were still there. Looking out through the glass window of his office, he could see the entire floor of the building. By this time in the evening most people had gone. It was about 7.45 and of the twenty or so employees and contractors who made up SLaM, only a couple were left. He looked over to Bridget's empty chair: if she were still alive she might have been sitting there right now, and he'd be able to ask for her advice; but now she was gone, and Alex was gone, and he felt the loss of his women keenly. His attention was diverted by Martin striding past his door laden with SEEKA posters and shirts.

'Bye, Lewis,' Martin's Cheshire cat grin appeared at the door.

'Bye, Martin. Have you got some more SEEKA mate-rial there?'

'Yes, I'm taking it to an event tonight. We have to keep pushing the brand don't we, and besides, I thought I'd help Dave out by spreading some of the promotional material for his magazines. He has got a lot on at the moment, poor old chap.'

Martin was basking in it; Lewis could almost smell the arrogance. The two men looked at each other. Lewis was tired, and for once, he couldn't be bothered to disguise his feelings. The look on his face was as eloquent as any words. Martin couldn't mistake the distrust, even hostility, and his features soured in response. In that moment, each of them could see what the other really thought. There was a sense of tension as they stared across the room at each other, and then something inside Martin snapped and he turned away, almost jogging down the corridor with his posters and T-shirts.

As he saw Martin disappear with his wares, Lewis had a sudden premonition that SEEKA would eventually destroy the company. He almost resolved to wind the project up right then.

* * *

Some hours later, in the darkness, pubs and clubs were gearing up for the weekend. For those who fancied it there was always the rave scene, and at venues across the country the SEEKA gospel would be preached. SLaM had developed a mix for the club DJs and they had taken it to the people with great enthusiasm.

At one venue north of the capital things were well under way. The house was packed, the air thick and heavy, and the revellers were moving along the contin-uum from disorientation to oblivion as they shook to the insistent bass thump of the dance music. There was little sign of alcohol: that wasn't what these people were here for. In quiet corners around the venue trade was brisk.

Martin surveyed the gathering. The music was powerful and the masses had been swept up by it. He had already been offered enough gear to knock him into the middle of next week. He wanted none of it, not tonight anyway. In fact he was concentrating, listening to the words whispered under the cover of the pounding bass line:

I am the SEEKA after the truth,
I want it now, I want to touch it now
I want to make my truth in this place now
Make your truth like mine,
SEEKA after the truth.

Yes, he was the man of the moment; he was the one at the centre, achieving the things that others only talked about. Through the shadows and the crash of the music, nobody could hear him speaking out loud the words that described his success. He wanted the money, true, and he loved the fact that he could influence people; that while they lost themselves in the most expensive of circumstances, he retained control. It was money and power. And whilst the likes of Darius Lench pursued their own weird agenda with the dressing-up and all the attendant mumbo-jumbo, this was the ultimate reward for him: the pride he felt at his own achievements.

This was the best night Martin had had for a long time, and bathed in a sea of self-congratulation, he moved around as if he owned everything he touched.

* * *

Some miles to the south, as the summer evening finally gave way to darkness, a lone figure sat at a desk and slid open a drawer. It was time to put his client's last wishes into action. A large envelope was placed on the leather of a desktop. From inside the envelope he took out a bundle of papers, and at the top of the papers were the photocopied versions of the two slim reports that Bridget had taken from Martin's office. One was the market research Martin had commissioned, and the other was the sales and marketing plan for SEEKA. Attached to the reports was a copy of the first section of an internal memo detailing how SEEKA could both feed on and encourage the rave culture.

Now he hesitated, either to consider the consequences of his actions, or perhaps to check some instructions. Eventually he took the copy of the memo, and placed it next to another envelope. Across the desk stood a pot of glue, some scissors, and a copy of *The Times*. Slowly, painstakingly, he cut out a series of letters and pasted them to a blank sheet of paper. Finally, he pasted the letters of a name and address to the front of the envelope and inserted the sheet of paper and the memo into the envelope. Applying the correct value in stamps, he took the package to a post office some distance away, and slid it into the post box.

* * *

Monday started badly for Lewis. He had been absorbed by the issues surrounding the company and SEEKA and in the process had managed to scratch his car as he parked at work.

That was nothing compared to what he found on his desk when he got into his office. Amongst the jumble of notes and letters there was a large brown envelope. Inside he found a single sheet of paper, a series of letters had been neatly glued in a straight line, they said: 'STOP SEEKA'.

Attached to the note was the one thing he had not wished to see again. When Martin had first mooted the idea of SEEKA, they had quietly commissioned some research – the results of that research with commentary on SEEKA's relationship with the drugs culture had gone into one of Martin's elaborate memos. Lewis remembered feeling uncomfortable at the time, with so much incriminating evidence on a single sheet of paper. He had asked Martin not to show it to anyone else. Now a copy of that same memo had come to him in the post – out of the blue.

Someone had seen this report; someone had a copy of it and now he was being blackmailed. Incredibly, it seemed as if they didn't want money. They simply wanted the project stopped. Lewis held his head in his hands and counted to five, slowly. He checked his diary and asked his new secretary to cancel his first meeting (in fact this was only a discussion with Dave Somerville). Then he called through to Martin.

'We need to talk as soon as possible, upstairs.'

There was a pause and Lewis heard Martin sigh, 'I'm actually a bit busy, Lewis, can we make it this afternoon?'

Lewis felt himself beginning to lose his patience. 'Now, Martin. This is important!'

A short while later Martin entered the room to find Lewis already seated at one of the chairs. There were a couple of sheets of paper on the table in front of him.

'Come and sit down.'

Martin looked at him, trying to gauge the tone of what was to come. There was just a hint of moisture across Lewis's brow, and his fingers were tapping lightly on the table, not very far from where Bridget had lain the last time she and Martin had had sex together. The thought made him start to feel uneasy, even vulnerable.

Martin tried to pull himself together: this was hostile

territory. Lewis had not asked him to come up here for a cosy little chat – that was clear enough. He reminded himself again of the fantastic success of the SEEKA project. Nothing Lewis was going to say could take that away. Smiling at his boss, he leaned against the side of the table.

'What's this all about then?'

'Look at this.' He pushed the mysterious note and the photocopy of the section from the sales report across the table. Martin picked it up.

'It's a copy of our note about SEEKA – so what?'

Lewis sighed. He was being reminded, again, of the limits of Martin's intelligence.

'It is a copy of your memo, Martin. A copy that has come to me from someone outside this office.'

Now, at last, Martin realised the significance of what Lewis was showing him. These were all his proud boasts about how much SEEKA could sell from the drug scene. He could feel his mouth go dry and he tried to weigh up the implications, to see the limits of his liability. At that moment, he could not do it. Fear started to eat away at the wall of confidence he had built around himself over the past few days, disrupting his thinking.

'Are you going to close me down, Lewis?' He sounded like a small boy reporting to his form teacher; inside himself, his pride wriggled at this new humiliation. Lewis looked at him for a moment. Martin had stood up and was pacing round the room.

'Your question is symptomatic of some of the problems we have here. Oh for goodness sake, sit down! I am not going to "close you down" as you put it, Martin. You are my employee: I can hire you and fire you, but I cannot "close you down".'

He went on before Martin could reply. 'If you mean will I be discontinuing the SEEKA project, the answer is no. But you must understand this: SEEKA is a part of SLaM. The money to get it started and the resources poured into it all came from SLaM. So, it is not just your project, but a collaborative venture between a number of areas of the business. Now I do not respond to threats, and I am not going to respond to this one. As far as I am concerned SEEKA is a good project and it is earning us good money and so we will continue to support it.'

Lewis leaned forward and looked Martin straight in the eye. 'I am not going to give up on a lucrative deal, Martin, but you need to understand this: SEEKA has cost the company a lot, and not just in terms of resources in preparation for the launch. I have lost at least one good employee over this project and it will need to continue to pay its way for a long time yet before the whole thing is worth the trouble.'

Martin heard some of the words, but all he felt was the relief at hearing that SEEKA would continue. Lewis was not going to pull the plug after all, and he would not have to explain it to Lench. Some of Martin's arrogance came back to him. Lewis thought he was hauling Martin over the coals, but this was nothing compared to a cross-examination from Lench.

'Martin . . . are you listening to me?' Lewis had been talking and Martin had lost the words in his own thoughts. 'Who else has seen this, Martin? Who else has a copy?'

'To my knowledge there are only two copies: the one that you have and my own. No one else has seen my copy.'

'How the hell do you know that?' shouted Lewis, at last losing patience.

Martin gave no answer. He could have escalated the argument, he could have asked Lewis why he was so sure nobody had seen his copy, but in a moment of discretion, he decided not to pursue the matter. Somewhere in the back of his mind, he remembered mentioning the report to Bridget, but it didn't seem like an appropriate time to bring that up.

'I want your copy, Martin, I am going to take both copies and destroy them – off site. Now as far as we are both concerned the report never existed. Have you got that? And while you are at it, wipe any copy of the report that you might have on disk. I don't want any trace of this report in the office. Go and do it now please.'

Without responding, Martin rose and left the room. He could feel his pride trying to re-establish itself and he was angry with Lewis. Although the project would continue, he had been made to feel small – and for what? It could not even be proved that it had been his report that had been copied.

Well it was something and nothing. He wondered whether he should tell Lench about it. Lench had asked him to phone in regularly with updates on the progress of SEEKA, and he had made it clear that it wasn't the financial returns he was interested in. It was getting to the stage where Martin couldn't even sneeze without Lench wanting to know about it. He resented both Lench and Lewis. Both were out to give him a hard time; both were in it only for themselves.

Martin stayed later than usual that evening. Of course, he was very busy, but there was also a sense in which he was postponing the inevitable. He had handed over his report to Lewis and left him to sort out the details. Now his thoughts turned to the phone call he would have to make to Lench.

The lay-by on the way back to his house was becoming a regular stopping point, and every call he made from there was an ordeal. He remembered with great clarity the moment he had vomited across the upholstery of the car when he had heard that Bridget was going to be murdered.

Steeling himself, he stopped again in the gathering darkness in the same lay-by. He knew the position of the numbers on his mobile; he didn't have to look any more.

'Hello.' The same precise civilised voice.

'Hello, it's Martin.'

'Hello Martin, how are things?'

'Very good. The sales figures continue to rise, things are going extremely well. We have had another two clubs sign up for the posters, the video mix, all of the stuff. It is spreading. . . .' There was a pause. Usually, Martin spent about a minute on the phone each time to Lench, telling him how wonderful things were. This evening he stopped after about fifteen seconds, and what he said was stilted. The silence continued.

He could hear Lench breathing on the other end of the line before he spoke again in a fatherly, almost tender, voice. 'What's happened, Martin? What is it that has upset you today?'

He always knew; the old man always knew. Martin reflected on it and almost smiled. He realised now that by gushing about SEEKA to Lench over the last few weeks he had made a rope with which he could be hanged. Now, he told him the whole story: the report, the discussion with Lewis. Lench asked Martin what had been demanded by the blackmailer.

'That was the thing: the note just said "STOP SEEKA" – there was no demand for money. I suppose we should be grateful for that.'

'Quite so, Martin.' Lench sounded supportive, but it was difficult to tell over a mobile phone. 'Well Martin, it does seem to be a bit of a storm in a teacup. I suppose we

shall have to wait and see what our supposed
blackmailer does next. By the way, who do you think it
is? Who had access to these reports?'

Lewis hadn't actually asked him who he thought the
blackmailer was, so it was something he had not really
thought about. In a sense, he didn't care because it
seemed that Lewis had dealt with the situation. If there
was no proof that the report came from SLaM then
whoever had sent the note held no threat for them.

'I don't know, perhaps it was Bridget, maybe with an
accomplice. . . .' He cursed his own feebleness. Was this
the best answer he could come up with?

'Very well, Martin, let's see what happens over the
next week or so. By the way, we are meeting again next
week at the usual place. I trust you will be there.'

'Of course I will be there. Goodbye.'

'Goodbye, Martin.'

Martin switched off the phone and sat motionless for
a minute. He had the feeling that he had been tested and
failed. It was a disquieting thought, and it made him feel
uneasy for about the fourth time that day. There was little more he could do now.

Starting the car he swerved, tyres screeching, into the
first lane of traffic. He realised that he had pulled away
with more than the usual aggression when from somewhere behind him a car horn sounded. The conversation
with Lewis came back to him. It was only now that the
import of one of Lewis's comments dawned on him.
What was it Lewis had said? *I have lost at least one good
employee over this project.'

He must have been referring to his PA, but why did he
say at least one good employee? Was it a reference to
Bridget's death? What else did he know? Martin cursed
into the wheel and longed for the journey home to be
over. All he wanted to do now was to get in, lock the

door, drink an excessive amount of alcohol, and listen to some undemanding, loud music. He wanted to hide, and this was the best he could do.

* * *

Lench sat at his study desk at home. He needed to come to terms with the fool in his Group. He had allowed Martin in because he perceived that he held a strategically important position in a company that could affect many young people. Surely manipulation of the culture had been one of his master's greatest triumphs, and this was a tactical activity in the overall plan.

Certainly, he had not allowed Martin to join on the basis of his commitment to the Group. Martin was just a common 'spiv'. Oh, for sure, it was all very strategic, and his role was important but, at heart, he was a stupid, greedy man who happened to be in the right place at the right time. He liked the sexual elements of what they did, but his heart was not really in service to the master. Lench had balanced this lack of commitment against the need for someone like Martin, the importance of a project like SEEKA. He had judged that it was worth the risk. If he had known what was going to happen he might have taken a different course.

He reflected on Martin's comments: *'That was the thing: the note just said "STOP SEEKA" – there was no demand for money. I suppose we should be grateful for that.'*

It was so typical of Martin, stupid Martin, to think that the worst thing that could happen might be the loss of money. If that *had* been the case, Lench would have been much happier. No, this person was an altogether more serious enemy; and very likely, the recipient of a package that the woman Bridget had sent before the assassin had got to her.

For the first time since the project had started, Lench began to weigh the value of the SEEKA project against all the trouble that it had caused. He had compromised himself badly when he had visited Alex Masters, but he felt he had to see her for himself. It was unlikely that she was the blackmailer: she would not have left her job and then started this. That would have made her the first suspect. It had to be a legacy of the woman Bridget, and therefore would be more difficult to deal with. It was, after all, quite difficult to threaten the dead.

So what was he to do? He looked at the phone on the desk and a number of options ran through his mind. They all led to the same thing: he needed to distance himself from Martin. It would be difficult, but it had been done before; and if the worst came to the worst there was always the assassin. He had always considered this option a very blunt and heavy-handed instrument, to be used sparingly. Deaths always drew a lot of attention, but if there was no SEEKA then there was definitely no need for Martin to be part of the Group.

He would start, anyway, by asking Martin not to report in every day. That could be disguised as satisfaction, and Martin would be too stupid to guess otherwise. Then he would have to decide whether to encourage the demise of SEEKA. He would have Martin's house searched for any connection with the Group. This was a familiar routine. Within a few days he could have put plenty of distance between himself and this weak fool. The idea seemed attractive, perhaps even necessary in the light of recent events.

Fifteen

The summer was proving to be an uneasy time for the people in Alex's town.

The young people gathered next to the supermarket, clustered together around a hi-fi system or an outsized stereo from one of their brightly-coloured, under-insured cars.

People walking along the high street looked on with a mixture of fear and confusion. Boredom induced a restlessness amongst the teens. They wanted to be together, but the street corners and the public benches were the only places to go. The girls seemed more bitchy and unforgiving, while the boys tended towards a motiveless aggression. There was nothing to do and nowhere to go. Some of the older ones managed to con their way into the pubs and clubs, but that was really only an option for anyone who was at least fifteen. Besides, it was expensive.

Alex walked down the street past a crowd of teenagers. She knew a few of them and they nodded to her. It was as much recognition as they would give when they were with their peers. She understood well enough and returned the compliment with a nod back, and walked on to her destination. Under her arm she carried a bundle of rolled up posters and some handbills.

That destination was, in fact, not far from one of the groups that she passed. She was going down to her café.

She unlocked the door and went in. The whitewashed windows had been cleaned, and a curtain now ran along the length of the shop frontage, shielding the inside from view. When she was inside, she closed the door and placed the posters and handbills on the counter. Then she stood and took a long hard look at the place.

The fixed tables and chairs had been laid out so that about a hundred people could be accommodated in the place. She had even prayed over the layout, thinking about issues like how many people the place would seat and whether there should be a little stage area for musicians and singers. The result was that the café had a serving area in one corner and a place for entertainment diagonally opposite it. The intervening space was filled with seating. In a moment of inspiration and foolishness she had painted the walls bright yellow, the colour of the sun, and she had then stuck some very large posters up. By the serving area she had pasted cork tiles over a bright red square she had painted on the wall. She intended to put up notices in this space. The first notice, in large purple letters on white card, was already up:

NO SMOKING
Thank you!

She was determined to have the will to enforce these rules. Her experiences with Daisy had helped her to decide that.

The ceiling was set with clusters of different-coloured lights that could be adjusted and angled so that they focused on the stage area. Surveying the place completely for the first time, Alex felt a sense of achievement. She had wanted this and now she had it; and with that came a feeling that some responsibility was being laid on her, and also a sense of humility. She had no room for personal pride: she served her Lord and if she achieved things it was through him and for him.

At her side, Angel looked on, sharing some of her sense of satisfaction. Had she been able to read his thoughts, she would have known that this feeling of responsibility was not just a passing emotion, but very real. She had been given much, and much would be expected of her. That was the way things were.

Alex walked around the back of the serving counter to the control panels for the café's sound system. She took a CD from her bag and slipped it into the player. There was the faintest whine as the disc started to spin, and then she heard the glide of a car outside, a sound suddenly cut off and obliterated as the impact of the music hit her ears. The whole place rattled as Alex reached for the volume and brought the thing under control. Of course, it wouldn't matter if she didn't have a CD, with MP3 files she could download and play anything she wanted. The Grand Opening was the following week, and she could put up her posters now, confident that she knew when the doors would open to the public. Each poster was in a different colour and announced the opening of the 'Salt & Light Café'. The proximity to 'Sound, Light and Music' of SLaM, was an irony not lost on her.

She drew back the curtain to stick the first poster onto the window, but the sight that greeted her caused her to drop some of the handbills to the floor. About half a dozen young people were standing outside. One or two now looked at her as if she were a rather impressive animal in a cage. She could only imagine that they had heard the music and, with nothing better to do, had decided to investigate. She smiled at them as she put up her posters, watching their faces as they took in the details: 'Live Music', 'Young People Welcome', 'Opening Next Week'. She opened the door and gave them each a handbill.

As she passed out the handbills, she could see from the corner of her eye a man walking down the street towards them all. He was some considerable distance away, and she didn't know why she had noticed him, but there was certainly an urgency in his manner which caught her attention. Although she did not recognise him, she could see that he was smartly dressed. He was carrying something, and there was something familiar about him.

The immediate demands on her, though, were from the young people in front of her; they were full of questions and each one wanted some of the handbills.

As she finished giving out her leaflets, a bus pulled into the stop a few yards down the road. One of the young people moved off to catch it and was joined by a couple of the others. The group dispersed, as those who were left started to wander off down the road together. She could see that they were in animated conversation and she dared to believe that they were talking about her café. In her heart, she felt the desire to see all of them, every single one, in here where they would feel accepted and welcomed and where something of the Saviour she knew would be communicated to them.

She saw the bus nudge out into the road and in the process, she caught a glimpse of the man she had seen earlier. It was Aiden, dressed as she had never seen him dressed before, in a smart suit. Usually in the evenings and at the weekends he wore dark shirts and jeans. If he had been wearing something like that this evening, she would have probably recognised him straight away. This was a different side to him: Aiden, the man who worked in some kind of investment job – she didn't know exactly what. She found herself not altogether disappointed by the identity of the mystery man. Without much thought she waved to him and he waved back.

Alex went back into the café and made sure the door was open to admit her visitor. She tidied her hair and then turned to the door, waiting for him to arrive. A mild sense of expectation went through her. It was not unlike the feeling she had had when John had visited her a few weeks before. The thought unsettled her. Was she going to be like this with every single man now, behaving like an excited school-girl, trying to make herself look her best? She did not want to let that happen; and yet she did want someone. And if she came across a single man who she liked and who shared her beliefs, then maybe something could develop between them.

'Hi Alex!'

She turned round. It was too late to think about it now, he was here.

'Well, I'm impressed. This is superb! You know, you really are going to be able to do some stuff for God here.'

Alex felt the most delicious sense of achievement and pride colouring her cheeks and making her feel shy.

Aiden laughed, 'Well I *am* impressed, Alex. In fact, I was wondering if I could help you at all. I mean in addition to the electrical work with John. Is there anything I can help with now?'

She looked doubtfully at his suit and tie, 'You're a bit smart for this sort of work, Aiden.'

'I've got some working clothes with me.' He held up a small sports bag, and she realised then that he really did want to help her. She was surprised at how moved she was by the offer, and she felt a moistness in her eyes. This was about as vulnerable as Alex wanted to be right now.

'Well you can always finish painting the office at the back – you can get changed there if you want.'

'Sounds good to me. I'll see you in a couple of minutes.' He disappeared into the office and Alex resisted the rather ridiculous temptation to follow him in there.

She was intrigued by the enthusiasm that he showed. He had helped out before, of course, but that had been with John, and he had been his usual reserved self. She needed to find out what had motivated him to rush down here tonight.

He emerged from the office still wearing the shirt but with an old pair of jeans and some overalls. Alex almost felt as if the real Aiden had suddenly emerged from the office, with the previous one cast in the role of an impostor. He smiled at her. 'Hand me that paintbrush and I'll get on with it.'

He made short work of the painting, and Alex thought he would probably go home having done his bit for the evening. To her surprise, he asked if there was anything else.

She decided to take advantage of the extra labour.

'Well there are these handbills to give out. I want every kid in the neighbourhood hearing about the café and wanting to come here. I suggest that we walk in opposite directions out of the café and just give out the fliers to everyone we see.' She looked at her watch. It was just after 9 p.m. 'We'll meet back here at 10 o'clock.'

'Okay,' he said, taking a pile of the handbills. With the same purposeful walk that she had noticed earlier, he headed for the door of the café. She followed him out and they walked away from each other along the length of the high street.

At 10.05 she arrived back at the café. Aiden was waiting outside. He had passed out all of the handbills she had given him.

'You got rid of all of them – well done!'

'Any time you want a hand, just ask and I'll help you if I can.' He went into the back office to collect his bag.

She had learnt to be wary of offers of help, but Aiden seemed to prove himself every time. He had offered to help with the rewiring and of course he had been a valuable addition to the youth club. Tonight, again, he had shown what he was capable of, and there were none of the emotional strains which dealing with John usually caused.

He emerged, and she looked at him again. He seemed to radiate calmness and a reassurance that made her own life seem giddy and insubstantial. She felt as if the floor beneath her feet was just beginning to tip to one side. In response, she had to hold on to the edge of the shop door. It was as much to do with tiredness as anything else. She had not taken a break in about ten days.

She realised now that she was scared, because she didn't want to be this vulnerable to anyone. Not when they were flesh and blood and could so easily be taken from her.

Aiden said goodbye and headed towards the door. There was almost a gracefulness about him that seemed unhindered by his briskness and determination. In that moment, Alex made a decision. It was a decision that she would not have made if she'd had any more time to brood on the situation. She decided that she would invite him back to her flat for coffee. He deserved at least a drink for his efforts, and maybe she deserved some more answers from him. In a sense, he seemed too good to be true. She wanted to see the vulnerable side to him, the weaknesses, the things that motivated him. So far, he had never let his mask slip.

'Come back for a cup of coffee, Aiden. You've done a lot of work and I'm grateful.'

Aiden turned to her without the hesitation she had expected. 'Thank you Alex, I'd like that.'

They walked back along the high street towards Alex's flat. Although Conner was staying over again, he would be out till late; he had gone up into town to listen to some band that Alex had never heard of. It was just as well, she wanted to question this man alone.

The first thing Aiden noticed when they walked into Alex's flat was the familiar sense of order that existed in this place. There was a kind of beauty here, a balance of peace. He started to relax and then, at Alex's invitation, he sat down in the same chair that John had sat in during his visit a few weeks earlier. He had the same view of Alex in her kitchen, making coffee.

He was struck by the energy she possessed. Even in such a simple task as making coffee, he could see the purpose, the drive within her. Here indeed was a woman who would get things done.

It was only then that he noticed a stack of CDs on the floor. They looked as if they had been propped against one of the chairs before they had toppled over and scattered across the carpet. It was an incongruous site amongst the symmetry of Alex's flat. She noticed him staring at them.

'Sorry, they're my brother's. He's staying here for a while to help with the launch of the café.' She scooped up the CDs and dumped them on the bed in the spare room.

Aiden was concluding that there was something very satisfying about being in this place without lots of other people. So far, he had only been here when the home group met. This time he had the place, and Alex to himself.

He started to soak up the detail. The light, warm colours suited the summertime and the aspect of the room. There were citrus yellows, with shades of sky blue reflected in the carpet and furnishings. On the mantelpiece were the ornaments that he had noticed on his first visit: three elephants and a number of other wooden carvings. Above them, on the wall, was a framed water-colour – a picture of a sunflower in bloom. The artist had captured the depth and richness of the yellow petals and the generosity of the bed of seeds contained within it. It was as if the whole room had been decorated to comple-ment the picture. Aiden felt a tangible sense of peace, and a kind of rich abundance, as if there were a very source of life here. In this environment Alex seemed to be transformed, within the warmth of the colours and the intimacy of the art and artefacts in the room she became more real, less another church member and more an individual, a woman in her own right.

Aiden found himself looking at her in a new light, and he liked what he saw.

She brought in the coffee and he savoured the warm aroma as he watched her sit in the chair opposite him.

'Why are you doing this, though, Alex? Why are you opening this café?'

'Because someone has to, so it might as well be me. You know what my passion is; you know what I want for the young people. I hate the fact that youngsters today are under such pressure, with school, friends, parents, drugs and sex – the whole thing. And then I had to get out of SLaM as well. The way the company was going was beginning to make me feel sick.'

'Like this SEEKA thing?' ventured Aiden.

'Exactly, it is evil, I can feel it – I couldn't stay there. Anyway, there is so much else to do, so much else I need to do.'

She leant forward and looked him in the eye. She was always like this when she got onto this subject.

'You probably know Alice, from the youth club. A few weeks ago, she came in with a fifty-pound note to pay for her sweets. She hadn't got it from her parents and it wasn't a birthday gift. So where did she get it from?

Thieving? Prostitution? The fact is, I don't know where girls of that age get that kind of money . . .' she paused. 'I have to do everything I can.'

Aiden frowned – there was probably a perfectly reasonable explanation as to why Alice had a fifty-pound note. 'She could have got it from anywhere; it might not be anything sinister.'

'No, there's something wrong. It's not just the money – it's the way she has been behaving.' Alex was frowning, as if distracted by a puzzle that she couldn't work out.

'What's happened to Alice is a reflection of what's happening in this town, and beyond. I am going to do what I can: first locally, with things like the café, and then maybe on a bigger scale.' She paused, realising that she was now talking about plans and ambitions that she hadn't shared with anyone else, ever.

'I want it to be big, Aiden. I want millions of young people to have an alternative culture, with everything that goes with it: fashion, music, literature, film, all of it. I want to invade this enemy culture with something that is credible and Christ-centred.'

She felt as if she had just revealed some of her most intimate desires to him, and it was terrifying.

'I'm sorry Aiden, you've got me on one of my hobby-horses. I really want to make a difference if I can, and this café is the start of it.'

He sat back and thought. He knew that soon he would have to tell Alex why he was here, but he was not really clear about his own motives. Up till a short while ago, he had been interested in Alex as a business partner. Now he was catching some of the infectious vision that she held, and there was something more. She was determined, strong, brave – and very attractive. He needed to decide why he was here.

Across the room, Angel stood with another of his own kind, the one who watched over Aiden.

Alex felt that she had said enough for now, so she decided to turn the conversation round. It was time for him to answer some questions.

'So, what about you, Aiden – what do you want from life?'

His smile made her think of a little boy who had been found out.

'The most important thing in my life at the moment is my work. I am with a company called Mustard Seed Investments. We specialise in finding fledgling Christian-run businesses for Christian investors. We have funds available at the moment and one of the projects I am interested in is your café. You have a vision and you have some finance, but you might need some more. I want to see if we can help you make this dream of yours a reality.'

Alex felt suddenly inexplicably alone. She wanted to scream at him, but could not. She felt hurt and offended, as if he had been unexpectedly rude to her. But of course he had not, and the offence existed only in her mind. She now realised that she had made some assumptions about Aiden's interest and she needed to take her own advice about being careful with her emotions.

After a few moments, she realised that he was staring at her.

'Are you all right Alex . . . you look a bit tired?'

She struggled for a sensible reply, but the space between them defied any answer from her. She smiled weakly, almost as an act of consolation for herself.

'Look, I think I had better be going – give you a chance to rest. We can talk again another time,' he said as he turned towards the door. This was not a situation that he wanted to deal with.

Maybe this was a unique combination of events; perhaps in other circumstances she would not have said anything and simply let him go, but the rules didn't seem to apply to Alex that night.

'Come back, Aiden.'

He froze, caught between her request and his own desire to get away.

'Yes, I am tired, so don't talk to me about your job, Aiden, talk to me about you – who you are. Talk to me about your hopes and your pain; tell me who you are.'

A sense of unreality swept over him. What was she saying? This wasn't polite Christian conversation; this was real and dangerous. He felt just the slightest tinge of excitement and his own desire to enter the arena.

'Okay Alex, let's you and I talk shall we?' He turned again to her, with exaggerated slowness, and now stood face on to her.

'You don't want me to talk business with you, but I'm not sure I want to tell you the kind of things you want to hear.'

'What do I want you to say, Aiden?' She felt the tension now, but she did not find it unpleasant.

'You want something of me – the real me. I think you want the short cut to getting to know who I am.'

Before she could respond he continued, 'My name is Aiden Stephen Kennedy, and my father moved here from Shannon before I was born. My parents live in the capital. I work as a business finance specialist, and I am currently single. I have a strong faith, but I haven't got everything worked out at all. There are times, Alex, when I wake at night and I scream, but it is a silent scream because my reputation with my neighbours does not allow me the luxury of screaming out loud.'

She looked at him, amazed that he would let her be a witness to his interior life. 'I am lonely, Alex, like you;

and I am wary, like you; and I will extend you every last piece of courtesy whilst I summon up the courage to be totally honest with you.'

Then he stepped up to her and hugged her, feeling the depth of the physical contact: her warmth, her scent, her presence.

Then, with no more words, he left her and made his way home.

Later that night, he awoke with a rush of adrenaline. In his mind were the ragged fragments of a dream. His first love had been there holding him and they had been sharing intimate secrets from the past with each other. Now fully awake he tried to store the fragments of the dream, desperately committing them to memory before he relaxed again into his bed and passed back into sleep.

Sixteen

Daisy had asked if she could help in the café over the summer. It wasn't because she needed the money, she just wanted to belong somewhere and Alex was the closest thing to family that she had. She was in the café every day in the week before opening, checking that all of the equipment worked, looking over the stock, and helping Alex with some of the last-minute details.

With a late burst of assistance from all sorts of people, Alex had her café ready before the official opening day. Laura had persuaded her to have an evening off and so some of the girls from the church had met in the centre of town and headed off to the cinema.

Conner had come up in the week prior to the opening day. That evening he said goodbye to Alex and slumped across the sofa in front of the TV. After ten minutes spent flicking through the channels, he eventually succumbed to his restlessness and headed down to the café where he knew Daisy was finishing off a couple of little jobs for Alex. He told himself that he wanted to try out the sound system and that was a good reason for going. He picked up his guitar and headed out into the warm summer evening.

At the café door, Conner rang the bell for an unreasonably long period of time and peered past the edge of the curtain. From behind the counter Daisy saw him and smiled. She considered Conner to be something of an enigma. He had sent her a letter reminding her that his big Christian event had stayed dry while the rest of the country was drenched. She was pleased for his sake that it hadn't rained, but it just proved that he was a bit odd. Maybe it was a 'bloke thing' as much as him being a Christian.

What she had found more intriguing had been the final section of his letter where he had tried to write about their evening together at Alex's flat. He had written about the fact that they'd had a good evening, then he had reminded her about how his big event had stayed dry (again), and finally he had written something about how he had enjoyed their time together (again). He had bumbled around in the words of this letter, not knowing what to say to her. Daisy realised that he did like her and, actually, she was beginning to like him. The next few weeks could prove to be very interesting.

She opened the door and let him in.

'Alright Daisy, how are you, mate?'

'All the better for seeing you, cousin,' she smiled at him.

'What? Are you really pleased to see me? Oh, say you are Daisy!' Before he had even walked through the door he had launched into song:

'Daisy, Daisy, give me your answer do.
I'm half crazy, oh for the love of you!'

She pulled him in and quickly closed the door, hoping that no one outside had noticed the noise.

'Shut up, Conner!'

'Oh okay, I'm sorry. Look I won't disturb you, I'm just checking the sound system.' He was still smiling as he got his guitar out and switched on the PA. After a few minutes of routine checks, he paused for a moment. He was quiet long enough for Daisy to look up from what she was doing, then he started to play again. He played a tune that she recognised from their evening together. She had to stop and listen as he played the piece with an intensity that made her spine tingle. She felt again the mix of feelings that she had experienced in Alex's flat those few weeks before. He looked up at her while he continued playing and, without thinking about it, he blew her a kiss.

Daisy felt a pressure on the sides of her head. It made her want to take Conner away from here and make love with him, right now. She almost felt ashamed for thinking such a thing. She put down the plates she had been stacking and walked over to the stage where Conner was playing. He continued with the piece as she moved over to him, and he afforded himself a good look at her.

She was wearing some very tight jeans that betrayed every curve that she had. She also wore a T-shirt that eased and moved with the curves of her body. There was a picture of a sunflower on the front of it. As his eyes explored the design, he almost lost his way and he had to close his eyes for a moment to refocus on what he was doing. It was a refocus that took in both his musical sense of direction and his moral purpose. As he pulled himself together and carried on with his sound check, Daisy took the final step towards him and, cupping his chin in her fingers, she kissed him on the lips. He heard himself play the same chord three times as if musically he was on hold while the rest of him dealt with this girl in front of him.

'You know, Conner, you could come back to my flat when you have finished.' She looked at the expression on his face. 'Oh don't worry, I'm not going to seduce you, and I know that you wouldn't get involved with me anyway because you are a Christian and I'm not. But we can be friends can't we?'

He didn't feel that he could decline. He was staying at Alex's flat but he had a key and could come and go as he pleased. Besides, he quite liked the idea of an hour or so with Daisy. In the back of his mind he repeated some words over and over to himself: 'I must behave myself with Daisy, I must behave myself with Daisy, I must behave myself with Daisy . . .' It was a mixture of self-resolve and prayer.

Conner finished his sound check. He couldn't concentrate any more anyway, so it was pointless to go on, and the system seemed fine. As he packed up his guitar and stored it in the office behind the counter, Daisy finished off her tasks and got ready to lock the place up. They caught the bus and headed off towards the centre of the city. It stopped a short walk from Daisy's flat.

The bus lumbered along the clogged streets of the metropolis, easing around parked cars and road works. Conner found himself wondering why he had agreed to go off with Daisy. He looked at his watch. It was about 9.45, and by the time they got back to her flat it would be nearly 10.30. They huddled into two seats at the back of the bus and Conner felt her leaning gently in to him. Was this a bad idea after all? Perhaps he should have said no. Still, it was too late to worry about that now. This sort of situation was a bit of a weakness of his: he would get friendly with a girl – just friendly – and then sooner or later they would get a bit carried away. Sometimes it meant the end of the friendship. He couldn't afford to let that happen with Daisy: she was family and also now perhaps a work colleague. It was no use, he really would have to try to keep himself under control. Absent-mindedly he wondered whether he was allowed to fancy his second cousin, or whatever she was.

He felt her lean towards him. 'Well, how is the band going, Conner?'

'We've got a recording of our work on CD, and a few small gigs lined up. We haven't got a contract though –

that's still a way off. The next six months are make or break. If we can't get a contract in that time then we will have to disband and start looking for some real jobs.'

Daisy laughed and patted his knee. 'If the others are as good as you, I am sure you will make it. So, are you all Christians, I mean do all your songs have a religious content?'

'To answer your first question, yes, we are all Christians, and to answer your second question, no we don't only do 'Christian' songs.'

The bus pulled up at some traffic lights, and he leaned towards her so that his lips were close to her ear: 'What about Alex's café then, what are you going to be doing there?'

'Well, college has finished so I'm going to help for a couple of months – a bit of cooking and waitressing, you know.'

'But why, I mean you know Alex is doing this as a subtle way to get the kids into Christianity. So why should you be party to that?'

'I'm not doing it for Jesus, I'm doing it for Alex.' Her tone was almost sharp. One or two of the other passengers close to them pretended not to notice the change in her voice. She continued, more quietly. 'It's work, Conner, and it pays the rent, and it keeps me in my little flat in student-land in a run down part of the city.' Despite the fact that she had recently received some money, she still couldn't get out of the habit of feeling poor. 'And I don't want to have to go back to my parents' house.'

They said no more to each other until they reached the stop near to Daisy's flat.

As they got off she turned to him, 'Look I'm sorry Conner, it's just that things have been difficult for me at home and I see the café as a means of escape. And I love

Alex. She has done a lot for me in the past few weeks. It's not so much Jesus I'm interested in as some of you nice Christian people.' There was just a hint of a cheeky grin on her face. Conner reflected on the fact that he hadn't felt particularly like family when Daisy had kissed him earlier. As they started down the road she took his hand, and he made no attempt to resist her.

They reached her flat, which turned out to be the top two rooms in an old converted Victorian town house. The place felt cold and damp: it was clear that the sunny weather of the past few days had not penetrated here. Daisy switched on the light. Conner wasn't sure what to expect, and he took in the whole of Daisy's living space in one go: bathroom off to the right, kitchen/diner and bedroom. It seemed like quite a generous set of lodgings for a student.

There were pens and pencils, cups and plates, papers and sketchbooks. They were scattered across the bed and on the table. An ashtray near the centre of the table contained the gathered remains of most of a packet of twenty. The strip light in the kitchen hummed when Daisy turned it on, making the room seem impersonal. Daisy noticed it as if for the first time, and, as if to compensate, she walked over to the little midi system sitting next to some cookery books and turned on the radio.

She asked Conner to find a CD while she swept the clutter off the bed and put the kettle on. Glancing at her collection, he found much that could be recommended. There were some things that even he would never have listened to, although there was enough for a genuine choice. In the end he opted for Van Morrison: it would set the right sort of tone for the evening – friendly, but not too friendly. Next, he looked around for somewhere to sit that wasn't the bed. Most of the available space was covered with books, sketches and papers; unless he sat on the floor, there was nowhere. He gave up and perched on the end of the quilt cover. She came through from the kitchen with some coffee, and sat down next to him.

Conner realised that this flat symbolised Daisy: hectic, disorganised, unsettled, and yet at the same time tempting, even sexy in a way that he could not fathom. They could be seeing a lot of each other in the next few months if they both worked for Alex in the café. For Daisy, the following academic year was planned out. She had got through her first year and had two more to go, but Conner had been on a one-year course, and that was finished. His future lay with the band.

'What are you going to do now, Conner?'

'Well, I am going to drink my coffee and try to behave myself!' There was a smirk on his face.

'No,' she slapped his leg and some hot coffee slopped onto his jeans. 'Oh God! Here, let me get a cloth,' and she hurried into the kitchen.

'I'm okay,' he said and he smiled as he wiped his trousers. It was uncomfortable, but he would survive. They both started to relax, and the CD played on, just loud enough to cover the drone of the fluorescent tube. Earlier, Daisy had wondered whether she was being a bit unfair on Conner by bringing him back here. She knew what she was doing, and she knew what she ultimately wanted. Now though, she didn't care. She knew that the most he would do was kiss her and so what if he did? It was safe, physical contact, so she reasoned, and that was something she needed right now. They talked for some time about Conner's band, and music, and the café, and Conner's faith, and her lack of it.

'I sometimes wonder whether Will was lucky getting out of this life when he did.'

Conner stared at her for a moment. 'How can you say that, Daisy? There is so much to live for.'

Daisy's response spoke of resignation rather than defiance.

'Is there? Do you really think that? "Choose life." Conner, is that what you're saying? Choose kids, and mortgages, and the rat race and the pointless striving . . . and for what? You might as well go out and enjoy yourself. And if you do get wasted, well, so what?'

She raised her voice as she continued to speak. The conversation had revealed an old source of poison, and she was leaning slightly forward, towards Conner, as if close proximity might help to reinforce the point she was making. He could sense her passion and it reminded him that they were both sitting on her bed.

He looked at her and shook his head.

'No, Daisy. No. I have looked at despair, and there is no glamour in it. I have seen what giving up does to some people.'

She looked at him, daring to confront him with her cynicism: 'Really? Is life so good? I've had life – I've had it for twenty years, and most of it has been rubbish. Nobody really cares; nobody gives a damn. It is just one long struggle – and for what?' She could feel herself slipping into the old rage that she used to feel. Anger at the injustice, the pain she felt at being unloved. 'Conner, if this is life, then maybe the alternative isn't so bad. Maybe getting stoned or tripped out or whatever, is just the best thing you can do. Some people are rather good at it.'

It was his turn to lean forward now. She could see that he was shaking slightly, as if he were about to burst. This was the first time she had seen him without the cheeky grin, the look of a comedian. She felt unnerved and excited by his passion.

'I'll tell you something, Daisy. You're right, there are some people who glory in the fact that they haven't chosen life; they have chosen something else. They have chosen to pawn every last asset until they are huddled in a room, curled on the bare floor like an unwanted foetus. And do you know what they do once they have sold everything they have? I'll tell you what they do: they start to sell anything else they've got. Their dignity, their moral values, their relationships – it all starts to go little bit by little bit, then when that is gone they start to find other people's stuff, other people's goods, and lives, and . . .'

Daisy tried to say something but he wouldn't let her.

'No, you can say your piece in a minute, when I have finished. I have seen this, you know. Real people with real lives – screwed up, wasted.'

He pointed at her. 'Just imagine you are huddled in a blanket, and you don't notice the smell any more, and the mattress is still there because who the hell would buy something that stinks like that? You've got nothing left, so you start to sell the things inside yourself, like what's right and wrong, and your family. And you have to start hating them so that you can sell the memory of them. It's all by degrees, so that you can sell it off bit by bit. It's like there's some maggot eating away at who you are, not in great lumps but in little bits so that every morning it doesn't take you so long to justify the next desperate thing that you're going to do. Then – when you've sold it all and the thing you're best at is justifying yourself – you get to the point where you have to justify the poverty of who you are. What do you say? You say it is worth it because the alternative is worse; because life is really greed and indifference, hypocrisy, and you aren't really missing anything worth having. And do you know what? If that were true – that life is just a scramble up the greasy pole followed by a slide down it into pointless oblivion – then maybe they would have a point. But that's not life, not real living. The way those people describe life – that isn't life, that's just existence. You know, if you convince yourself that the choice is between 'E' and existence and you chose 'E', well who can blame you? You've got a point haven't you?

'But you don't have to exist, you can choose life, real life, and that's better than anything you can swallow or shoot or snort. So, when I chose, I didn't choose a trip, or the rat race – I chose life, and I will keep on choosing life. Do you know why? It's not because things aren't difficult, not because things aren't unfair and painful and unjust, but because I realised that I wasn't alone after all. There is love, and there is purpose, there is more than all this scrambling around in our own muck. Otherwise we all might as well shoot up or sleep around or whatever we want to do.'

He stopped, as if all the breath and energy had gone from him.

'I know love here inside myself.' His voice grew softer now. 'My life is relevant, I am loved, and I matter. And so do you, Daisy, so do you.'

He stopped and looked away from her. Daisy had forgotten what she was going to say, overcome by the spectrum of emotions he had shown, and the intimacy with which he had finished what he was saying. It had not been a particularly eloquent speech, but it had been from the heart.

She was just wondering whether he expected her to answer when he spoke again.

'So what are you going to choose, Daisy?'

She felt exhausted just listening to him. There was little she could say. He was asking her, forcing her to make a decision that she was nowhere near making, and she didn't understand anyway.

'I don't know what you and Alex and all the rest of you have found that gives you so much passion and so much . . . discipline.'

He laughed at the word 'discipline'.

'What do you think I've found, Daisy?' He looked into her eyes and, for the first time, he thought that he could see into her soul. It was a crowded place, but there he saw a longing, a hunger for reality. She really wanted to find the answer. This was no feint, no game. As the truth seeped into his mind, he put his arms around her shoulders and held her as gently as he could. In the end, she felt such compassion coming from him that she had to push him away. She could not yet face such love as this – she did not feel worthy of it.

But she could face opening up a little – she trusted him that much – so she talked about the wreckage of the first years of her life. She talked about her loveless childhood, some of her father's superstitions, the way he sometimes sought out mediums and astrologers for advice. Then there was the pain she felt sometimes, the anger and self-pity. Although the mood had calmed down, this was still a groundbreaking conversation for her, and it could only have happened in her flat, on her territory.

'Alex has helped me a lot though,' she said. 'My time with her was like a healing process. I think there's more though.'

'What do you mean, more?'

'It's still there, Conner. Deep down in myself, I can feel a darkness. It makes me feel self-pity. It's like an enemy inside my head, damning every action, telling me how I am used to the indifference and the distrust. I can't cope with being loved!'

Conner leaned forward and kissed her forehead, lingering for a moment as he took in the scent of her hair. 'Sometimes when I can't cope with things I just . . . go away. I finds it's always best – I just disappear.'

She smiled at the endearing, foolish way he seemed to deal with life; 'Okay, Conner, so where do you go?'

He was silent now, as if to tell her would be to give up something precious.

'Look at me, Conner.' She faced him with her blue eyes searching out the secrets within him. 'Where do you go? Tell me where you go to find peace.' Daisy wanted to be in a place like that. She had never known peace in all her life.

He let out a long sigh, and the cheeky smile returned to his face. 'Maybe one day I'll take you there.'

'Promise me you will, Conner.'

'Maybe.'

Then he took her in his arms and held her as if he loved her. He didn't know why he did it – perhaps it was because he knew that he was going to hurt her with what he said next.

'Daisy,' he looked at her. 'Let me ask you one question.'

'Yeah sure.' She felt as if an already deep conversation was about to go one step deeper. He had proved to be so unpredictable that she didn't know what to expect.

'Do you believe in demons?'

'What?'

'Do you believe that demons exist? I mean really exist?'

She laughed: a short, rather derisive sound that suggested that this was territory that she did not want to cover. Within herself, she suddenly felt very uncomfortable.

'No, of course I don't! Why? Are you going to suggest that I'm possessed?' An uneasy smile crept across her face.

'I don't like the word possession: I think sometimes demons hang around people, like unwelcome guests.'

'Are you saying I have one of these things around me?'

'Maybe . . . I don't know.'

It was too much for her. How could he suggest such a thing? How dare he spoil the evening with this sort of comment?

'Who the hell do you think you are, Conner?' She could feel the release of adrenaline, and the background panic. She sat back from him and put down the mug she was holding, because her hand shook. 'What do you think you're doing, talking to me about demons?'

Conner sat up and sighed. Perhaps he'd just done something really stupid, he just didn't know. 'I'm sorry Daisy, you know how I say things without thinking too much about them. It's just that it's not you. I mean the intensity in you, the unease – I can feel it coming from you and I am sure you can feel it inside.' He looked at her as if he was pleading for support. Did he really expect to get it from her?

'I can't believe you can say this sort of thing! I mean, I don't even believe in all this stuff. Who do you think you are; who do the lot of you think you are? I suppose you think I'm going to hell don't you. Well damn you Conner!' She was angry now. She had raised her voice and she was standing up. At the back of her mind, though, hidden away, the awful plausibility of what he had said started to gnaw at her. She didn't believe it, and she didn't want to know, and she hated him for being so observant. She felt like a cornered animal, and because it just might be true, she was even more vehement in her denials.

'I'm sorry Daisy,' he replied, sensing that a quick exit might be the best course of action. He got up, placed the mug on the side of the table and started to walk to the door. She watched him through the moistness of her eyes, the outline of him blurred with tears. She hated him and yet he was like a lifeline. Although she wanted him out, she also wanted him to stay. She felt like a wire pulled in two directions and tightening with every moment.

Not for the first time, Conner wondered whether he had mistaken a word which God had wanted him to say for putting his big foot in it. When he got it right it had a deep effect on the person he was speaking to, but when he got it wrong, he made a complete fool of himself, and often upset the person in the process. What had he done here? He just didn't know.

He turned and she saw his features through the blur of her tears. 'I'm sorry Daisy . . .' he hesitated, and looked away from her. 'You see, I love you, and I want the best for you.'

She told him what he could do with his love, and he turned again and went to the door. This was no phoney exit, and he was already checking for the change in his pocket, hoping the bus wouldn't be too long.

As she watched him leave, Daisy knew exactly what she wanted to do. She wanted to laugh at him and despise him and flick him away like an insignificant little insect. But she could not. She could not make her anger fit with the respect and concern he had shown her. She desperately wanted to call him back, even if she ended up shouting at him again. At least he would be here with her. But if she called him back she was admitting the possibility that what he had said might be true, and she didn't want to do that. She could hear him walking down the stairs – he would be at the front door of the house in a moment. This religious nut really loved her. He was a fool to say what he'd said, and he was a fool to love her. She wanted to hate him – not really because of what he had said, but because he both cared for her and hurt her. He asked things of her that she couldn't give him. But if he was right, what then?

She heard the front door slam. Something that seemed beyond her own volition launched her towards the kitchen and over to the window above the sink. She pushed up the old sash window which creaked in protest. She could see him, a receding figure heading for the bus stop.

'Conner, don't go! Come back, please!' The entire street must have heard her, and she was suddenly aware of how loud her voice could be when she really wanted to get someone's attention, and how urgent she sounded.

He turned around in the middle of the road and looked up to her window. Not wanting to make any more noise, she beckoned to him. He waited a moment and, as she beckoned again, he turned and headed back to the flat.

She was in the kitchen making some more coffee, trying to work out what she could say to him. He pushed the door shut and walked back to the bed where he had been sitting a few minutes before.

'Listen Conner, if you don't talk about demons again tonight, I won't spill coffee on you – is that a deal?'

There was a moment of silence between them, and the sound of Van Morrison floated in from the other room. She didn't deserve to be upset any more this evening.

'It's a deal. But can I ask you one more question?' He looked at her with his cheeky smile. Inside himself, he wondered why he was always pushing his luck; why he couldn't just sit here and be neutral for a couple of hours. He would never be like that.

She was facing him now, handing him a fresh mug of coffee.

'Go on then Conner. I suppose this is going to be a bit more religion, but I warn you, this is the last one.' There was an edge to her voice. She had clearly had enough for tonight.

He tried to look as serious as he could: 'Who do you think moved the stone?'

Daisy traced back their conversation to see if there was something she had missed, some issue or question that had gone unanswered. She could think of nothing. 'What are you talking about, Conner?' He was always talking in riddles; no wonder she felt so nervous with him.

He sat up slightly and took her hand. 'The stone in front of Jesus' grave . . . who do you think moved it? The Romans, the Pharisees, the disciples . . . an angel maybe?'

He half expected her to ignore the question, but to his surprise, she smiled.

'Ah, now I know the answer to this one. It was none of them! You see, Jesus was actually an alien and after they buried him, the mother ship came down,' she looked at him in mock seriousness, 'and a party of aliens came and beamed the stone and took him away. That's what happened.' She smiled a knowing smile.

'Really?' Conner was incredulous.

'Really.' She sat down on the bed next to him and looked him in the eye. They sat staring at each other for a full ten seconds before Conner gave in and burst into laughter. Then she laughed, and there was such a sense of release in laughing with him that she nearly started crying again.

As the laughter died, he stood up and moved to the other end of the bed where he sat down against the wall. Then he held out his arms and she lay back against him. From where he was sitting, he could cradle her, and she felt as if she were a child again, receiving the love that she had craved. It was an indulgence that she would never have allowed herself, even a few weeks ago. But now she didn't care. She was too tired to resist it, and besides, he wasn't going to hurt her. He had taken a risk with her like Will had taken a risk, although Conner's had been the greater of the two. As far as Daisy was concerned, it didn't matter whether he was right or wrong, she had learnt that people who took risks for her were the ones who loved her.

Time eased by, and only the ending of the CD brought them out of their reverie. Conner went to the bathroom and thought about putting on his coat and going. The last bus home had probably gone by now.

'I suppose you should go,' she smiled at him. She didn't feel so much like a child any more, and she wanted to take him into her bed with her to enjoy the intimacy further, but it wasn't going to happen.

'Oh stuff it!' He sat back down on the bed and she lay in his arms again.

In his mind he played through the tune that God had given him in Alex's flat a few weeks before. The notes tumbled through his mind, and then he thought he heard Daisy singing along to it in a language he didn't understand. Gradually the language changed and she was singing his name. *'Conner, Conner* . . . Conner!'

He woke with a start, and at first, he didn't even know where he was. His neck was aching and his back hurt. She was sitting up next to him.

'Wake up, Conner,' she laughed. 'We both fell asleep. It's 6.30 in the morning.'

This was one of those rare occasions when words just failed him. He got onto his feet; his body ached and his mouth was dry. Taking a deep breath, he swayed off to the bathroom again. When he returned Daisy had made some tea.

'Well how about the first bus instead of the last one?' She was smiling at him. He smiled back, but remained silent, his mouth felt like a piece of carpet.

They sipped their tea in a kind of disorientated silence for a couple of minutes and then Conner slowly got to his feet again.

'I don't know what Alex will say,' he managed a laugh. 'I think I'd better go. I'm supposed to be helping her later on today.'

Patches of the previous evening's conversation were coming back to him. He remembered the comment about demons, and Daisy's explanation of who moved the stone.

'That gravestone thing, Daisy. . . . I shall be back for a real answer one day, but until then, here's to the mother ship.' He raised his mug in mock salute.

Then he came to her and they embraced. He felt like falling asleep again in her arms. Daisy relaxed as well, and if they stood here long enough one of them was going to fall asleep. He released her and headed towards the door, blowing her a kiss as he went.

She looked out of the window in the kitchen onto the street below. He was walking towards the bus stop at a brisk pace, and the sunrise picked him out as a dark figure on the pavement. She judged that the bus would be along in about quarter of an hour. Just as she was going to pull the curtain, he turned and waved. She waved back and blew him a kiss but she thought that he was probably too far away to notice.

It was only when he had walked round the corner and disappeared from view that she realised that she had been standing on tip-toe to get a better view of him, and the arches of her feet ached. She started to tidy up the room for something to do, walking the sensation back into her feet. When she picked up the cup he had been drinking from, she spoke aloud to herself. 'Who moved the stone? You will get your answer one day, Conner. Soon, but not yet.'

Seventeen

On a bright summer morning, Alex Masters opened her café.

A small crowd had gathered outside the place. Some were church people who were around and wanted to show some support. Some were kids who were either in the youth club or hung around on the street and had heard about the place. A rather flustered man with a pencil moustache turned up from the local paper. He demanded that Alex stand in front of the café with a big grin on her face holding one of the mugs. As the photographer worked, Conner stood just behind him pulling the most ridiculous faces and extravagantly photographing everyone with an imaginary camera. Alex, initially distracted, ended up laughing. The man from the papers promised a nice shot and a small piece in the local news section, around about page thirteen or fourteen.

Daisy and Laura were on for the first shift of the day. Alex would take over later, but for now, she wanted to be amongst her first customers. The place filled up quickly, and the music was upbeat gospel, full of the promise of forthcoming victories. It was not to everyone's taste, but you had to start somewhere. Some notices had gone up on the board: details of different bands that would be playing in the café over the next few months, information about activities in the church, and the boldly-coloured 'No Smoking' sign.

Alex had spoken to most of the people in the café when Aiden appeared. He was dressed in his suit and obviously on his way to work. A little fish symbol stood out on the material of his lapel. He waved to Alex and went over to the counter to get a coffee.

Alex looked at him for a moment. Here was a man who had suddenly come into focus for her. She had not paid him much attention because she had been so wrapped up in her feelings for John. Now she was beginning to realise what she had been missing.

She moved across in his direction, chatting to customers on the way.

'This is a great day for you, Alex.'

'Thanks, I just can't believe that it is all happening now.'

Aiden leaned forward, 'Well it is happening, and only you could do it – certainly here in this town. It's going to be good, Alex, very good. Listen, I know I can't help much in the café with my job as it is, but if I can help you, I will. You just need to ask, okay?'

'Thanks, Aiden. I do appreciate the support you have given me,' she placed her hand on his arm. She seemed to watch herself do it as if it was someone else's hand, but then he placed his hand on her and she felt herself travel through an emotional landscape from acquaintance to friend and then on to new territory. She realised again how much this man was beginning to mean to her.

He was about to speak when a woman, whom Alex vaguely recognised, interrupted them. She was dressed in a beige jacket, skirt, overcoat and gloves. There was a rather elaborate brooch on the lapel of her jacket. Her clothing suggested self-importance and social superiority, but her face suggested the weight and horror of an appalling worry.

'Are you Alex Masters?'

'Yes, that's me.'

'I'm sorry to trouble you, my name is Brenda Marsh. My daughter, Alice, goes to your youth club. Well, Alice has disappeared. She went to school on Friday, and she went out on Friday night – I don't know where, she got back quite late – and then on Saturday morning she just went off, and I don't know where she is. We can't find her – none of her friends know where she is. Do you know where she might have gone?'

Mrs Marsh was turning paler by the moment, and her left hand was trembling. Aiden got up from his seat and invited her to sit down. She accepted his offer, and sank into the chair. Brenda Marsh was an uneasy mixture of civility and panic. She wouldn't normally have come into a place like the café, but the veneer of respectability was starting to wear thin.

Once seated, she removed a small hanky from her pocket. She looked as if she had had little sleep in the last couple of days, and dark, brown-grey rings circled her eyes.

Alex felt a wave of compassion for this woman, who clearly loved her daughter. 'Let me get my friend here to bring you a cup of tea, Mrs Marsh, and we can think about all of the places where Alice might have gone.'

She nodded to Aiden who promptly went off on his errand. Alex turned her attention back to Mrs Marsh.

'Have you informed the police?'

'Oh yes, but what can they do? Loads of kids go missing each year. She was only fourteen you know.'

Alex tried to mask the shock at hearing this woman refer to her daughter in the past tense, as if she assumed that Alice was already gone forever. She cast her mind back over the past few weeks. Alice had been to youth club occasionally and, yes, she had seemed a bit withdrawn. She remembered the fifty-pound note: Alice had been very agitated the night she had used that note to buy sweets. Did that have anything to do with it? She made a mental note and listened as Mrs Marsh seemed set on telling it all.

'There's more,' she whispered. 'We had had an argument on the Thursday, about this . . . .' She produced a little packet from her handbag. It contained a tiny pill with a $ sign imprinted on it. 'I found it in her room.' Alex stared at the pill as if it were an exotic species of insect, a beautiful and dangerous enemy.

'I'm afraid I don't know what it is, Mrs Marsh. I suggest you take it to the police station.' Then on impulse she said, 'I could ask one of my friends here. Can I borrow it for a moment?'

'Of course.' She handed over the packet.

Alex took the little pill and walked over to the counter where Daisy was serving.

'Daisy, can I have a word with you out in the office for a minute.'

They left the customers and Alex showed her the pill. Daisy looked at it and squinted at the design.

'Well it's probably 'E' – you know, Ecstasy. I haven't seen this type before, but it might be popular round here. Where did you get it from?'

'I've got the mum of one of the kids in the youth club out there saying her child has disappeared, and she found this in her bedroom.'

Daisy frowned. 'The poor kid could be anywhere. She might be hiding, or she might have gone up to the city. Anything could happen to her there.'

Alex sighed. This was not the message she wanted to take back to Alice's mother.

'I can't believe it. She was in our youth club a couple of weeks ago.'

'Well I think you should give the thing back to her so that you're not done for possession on the day your café opens, and tell her to go to the police.'

Alex looked at Daisy and then at the packet in her hand. This was the last thing she needed today.

'Isn't there anything we can do, Daisy?'

'Like what? Do you want to go driving round the streets at night on the off chance that you might see this girl?'

Alex stared at the tiny packet in her hand.

'Yes Daisy, if that's what it takes I would drive round the streets and look for her.'

Daisy looked at Alex, and realised, yet again, why she had chosen Alex as the person to talk to, the person to be around. This was a type of compassion that she had never seen before.

Daisy sighed. 'Look, Alex, be careful: if you do find her, there might be others with her. These people are not nice . . . do you know what I mean? Anyway, perhaps she wanted to get away – it does happen.' Daisy turned round and went out of the office.

Alex was alone. She looked out of the office window and saw Mrs Marsh sitting at one of the tables, staring into space. She also looked like a lost child. She had left Aiden with her, and he looked as if he was gamely trying to make conversation. She would have to go back to them both soon.

Before she did go back, she turned the key to the office door and knelt down on the floor. Clearing her mind of other considerations, she asked God for some guidance in the matter.

'Lord, what do you want here? Should I get involved; can I help?' She closed her eyes and waited. She could almost feel the second hand of her watch ticking round. Aiden and Mrs Marsh would be waiting for her. The café needed her presence; this was the first day.

Any moment someone would come looking for her.

She continued to kneel on the floor, while the muffled sound of the café came through the wall

'Jesus. . . .'

A voice or a feeling, something inside her, spoke to her: *'Leave it alone.'*

That was it: a rather depressing response, but she knew by now that when she asked for an answer she should be satisfied with the one she got.

Alex walked back out into the café and went to the table where Mrs Marsh was sitting. She handed back the packet.

'You should take this to the police, Mrs Marsh. I think that's the best thing to do.'

'Thank you, yes, I'll do that.' Even Mrs Marsh had some idea that the pill was a drug of some kind. Alex saw her put the pill back in her bag and, again, felt a sense of compassion for this woman. She was having to come to terms with the fact that her daughter was not only missing, but also a potential drug addict.

Alex watched as she eased out of the chair and walked towards the door.

'Mrs Marsh,' Alex wanted to offer her some crumb of comfort, 'if I see or hear anything I will let you know.' Brenda Marsh nodded and walked out.

Alex and Aiden watched her as she walked out of the door and disappeared down the street. Aiden picked up his case.

'I'm sorry, Alex, but I have to go.'

'Of course. Thanks, Aiden.'

He smiled, 'I will drop by later if that's okay with you.'

'Yes, please do that.'

She smiled and on impulse reached out and took his hand. He drew her to himself and hugged her, whispering as he did so: 'I will pray for Alice, I'm sure they will find her.' Then he picked up his case and walked out onto the street towards the station.

* * *

That evening, Conner and his band played two half-hour sessions in the café. They very wisely avoided some of their original and rather obscure material and stuck to the cover versions. They also mixed in a couple of the latest worship songs.

The café was packed, and there was a spill of young people out onto the street. The smokers hovered near the entrance leaving a litter of cigarette ends at the front of the café.

Alex had suspected that this might happen and she was trying to find someone to clean up outside after the café closed. There was no one else around, so she was left to do this herself. If there was ever any danger of the whole thing going to her head, it was dispelled by her last little job of the evening – clearing up the fag ends from the edge of the door and the road outside.

For all that, the first day of opening for Alex's café was a great success. The novelty would wear off, of course, but Alex felt satisfied. The dream was becoming reality – yet there was still much more to do.

* * *

Later on, exhausted and in bed, she thought about her day. The press had been there, the kids had turned up, the staff had turned up, there had been no trouble, and everyone had gone away with a little card telling them what the café was there for, and why Jesus was real and relevant to them today. It had all been a great success, but Alex knew that she could not celebrate that success now. There was no joy within her as she tried to settle down to sleep.

She turned over in her bed, just picking out the tune from a CD that Conner was playing in her lounge. To this day, she didn't know how he managed to stay up so late. She whispered the words to herself: 'It has all been a great success,' and she turned again trying to find a comfortable position. But the tears trickled down her cheek and onto the pillow, because the last thing she thought of as she finally drifted off was the thing that had haunted her mind all day, deeper even than the distraction of Aiden – Alice.

Alice, one of 'her' kids, had disappeared. Possibly, even now, Alice was having to work for some pimp up in town. Alex shut her eyes tight and squeezed out the tears. She had to express her sorrow before the sleep came.

'It has been a terrible day, Lord. Please God help the young people; help Alice.'

Eighteen

Down at the police station, Richard Riches was helping the force with their enquiries. A long night lay ahead.

The smell in the interview room was starting to seep into the corridor outside. Two officers, shirtsleeves rolled, sat behind a table. The larger of the two, an inspector, had interviewed Richard 'Ricky' Riches so many times that they were on first name terms. The other officer was a sergeant, contributing to the process of making the suspect sweat. Ricky was a small cog in the large machine of organised drug crime.

They had been sitting here for nearly an hour. One of the officers sighed and leaned in towards the table, the chair he sat on creaking under his weight. On the table was a large ashtray, two empty cups and a search warrant.

'Come on Ricky,' said the inspector. 'Just look at yourself – nobody knows who you are and nobody cares, except us. But if you don't start talking soon me and my colleague here are going to take this warrant, and we are going to crawl all over your horrid little flat. Now you think about that, Ricky; think about all the little secrets you've got hidden away.'

The other officer, who was learning fast, leaned forward to join his colleague. 'We can be very thorough if we need to Ricky, but I think you know that.'

'Now I'll tell you how it is, Ricky,' continued the inspector. My governor, he wants to nail you for good this time; and who can blame him with your sort of form? He wants us to get the rubber gloves on and have a good old rummage around, know what I mean? All the little nick-nacks you put in the drawer with your y-fronts, all the little packages behind the sideboard, in the cistern, under the floorboards, perhaps a little something in the fish tank. A thorough check-up you might say.'

The inspector leaned forward and reached for another cigarette. He offered the packet to Ricky, who sat opposite him, hunched over the table, staring at him from the edge of insanity.

'I need to go to the toilet,' growled Ricky, taking a cigarette from the packet.

'Come off it, Ricky, that's the fourth time in the last hour,' said the sergeant

'Suit yourself, I'll just do it on the floor.' The figure grinned, showing his teeth, shot through with decay.

The inspector bowed his head and sighed. 'Interview terminated at 22.14. Mr Riches is visiting the lavatory.' The tape clicked to a stop. 'Take him out, Al.'

Ricky Riches, a veteran of police interviews, rose from his seat and stretched. He looked as if he didn't have a care in the world, shuffling over to the door, nodding to the inspector as he went. But inside his brain there was feverish activity: all the deals and all the favours, all the contacts that he had made over the years – and now the police had managed to pick him up just when he had been loaded up with gear: smack, 'E', dope, the lot.

What was worse was there was more at the flat, much more, and they knew it. If they went through the place properly, they would pick up enough stuff to make the early evening news. He could just imagine some top brass copper standing at the table with the cameras rolling over bags and bags of the stuff, giving some lecture about a breakthrough in the local fight against drugs.

He knew that they had him this time – they really had him. But of course it wasn't really him they wanted, it was his boss, or his boss's boss. Ordinarily he would have told them where to go. He'd done time before and it was no big deal. But this was different, and there were two factors that made it different. Firstly, the amount of gear they had found on him made it likely that he was going to go down for a long, long, time. Years – a lot of years. Secondly, and this was worse, he was outliving his usefulness. The people he worked for were getting fidgety, questioning his methods, making noises about how he was getting sloppy and unreliable – and they had a point. He was getting to be so messed up that he had to think for a couple of seconds before he remembered his real name. If he didn't end up in jail this time, he would probably soon end up dead.

As he neared the door, the inspector rose sharply from his chair and stood in his path.

'Al, I think Mr Riches wants a drink of water. Could you get it for him, please?'

The three of them stood for a moment, as if trapped by the intensity of the situation. The tape was off; this conversation didn't exist. That gave certain advantages to all parties. The sergeant nodded and left the room. Ricky felt the kind of fear that he usually reserved for his bosses. If he hadn't really wanted to visit the bathroom before this, he certainly did now. The inspector, a taller man than he was, looked down at him and then moved round so that he was standing side-on, about six inches away from Ricky's ear.

'Don't disgrace yourself on my floor, Ricky. I'll let you go to the lavatory in a minute. Now you listen very carefully to me because you are running out of time. You deal with me, Ricky, because I am ever so much nicer than your bosses. I think we both know what I mean. So while that nasty old tape machine is off, why don't you have a little word in my ear.'

'And if I don't?' Ricky screwed his eyes round to see the glistening face of the inspector.

'If you don't, I'm going to take my rubber glove and put it in places you don't want me to put it. Then, when I'm finished, I'm going to put you inside for a long, long time, if those who pull your strings don't get you first. I understand your card is marked anyway, and when you lose them all this gear, well . . . .'

Ricky could feel the ground moving under him. His life was about to fall apart. He was getting close to the point where he had to take the risk.

'So, what if I tell you something?'

'Well, if you do then nobody else heard it, you know what I mean; and I'll give you a bit more reassurance. We have had four or five dealers in here today and we've heard all sorts of things, so you can tell everyone that you've said nothing, and it'll be believable. Besides, we don't have to put the gloves on, do we? Perhaps we'll just forget searching your place for twenty-four hours and have an early night.'

Ricky didn't like to think about this sort of thing for too long. He whispered in the inspector's ear – something about an event happening that night – and then wished he hadn't said anything. And then he didn't care. They took him to the bathroom and they gave him some water, and then they took him back to the cell where he paced around for two hours before he fell into a fitful sleep. True to his word, the inspector let it be known that Ricky had said nothing and would soon be released for lack of evidence. If there was anyone in the station who had a tendency to talk to the other side, that was the message they would get.

There was to be no early night, however. They had work to do. In an office above the cells, the inspector was

briefing his team. Ricky's fragmentary confession was
not the only thing he had to deal with, he was also
getting some pressure from his governor about a new
trend on the rave scene. Some idiot somewhere had
decided to market drug-related merchandise to the
punters, and his superiors wanted it off the streets.

'So when we go in we're not just looking for the usual
stuff, we want to pick up anything with this design on
it.' The inspector showed his team a range of items, each
with the SEEKA emblem on them. 'The DCI is collecting
all this SEEKA gear at the moment – whoever's producing this stuff is on his blacklist. Any questions?'

Everyone was silent. They had been through this sort
of operation plenty of times, and they knew what they
were doing.

* * *

'Don't worry about it, Dave.'

Martin Massey, true controller of the SEEKA machine
indulged in a little self-admiration as he calmed another
of the troops. In a private fantasy of his own, he saw himself as the head of a media empire with everyone around
him (including Lewis) acting as officers of various rank
and privilege. Occasionally, he would indulge in an even
more ludicrous fantasy where he appeared as the sun –
the bright star at the centre of a solar system of other
planetary workers. He was in a 'solar system' mood
today: Dave stood in front of him fiddling with a
magazine and getting into a flap about some aspect of
SEEKA publicity material. Within his own firmament he
called Dave 'Mercury', not because of any vigour or energy that he might show, but because Martin saw Dave
floating round near the centre of things, but turning out
to be rather burnt-out and irrelevant.

As he was about to dispatch Dave, the phone rang. Now here was news: one of his friends was organising a rave for that evening and he was being told the location in advance. He confirmed the venue and scribbled it on a piece of scrap paper in bold letters as he finished the call. He wanted to bring the discussion with Dave to a close – the points had been made and noted.

'So like I said, Dave, I will deal with it. Don't worry.'

But Dave was already leaving, making his way out of Martin's office. Martin watched his colleague disappear and murmured under his breath: 'You have flown too close to the sun my friend, and like an Icarus, you will fall.'

He placed the remaining files on his desk into a drawer and locked it. Then, taking his coat, he headed out to another night of the life he loved.

He followed a well-worn path to the venue: something to eat, something to drink, then off to a mindless rave somewhere. They were all sharing in a kind of amoral despair, that was true enough, but the difference was that he was making money out of it.

It was a good night: hot and steamy, and anonymous, with everyone losing their identity within the beat and volume of the music. After a while, he joined his associate on a stage area at the front. They nodded an acknowledgement to each other, but there was no further exchange as the sheer volume of the music precluded anything but sign language.

He surveyed the crowd: waves of heads and arms silhouetted against the different-coloured lamps. The noise was driving even him out of any sense of reality.

He was just weighing up the offer of a little something to improve his mood when his eye caught a tall man moving with almost athletic speed through the room towards them, scattering the ravers as he went. He was about fifteen yards from the stage when he held up both arms as if trying to send a signal of some kind.

The man standing to Martin's right moved with such violence that Martin was shocked back into reality. The music suddenly cut out, as did most of the lights. There was a noise across the whole venue like the wailing of a dying man.

'Police! We are leaving now!' Someone took his arm and he felt himself propelled backwards to a door behind the DJ. As he turned, he saw a team of about four or five people running with the DJ's equipment. Then he was out in the open night and he could see a group of vehicles off to his right. There was a flicker of blue light.

As the team threw their equipment into the back of a waiting transit, he was bundled into another vehicle. The door slammed against him, wedging him between the handle and the tall man who had given the signal; there were three of them packed into the back of the car. He looked out into the darkness as the driver brought the engine of the car to screaming pitch, encouraged by Martin's associate in the passenger seat. They lurched forward towards the track they had come along earlier. Out of the window, Martin saw a police car swing round to intercept them. Judging the distances, he figured that they would get caught. His first thought was Lewis, and his second was Lench. He closed his eyes and cursed.

He still had his eyes closed when there was an explosion of light just outside the window. It was followed by at least three others in quick succession. His eyes were watering, but he could just make out a crouching figure, now some way behind them.

'Go, go!' hissed a voice within the vehicle.

In response, the driver pumped the accelerator with renewed vigour and they bounced along the track for another two hundred yards before swinging out onto the main road.

The car slowed to about sixty. Nobody spoke for about five minutes.

'Someone knew,' said Martin's acquaintance.

'Yeah, like who? Nobody knows until we put it out on the station. Then everyone knows.' This was from the man next to Martin. There was a smell about him that Martin couldn't quite place, it reminded him of chemistry lessons at school.

Another voice broke in: 'Well this is the life we lead isn't it!' the voice paused. 'And what was that flash? Some photographer or something?'

The driver laughed nervously, 'Like we are all going to be on the front of the nationals tomorrow.' Everyone grinned, then the man next to Martin gestured towards him.

'If they got anyone it was your mate here.' He turned his head so that he faced Martin more directly. 'Something for your West End friends to look at over lunch, eh, darling?'

This provoked a laugh and Martin felt a tinge of anger. These people had no clue to his significance, but for the moment, there was nothing he could do.

* * *

Down at the station the inspector erupted.

'Who invited the papers? Who? We had a carload of suspects, the cream of the crop, and because some idiot with a camera got in the way, they got away! We lost them! Why?'

The sergeant considered pointing out that they did have a car registration number, but that was not going to console his boss right now, so he remained silent.

'Okay,' said the inspector, 'let's have a look at what we did manage to get.'

A large plastic-topped table, loaded with little packets and bottles dominated the room. It looked like some kind of travelling pharmacy. In one corner, there were some posters and a couple of CDs marked out with the SEEKA logo. It was some consolation. The haul of goods was impressive enough, but the haul of suspects was lousy.

Five minutes later, down in the cells, the inspector was shouting into Ricky's face. The light was on and Ricky was staring at the inspector through bloodshot eyes.

'Was it you Ricky? Invited half of Fleet Street to our little party did you?' The inspector could sense himself losing it. He breathed deeply and stepped back.

'What you talking about?' squeaked Ricky who had never seen the inspector so angry. He wanted desperately to put a lot of distance between himself and this man.

The inspector gave Ricky a summary of the evening's events: an excellent police operation marred by the arrival of press photographers, so that suspects escape in the ensuing chaos.

Ricky's brain dragged itself into first gear.

'How could it have been me? I didn't tell you anything till you had me hanging by a thread. Do you think I would have told some miserable journalist for a couple of hundred quid or something?'

The inspector paused. It was true. Ricky Riches would never have told the press anything – it was not his style. Someone else had let them in on the game. But who?

As he left the cells, he thought back over the events of the evening. Nobody in the station could have sold that information because up till the moment they left he was the only one who knew where they were going.

The team went back to their homes, and the inspector wrestled with a problem that he would never be able to solve.

* * *

Across the capital, a journalist looked down at a set of prints, a gift from his colleague sent through the miracle of wireless technology. He shook his head and smiled. Some of them of course were rubbish, really rubbish. They could have been snapshots of his granny! But a few were really clear, including an atmospheric shot of one of the blokes in the getaway car. It was an absolute gift! Getting the tip-off about the rave had been useful, finding the police had become involved made it even better, and getting a picture that was probably of the very guy they were trying to track, that topped it all. On this occasion, he placed the others in a drawer and took the one of his intended victim to a woman sitting down the corridor from him. The image was of a man with a rather long face and short hair. The expression on his face suggested that he had been captured for immortality just as he had heard some terrible piece of news. His mouth was half open in preparation for a howl of anguish, and the right hand was shielding one eye, while the other was wide open, perhaps in terror. The thing taken as a whole suggested a nice mixture of fear, a desire for privacy, and confusion.

'Go on Jo, it's got to go in. Look at the poor devil – he looks like a rabbit caught in the car lights! It fits that piece we are doing on the drug culture. We even know who this guy is.'

The woman looked down at her colleague and then at the photo.

'How can you be sure you know who that is. It's a great shot, certainly, but it could be anyone.'

Her colleague looked disheartened: 'It's got to be him, really Jo, we know he was there.'

'Legal, bless them, would hang me out to dry if we printed this with a name.'

'How about if we just use it without the name, that would work.'

'Okay,' she held up her hands, 'you've sold it to me. Go on, get it down to features before I change my mind.'

Sean took the print and walked briskly down the corridor. Later, as the presses started to roll, he wandered off to the end of the foyer on the ground floor. He never minded phoning people at unsociable hours if it was good news. Tapping on the buttons of his mobile, he scanned the waiting area: just a single security guard, adopting that pose of semi-conscious alertness that veterans of the profession are so good at. Outside in the darkness a car moved past.

He was through.

'Hi, it's Sean. Yes, I know what time it is, but you're going to love this. Your lucky guess, yes it couldn't have gone better . . . Yes, he'll be in there, but get this: the police raided the joint at the same time. I nearly got run over! What? . . . No of course I didn't tell them, they must have heard about it from some other source. . . . Yes, they'll be furious. I think the organisers got away but they must have taken a load of this SEEKA gear . . . No you don't need to worry about the payment, it will be with you as arranged. Look, I've got to go but I just wanted to tell you. . . . Hey, get a copy tomorrow morning, page four I think, it will make your day. . . . Yeah, bye.'

Back in the office, Sean gathered his papers together and looked at his watch. He couldn't believe it was nearly two in the morning. The taxi would be here in about ten minutes. It had been a good day for the great British press, especially for his little bit of it.

Nineteen

Alice was lying on a hard surface. She knew she was on her back, but she wasn't in bed. In fact, she didn't really know where she was.

She concentrated on the surface beneath her. It was hard, and the air smelt like she was outside somewhere. She knew that when she started to move she would feel pain; she would feel a hard surface where there should be something soft, and cold where there should be warmth. In the last couple of days, she had learnt to value the comforts she had taken for granted; and she had learnt how fragile her body was. She had run away on the Friday night with some cash and a head full of defiance. By Monday evening she was cold, tired, wet and frightened. She had just bought some food and some drink and walked around the city. On Friday night she had slept at a railway station near where she lived. Amazingly, nobody had seen her and she had caught an early train into the city on the Saturday morning. She had nearly turned back then and gone home. For the next three days she had walked and slept in the city. She had befriended a former prostitute who had been sleeping rough for eight years. It was this friendship that had saved her from anything worse than the aches and pains she now felt.

Those aches and pains were becoming more real as Alice woke up: one type of pain around her neck and head, another type in her stomach. She tried to open her eyes; her vision was blurred but there was some daylight.

She lay still for a moment, concentrating on the noises that were coming to her. It seemed that even in the last few minutes the amount of noise had increased; cars came into and out of her range of hearing; people were walking past her on the street. Reality seemed to be breaking into her world and she knew that she was outside, probably on the pavement, but she didn't know where. She did not have the will to try and open her eyes again just yet. Then, suddenly, she heard a very distinct sound: a voice, old and kind, and resonating with an acceptance that she found immediately attractive.

'Hello my dear, are you all right?' It sounded a bit like her granny's voice calling to her.

'Hello,' she croaked back. She imagined her grandmother joining her on the pavement, keeping her company.

'Oh my dear, you are in a bad way aren't you. Here, let me help you.'

Alice opened her eyes just a fraction to see a face looking at her. She was indeed outside, but not on a pavement. Rather, she was slumped in a shop doorway. She tried to focus on the person who was speaking to her but she couldn't. She noticed that the face had something growing out of the top of it, like a maroon-coloured bubble, most odd. She closed her eyes again and then with rather more effort re-opened them.

The face was still there, with its maroon attachment. She tried to sit up.

MISTAKE!

Her head screamed as the world swivelled around in her eye sockets. She would have lain down again immediately but now there was an arm to support her. As she moved, her stomach churned.

It had certainly been a mistake to get up quickly. She felt herself start to retch and she turned to one side. The mixture seeped from her mouth and made a pool on the ground beside her, while some ran onto her clothes. The face spoke again and someone wiped her mouth, and then there were two voices. When she looked round there were two faces and each one had a maroon bubble above their heads. They seemed to be discussing her plight.

'No, I think she's under sixteen; probably run away from home,' this was Granny.

'Well we should take her in and see what we can do for her,' said the other one.

Alice looked at the faces, one an older woman (Granny), the other a younger man, and she could see that the maroon bubble was actually a crest of some sort, on a black hat. These people were wearing uniforms.

'What time is it?' Her voice sounded like she was speaking from the grave.

'Its just after eight in the morning, my love, and I think we need to give you a bit of a hand. Can you tell me what your name is?'

'Alice: I'm Alice, and I've left home.'

'Well, Alice, let's see if we can help you out here shall we?'

She knew she wanted their help. Now the defiance and frustration were dissipated; and hearing a voice that reminded her of her grandmother made her think of herself as a little girl again. Some minutes later she was in a vehicle like a small bus, heading across town. She knew this was London, but she didn't know which part. The traffic was very busy now.

They took her the short distance from the West End street where she had collapsed the previous night, to Hopetown, a residential centre for homeless women amongst the sari shops of Brick Lane. She had a bath and something to drink and they gave her a change of clothes. The clothes weren't what she would have chosen to wear, but they didn't smell as much as the things she had been wearing.

She still didn't want to tell anyone who she was; so they allocated her a room and let her get some sleep. She lay in bed, experiencing the sensations she was used to; the smell of clean sheets, the softness of pillows and blankets. She was just beginning to lose herself again when some curiosity made her open her eyes. There was lettering on the blanket. She picked out the letters that were not covered up.

'L V A T I O N A R M'

Of course, now she understood it. She was in the hands of the 'do-gooders'. And they were indeed doing her good, and it felt okay. When she had been a little girl, she had sometimes put money in a tin for the 'poor children', as her mum called it. Now she was getting the benefit; she had become the 'poor child'. With that thought in her mind, Alice Marsh, recent escapee from family life and now a rather wiser person, closed her eyes and went to sleep.

She awoke late in the afternoon, and by then she had forgotten why she wouldn't tell them her name and address. After tea, she rang her mum. She could tell her mum had been worried sick – she could hear it in her voice. They talked about the tab that Mrs Marsh had found. They talked about the two other little pills that Alice had with her. She hadn't even taken the drugs she had purchased with the cash from the building society, the same cash she had used to buy a few sweets at the youth club. When they'd finished the conversation, her mum told her that she loved her, and Alice cried.

She went home the next day and it was only when she got back home that she realised how much she was still a child, and still wanted to be a child.

She was going to enjoy the good things about coming home: real food, real love, private space, warmth and softness. There were some things that her mum would never understand, like why she didn't completely regret what had happened, but she did love her all the same. Then there was the club, Alex's club. She realised now that the club was a place to grow up in; it was an environment where she could work out how she felt, a place where she could work it all out in her own time. She was looking forward to the next Friday evening.

Twenty

Lewis Ashbury looked at the newspaper photo once more. There was a chance, and it was a slim chance, that the picture he was staring at was not Martin.

He reflected on the fact that if this had happened even a couple of months ago he would probably have laughed about it and thrown it in the bin. But this was not two months ago, this was now, and the pressure was on. Someone was trying to blackmail him into halting the SEEKA project, and using the fact that SEEKA and the drug culture fitted hand in glove; there had been an article in the press recently portraying SLaM and other organisations like it as parasites, feeding off the lives of young people. The popular discontent was growing in the summer heat. Given the context, this picture of Martin was unfortunate. If the blackmailer saw this photo and knew who Martin was, he could sell an absolute gem of a story.

He sat back and removed his glasses. With his eyes shut, he could see images of newspaper headlines: 'SLaM – The Drug Connection'; 'SLaMMED – Media Firm Accused of Encouraging Drugs Amongst the Young', and so on. Doubtless, these articles would include the picture of Martin driving away from some rave – and not just any rave but one that the police had raided. The article didn't expressly mention any SEEKA material, but Lewis could see that it was only a matter of time.

With a mixture of regret and relief, he finally made his decision. It was the end of SEEKA; the best thing, the only thing he could do. It was going to be a very expensive business but he felt that he had no choice. He scribbled some notes into his diary. There were some financial arrangements that he would have to make first thing in the morning.

Putting his diary down, he sat back in the chair and sighed. He was sitting in his study alone in his house, and he felt isolated. There had always been that nagging doubt in the back of his mind, something which told him that a lot of what he did, a lot of what SLaM did, was actually harmful to young people. Maybe his life wasn't all just fun and glitz; people did actually get hurt as he made his money. That was especially true of SEEKA.

He suddenly felt very tired, weary of all the worries and concerns that had crowded in on him. As he closed his eyes he imagined thousands of parents ranged against him, people of his generation, in their thirties and forties; people with children whom they loved, children who were not just being poisoned by drugs, but were being encouraged, actively encouraged, to poison themselves. And he didn't have any children who could be harmed by the very things he was producing. He could almost hear the mothers and fathers now, anger in their voices at the ruined lives of their sons and daughters.

He had never felt like this before. It crossed his mind that he might be entering some sort of mid-life crisis. Then again, perhaps he was just beginning to realise how much damage he had done. He felt completely alone, and he *was* completely alone. An unfamiliar sting in his eyes reminded him of what it was to shed tears.

On impulse, he opened one of the drawers of his desk. Pulling the drawer out with some violence, he tipped the contents onto the floor. He spread out the papers and photos and just as his search was turning to frustration, he found what he was looking for. He picked up the brown hard-backed envelope and tipped the contents onto the desk. He looked down at the two pictures and the sting in his eyes intensified.

The first showed him holding a champagne glass standing next to a huge card. The caption, 'Good Luck SLaM', could be seen even in the grainy medium of this snapshot. On the other side of the card stood Bridget, also holding a champagne glass. This was how he would remember her: glamorous, determined, sensual. The photo didn't really do her justice, although he could remember the day well, the very start of SLaM when there had been just him and her.

He looked at the other photograph. This was a larger print and the quality was much better, but then this had been a publicity shot, taken in a studio. This one showed Bridget a few years earlier striking an alluring pose over the bonnet of an Aston Martin. Lewis found himself grimacing at the irony of the name. The photo showed all the elements that had attracted him in the first place: the mouth, a mixture of desire and strength of will, the form of her body, her gorgeous chocolate-brown skin.

The tears came at last, and he felt a tremendous sense of release as the drops hit the surface of the desk. He was alone, nobody could hear him, and in the luxury of his solitude he cried as he had never cried before, astounded by the poverty of his situation. He felt like the man who had gained the whole world, but had given up his soul in return.

* * *

Some fifty miles away, Lench sat back and lit a cigar. Circumstances, for once, had simplified things for him. At last, events were playing into his hand rather than causing problems. The photo in the paper was the excuse he needed to close down the whole Martin Massey/SEEKA thing. Martin was drawing attention to himself – unwelcome attention. It was likely that the SEEKA project would be next, and that meant that both it and Martin had to be jettisoned without further delay.

Lench tried to see a positive side to the proceedings. At least this was familiar ground and it was unlikely that Martin would even need to be removed completely. He just needed to be reminded that it was in his best interests to remain silent now. The mobile number would be untraceable by tomorrow, and he would get the assassin to clean things up a bit at Martin's house. Clearly, they would have to relocate the Group meetings, but that happened on a regular basis anyway. He had been delaying the next move for precisely this reason.

Cigar smoke spiralled gently into the air and Lench tried to relax. This project was over and, phoenix-like, a new one would rise from the ashes. Martin would disappear from the theatre of operations, and maybe a new character would appear. The agenda would be the same – the glory of his master, the defeat and humiliation of the opposition.

But it was not as simple as that.

He wanted to believe that SEEKA had been a success and, to an extent, it had, but things had got complicated, people had made mistakes and the centre of the whole job, this idiot, Martin, had been found out. He was sure that he was safe and the Group was safe, but how had this episode affected the wider strategies? He could only speculate on that. Then there were the others: people who had heard his bragging; people who were watching this project of his. Their envy and admiration would turn to derision and scorn if they knew the extent of his failure. Some of his associates had also worked hard to take the Christian values out of the culture and inject something quite different. It would be very embarrassing if SEEKA backfired to the extent that their enemy started to reclaim some of that ground.

He thought through the implications and he did not like what he saw: there was complexity at every turn. His struggle came to a premature halt as his eye caught sight of a grey mass falling from the end of his cigar. The ash fell and broke into pieces as it hit the carpet. Lench cursed. He would have to demean himself now and find a brush to sweep up the mess.

Twenty-One

Aiden and John were sitting in the beer garden of a local pub. They had found an evening to get together and chat. Each of them was wondering what the other could bring by way of insight and wisdom for their own personal situation.

John was returning from the bar with the drinks, Aiden was browsing through his paper. One story, together with the photograph that accompanied it, caught his eye. Apparently, there had been a big rave at a farm warehouse and the police had been tipped off and raided the place. The story was credited to 'our reporter at the scene' who had, presumably, also been tipped off. What was really interesting, though, was the picture: it showed a vehicle, probably moving at some speed, with a pale horrified face looking out through the passenger side window. Aiden had showed the picture to Alex and her eyes had widened with amazement as she looked at a picture of one of her old colleagues. The caption beneath the picture read: 'Rave organizer escapes as police close in.'

'He looks a bit like that figure from *The Scream* doesn't he?' said John, peering over Aiden's shoulder and looking at the newspaper. He placed the drinks onto the wooden table.

'You mean that painting, the guy on the bridge – who's that by now?' said Aiden.

'I don't know,' said John. 'Norwegian wasn't he? Anyway, cheers!' he raised his glass to his friend.

'They found that girl, Alice, that went missing,' said Aiden.

'Yes, thank God for that,' sighed John. 'I'm pleased for Alex's sake. She's was devastated by the whole thing. I've never seen her so withdrawn, and . . .' John was trying to find the right word.

'Angry?' suggested Aiden.

'I guess so,' said John. 'Maybe she was angry. She just feels so passionate about the young people, that's the way she is.'

'You know her pretty well, don't you,' said Aiden.

The warning lights in John's brain flickered for a moment. He recalled the home group where Aiden had seemed so perceptive, evaluating the relationship between Alex and himself, and getting pretty close to the truth by the sound of it. He didn't mind telling Aiden about it all, especially now that the issue seemed to be resolved, but it was a subject that needed to be approached with caution. 'Alex and I are close,' he said. 'But if you are going to have close women friends, you have to know how close you can let them get – do you know what I mean?'

'Yes,' said Aiden, 'I think I do.' They both pretended to take an interest in the gardens around them for a moment, sipping their drinks

Aiden eased towards John and spoke quietly, 'And how close can you let them get, John?'

John thought about his answer. This was like tiptoeing through a minefield. 'Well, if you're married then you don't sleep with them for a start.' He smiled as he continued, 'And if you're not married you don't sleep with them either, but you can get more emotionally involved. What I mean is, if you're single and available then it's okay to get involved.'

'Surely though,' said Aiden, suppressing a smile, 'once you're married you never worry about other women.'

John looked over the rim of his glass at his friend. It really was too much for Aiden to be playing these games with him.

'Aiden, you never stop worrying about women, wife or otherwise. There is always a woman to worry about – a partner, your mum, a daughter, the girl you don't want to fancy but you do, the girl who fancies you.'

They returned to their drinks. Above the intermittent rumble of vehicles from the high street, they both listened to the bird song from the trees around them. John knew what was coming, but he wasn't going to make it easy for Aiden. He had to ask this in his own way.

'What do you really think of Alex, John?'

'She's great, really. I mean, she's driven through this café project of hers; you have got to admire her for that.'

'You know I sometimes wonder whether you haven't got a soft spot for her. Do you know what I mean?'

'You want to be careful who you say that to, Aiden. People could get the wrong idea.'

'I'm saying it to you, John, and only you. I'm not saying it to anyone else because it's nobody else's business. Look, you can tell me to mind my own business if you want to, but I am your friend, and I'm not here to gloat: I want to learn from you.'

John laughed. 'You want to learn from me! How?'

'How do you cope, John?'

'Cope? Cope with what?' said John.

'The Christian sister who you feel attracted to, and the feelings are mutual, and yet you both want to do the right thing . . .' Aiden picked up his glass and sipped again.

'Are you playing games with me, Aiden? If you want to ask me about Alex . . .' he made a conscious effort to lower his voice. 'If you want to ask me about Alex, then go right ahead.'

'Okay, how did you stop yourself from having an affair with her? I assume you haven't had an affair with her,' Aiden added, looking across with a steady and patient gaze, and John realised that he should actually be grateful that he had friends who were prepared to challenge him like this.

'Only in my emotions, Aiden, but that was bad enough. The feelings I had for Alex worked their way into my heart, and it was a problem for a while. But not any more. The thing with Alex – what I felt for her – it's gone now, gone for both of us. We just decided, both of us just decided to serve the Lord and do the right thing.' Then he added, 'I'm telling you this in confidence, Aiden, okay. Not even Laura knows all of this.'

'Of course. If I get you another drink, will you tell me more about it?'

'Yes sure . . . maybe you will learn something.'

Aiden disappeared off to the bar. John suddenly felt as if everyone was looking at him. He glanced around the beer garden and was almost surprised to see that nobody was taking any notice of him at all. He could just pick Aiden out at the bar. He prayed for wisdom, as his friend sat down again.

John had gone too far to hold back now, so he related the events of the evening he had taken the home group notes round. He almost floundered as he tried to describe the feelings he'd had when Alex was in the kitchen, but Aiden gave him some gentle encouragement. They agreed, in the way only men can, that she had a stunning body, and that there was something else, something indescribably attractive about her determination, the intensity within her that drove her to achieve her dreams.

Having gone this far, John was ready to tackle the other encounters. He talked about the home group evening, and then finally the encounter in the café when he had called round to help. By the time he finished his narrative he had achieved such intensity that all they could do was fall back into silence.

'Bit of a close thing then, John,' Aiden smiled.

John laughed. 'The thing is, I don't know why I did it. I am perfectly happy with Laura, and I know the difference between right and wrong. It was as if I was getting involved, really involved, and there was nothing I could do about it. I felt like one of those insects that crawls round the edge of a pitcher plant, and its easy to go just a little bit further in, but so hard to get out again.'

'But you did get out – you escaped. Well, you both escaped.'

John sighed, 'It was Alex really. She was the one who in the end said, "No!" I can remember standing in that office and she was leaning against me. I knew that if she didn't stop it, well I didn't know how far I would go. Then she just stood up and looked at the wall. She had the strength to break the spell, and I thought, "Thank God, just thank God".

'I tell you, Aiden, after that moment I felt so free, as if someone had taken a huge weight off my heart. I went home and I bought some of Laura's favourite ice cream. I think she sensed that the battle was over. I still don't know whether she realises what went on. And Alex is her best friend!'

'So how are things now?' asked Aiden.

'We're okay now. It's finished. I've even talked to Laura about how I felt.

John had said all he wanted to. At first he wanted to tell Aiden all about how he and Laura had made love that night and how good it had been, but then he realised that it was a part of his life that was private: he had indeed said enough. If he had learnt nothing else from the whole business with Alex, at least he could point to a new awareness of just how precious his relationship with Laura was, and how, together with Josh they made that most delicate and valuable of God's creations: a family. The thought of the two of them now, even as he sat here with Aiden and with his drink in his hand, almost brought tears to his eyes.

After that, the balance of the conversation swung away from John's experiences and towards Aiden. John had realised some time ago that Aiden was not the disinterested observer that some people thought he was. Certainly, he was very controlled and cool on the surface – an act he had perfected over a number years – but beneath that smooth exterior, there was a passionate heart, and all this talk about Alex had made John curious. It was time to put his friend under the spotlight.

'So what do *you* think of her then, Aiden?'

Aiden placed his glass on the table and looked with a half-smile at John. He fingered the wood of the table they were sitting at. When he spoke, his voice had a dreamy quality, as if he had just glimpsed another world, or a place far away.

'She has vision, and passion and determination. She cares, she loves, she wants to achieve things for God, and yet she is also vulnerable. She not only gets hurt, she chooses to be hurt as a part of her work for God.'

'Yes, yes,' said John impatiently, 'but what do you *think* of her?'

His friend smiled with disarming honesty: 'I don't know. If I'm honest, I'd have to say that I don't know what I think of her. I know she's scared, and she has a bit of a past, but maybe I do too.'

'Do you?' said John. 'What's in your past then?'

Aiden winked at him and drank from his glass. John waited for a moment and then said: 'You really do like her, don't you. Well good luck to you mate, she's lovely, and I can say that now. And she likes you too, you know.'

'Yes, but there is a problem,' said Aiden, shaking his head.

'Well solve it mate, because she is gorgeous!'

'It's not as simple as that. You see, my company is looking for Christian businesses to invest in at the moment, and Alex's café could be a good proposition.'

'Oh, I see,' laughed John, 'and you don't want your personal feelings to compromise the business deal. Well, if I were you, I would forget the business opportunity and get the girl. There will be other investments, but only one Alex Masters.'

'I know, John. You're right of course, but I am scared. I don't mind admitting to you I am frightened by this.'

John leaned forward. He was inches away from Aiden, whispering, 'If I was not married, Aiden, I would be trying to have a relationship with Alex. She is exceptional – I mean it, she is. But you, you are not married and if you see a girl and you like her and she likes you, well isn't that the way God intended it? Look, this is your life, Aiden. Where do you want to be in two or five or ten years? All I would say is this: don't idealise the whole thing too much. A relationship is hard work, you know. I'd say it was 80 per cent routine, 15 per cent grafting and 5 per cent romance.'

'Really, is the romance bit as much as 5 per cent?'

'Well,' John slumped into his seat a little, 'let me give you my best bit of insight on Alex. She is a paradox: she is brave and shy, courageous and unsure, strong and weak. Do you understand what I am saying? She has within her the potential to do great things, and nothing. If you can find a way of encouraging the best out of her and still being there when she is at her worst,' John spread his arms wide, 'she will be yours, my friend; she will be yours.' Then, as if on impulse, he got up, drained his glass and said: 'Come on, let's go over to the café. You know she's working there tonight.'

'Hang on, John, why should we go to the café this evening? I wanted to spend some time talking to you.'

'We've talked enough, come on.' John led the way out of the pub and up the high street towards the S & L Café. It was about 8.45, fifteen minutes before the place closed for the night.

'I shouldn't be letting you do this to me, John. I mean, what am I going to say to her when we get in there?'

'Well how about, "Hello Alex"? Look, I know for a fact that she won't have eaten yet, she never does when she's there in the evening, so take her out somewhere and give her a decent meal.' They paused for a moment just short of the bus stop. The café was just yards away.

'Aiden, my friend, seize the day! You know she feels something for you, and I know you feel something for her, so why don't you just go in there and relax, have a coffee and then suggest that the pair of you get a bite to eat. The rest, as they say, is easy.'

Aiden screwed up his courage and was about to walk in the direction of the café when he was caught in mid-stride by the realisation that John had dropped behind him.

'What are you doing, John?'

'I'm waiting for the bus.'

'Aren't you coming in here with me?'

'No, I'm not. I have a gorgeous woman to go home to and being with her is infinitely preferable to watching you and Alex making small talk together. Go on, Aiden, I've got a woman and you haven't – so go and get one!'

John had enjoyed himself enormously. Usually it was Aiden who was dispensing the wise advice, but in this arena, John had the edge. He watched Aiden walk with an almost comic boldness up to the door of the café. In his enthusiasm, he almost crashed straight into someone coming out of the doorway.

'Oh, sorry!' He stepped to one side. The figure, a boy of about fifteen, mumbled a word, which might have been 'alright' but had dissolved into a kind of affirmative grunt very popular with the young people of the area. The boy disappeared and Aiden entered the café. He looked around at the mixture of customers: a few older people, mostly men, who seemed to be in there for a meal and some youngsters grouped in the corner where the stage area was. Really, it was quite quiet. He went up to the counter. Alex was there with a couple of other people, neither of whom he recognised. He ordered a coffee.

'Aiden!'

She looked very pleased to see him. She came round to the front of the counter and gave him a brief hug. Suddenly he couldn't remember any of the things he was going to say and he stood staring at her for a moment. He was reduced to listening to the music playing in the background. Then some part of his brain, he wasn't sure which, managed to kick into gear.

'I was with John and he has just caught the bus home so I thought I'd drop in and see how you were getting on.'

'Oh, that's kind. So have you had some dinner with him?'

'Pardon?'

'Did you have dinner with John?'

'Oh, no I didn't.'

'Well if you're not busy we can get something and eat it at my place, if you want.'

Once again, Aiden was thrown. He was supposed to be asking Alex out, not the other way round. He decided that the bold approach was required: it was now or never.

'Alex, come out to dinner with me this evening. Let's not just get a take-away, let me take you out and buy you dinner.' Alex's co-workers had heard the conversation and glanced up to her to see what the verdict would be. The expression on Alex's face was a prelude to an emphatic 'Yes', but she never uttered the words.

Instead, her attention was diverted to the door of the café. A man had walked in. They had not seen him before, but his presence seemed to change the atmosphere of the place. It was not that this man was large or imposing, but there was something about him that made Alex uneasy. He reminded her of the encounter she'd had with the man in the suit outside her flat.

The man walked over to the counter.

'Tea.' He had a mackintosh on with the collar turned up, and a scar snaked across his face as if he had been slashed quite recently with a sharp knife.

The mood of the place changed, inexplicably, like the sun disappearing behind a cloud. Everyone felt uneasy, and some young people in the corner started to shuffle towards the door. Some unconscious decision had occurred amongst them and they left, clattering against the tables and chairs as they went.

The figure in the mackintosh took his tea and sat down in the centre of the café. The new visitor looked around the place, quite satisfied with the effect his entrance had had. This was going to be very amusing.

This was the assassin, revelling in his freedom: out and about again after a short period of confinement. He had been doing a bit of 'freelance thinking'. That was what Lench called it. He wasn't sure what it meant exactly, but Lench tended to use the phrase when he was reprimanding him for doing something outside of his express orders.

But, he had been locked up for long enough. He had heard Lench talk about this woman, Masters, and her 'Jesus Café' and, with time on his hands, he had decided to pay them a little visit. Who knows, he might even have to kill her one day. This trip could be thought of as a bit of reconnaissance.

He recognised her instantly, as the description Lench had given him had been thorough and they had a slightly grainy photo that someone had taken a few weeks ago. He was looking at her now. She had a nice figure and quite a pretty face. As a rule he didn't like killing pretty women, but he would deal with her if he had to. He wondered whether it would come to that. He felt no fear in this place. Look at them all – a few girls behind the counter and a couple of other punters who looked as white as sheets. The assassin stretched out in his chair. He was really tempted to cause some sort of scene, but he remembered that this was reconnaissance, and he probably shouldn't even be there.

In the spirit world, Angel was able to see both the man and those who accompanied him. The sight of them was an offence to Angel and he turned slightly from them in disgust. One was clearly in charge of the rest: it reared up and approached Angel. Standing face to face with him and screaming at his face, its whole torso and head shook with the absolute rage and anger that consumed it.

'WE ARE LEGION, AND WE BRING THE LOVE OF VIOLENCE, AND THE LOVE OF MURDERING,' it screamed with a piercing, yet aching cry.

Angel stood motionless, unafraid of the violence and desperation that had appeared before him. He almost felt a kind of pity for them, but he knew that the Lord would deal with them all as he saw fit.

Again the demon crept up to Angel, arched its back and then threw itself forward with all the malevolent strength that it could muster, screaming obscenities at its angelic opposition; its comrades crowded round, goading Angel into some reaction.

But Angel had discovered a profound sense of peace. He felt none of the apprehension about this encounter that he had felt when Alex had met Lench, or when Alex and John had been alone in the café. He stood his ground as the spirit threw itself at him. The thing grew even more angry and started to utter every blasphemy it could think of in every language that it knew. Still, Angel watched and waited.

In the café, the arrival of this man had made Alex's spine tingle. She felt as if she were engaged in battle with him even though she had done nothing but watch him walk in. A kind of uneasy truce, really more like an impasse, had occurred. The man was evidently enjoying it all. She watched him as he sprawled out at one of the central tables. He had started to take the sugar sachets out of the pot they were stored in and was tearing them open one by one, spilling the contents onto the table.

The atmosphere in the room thickened. Everyone was looking at this figure who had, no doubt, sat at one of the tables in the middle of the café to reinforce the fact that he wanted to be the centre of attention.

The spirit that had been attacking Angel, to no avail, now restrained itself and, with a voice like gravel, spoke into Angel's ear.

'Angel, look how our man sours the place. That is the power we give him, the power we have in him. WHAT HAVE YOU GOT?'

It gibbered to itself for a moment before going on. But now Angel was not listening. His attention had been caught by a thin shaft of light that seemed to appear from a ceiling tile and descend gently downwards, until it landed on Aiden. Of course, the people who were present in the room would not have seen it, but Angel had, and now he expected something to happen, and that something would involve Aiden.

The spirit had stopped talking and its eyes had widened at the sight of this beam.

It was Angel's turn to respond: 'Spirit, you should know that the man who controls your host has already passed this way, and he was defeated. Your man will now have to leave and all of you with him.'

'No, he will not!' The spirit raised itself up to its full height. It towered above Angel and screamed out its ancient rage once more, but it too had noticed the beam of light and it knew what it meant. Some of the other lesser beings that accompanied it began to whimper. They collected round their champion like frightened children might crowd close to their mother.

In the café, Aiden felt an idea form in his head. The idea galvanized him into action. Watching the figure in the mackintosh as he finished his destruction of the packets of sugar, he walked, without haste, to the central table where the assassin was staring at him.

'You must have really made her angry.' His voice held no fear, and he spoke clearly above the music so that everyone heard what he said.

The assassin was so surprised by Aiden's comment that he dropped the debris of the sugar packet he was holding and little brown grains scattering across the table.

He was suddenly very aware of his scar. Almost by habit, he scanned the room again. There were three women at the counter, including the woman, Masters. Then there were two other customers, one middle-aged male watching him, and an older male, perhaps sixty, ignoring him and intent on finishing his dinner. Then he noticed that another male, perhaps in his thirties, had entered the café. He was now standing between the assassin and the door, a complication he did not welcome. Aiden and John acknowledged each other with a brief nod. The assassin looked at John and then at the door. Situations like this made him nervous. Someone was juxtaposed between him and a means of escape, and for the first time he started to feel the prickle of tension at the back of his neck. One of the staff turned down the music.

'Yes, she really must have been angry.' Aiden's voice was quite soft, but quite audible. There was no other sound in the café except the rush of traffic outside and the clink of cutlery as the older customer continued with his meal.

Under her breath, so that only she was aware of what she was saying, Alex was praying that Aiden would come to no harm. At her side, Angel had seen the forces that had railed against him return to their host, and then face Aiden. A form, completely intangible, surrounded him. To Angel it looked rather like a cupped hand, and he knew exactly what this was – who this was. The spirit that had assailed him earlier recoiled and battered against the hand, but to no avail. Aiden's own guardian stood with him.

'Excuse me, friend?' The assassin spat the last word out like a blasphemy.

'That scar. It could not have been accidental, and it could only have been administered by a woman.' Aiden looked down at the assassin with perfect equanimity. 'If it had been a man he would have killed you.'

The assassin looked at Aiden as if he had just spoken in a foreign language. What did this man know, that he should be so sure that a woman caused this scar? The calculations went through his mind: five witnesses . . . exit six metres away . . . who was this guy, what did he know? . . . three tables, two to the left, one right . . .

Suddenly, the assassin sprang up with astonishing athleticism, judging his moment to perfection. Even as his brain wrestled with the near panic of the situation, his body responded and performed as required. He landed just past Aiden and took two loping strides to where John was standing. With his momentum carrying him, he tapped the centre of John's chest just hard enough to make him step back a pace. In that moment, his fourth stride took him to the door. He turned right on the pavement and started to run down the street. As he had expected, everyone in the café simply stood and watched the spectacle. He lengthened his stride and put distance between himself and the café.

A clean getaway hadn't altered the fact that this encounter had ended in defeat for him. The defeat had occurred on a level that he couldn't really understand. It must have been some sort of 'spiritual' thing. More urgent now was the question of whether he should tell Lench about his little visit – his piece of 'freelance thinking'. His thought processes were interrupted by the sudden explosion of anger inside his head. He almost had to check his run as voices in his head seemed to scream in a chorus of frustration and madness. Now he was sure there must have been some spiritual dimension to the comment about his scar and who had caused it. His enemies had tapped into the unassailable resource that always seemed to be open to them. Just like Lench, he had been outgunned by the opposition.

As he reached the end of the high street, he turned a corner and then, within a few yards, he came to an alley. Although he was clearly not being pursued, he continued to run until he reached his car that was parked in a side street at the other end of the alley. He leaned on the roof of the vehicle and cursed under his breath.

The throbbing clamour inside his head had not yet subsided. The intensity was such that he was in danger of vomiting into the gutter by the car. At least there had been no pursuit. His head felt as if it contained a dozen insane captives, each one trying to break free. He cursed them all and then, inevitably, he found himself bent double over the edge of the pavement, disgorging into the road. At that moment, he admitted to himself that coming here had been an unwise act: 'freelance thinking' was not his strong suit after all.

Everyone in the café stared at each other. Alex and the other staff were motionless, while the CD played on.

Aiden looked up at them all as he scooped the remains of the packets of sugar into his hands.

'I have no idea . . . I have never seen him before.'

'How did you know that the scar was caused by a woman?' said the waitress who had spoken first.

'I don't know, I just knew that it was true, I just had to say it.' Aiden walked over to the counter with his hands full of sugar packets. 'Is there anywhere I can put this?'

Alex pointed to a bin near the counter.

'Come and wash your hands,' she said gesturing to Aiden to come out through the office. He could have done it in the customer toilets, but Alex wanted to talk to him. In the office, Aiden washed his hands at the small sink in the corner and, at Alex's invitation, sat down.

'You don't know who that was, Aiden?'

'No, I have never seen him before in my life.'

'He seemed strange . . . evil.'

'He was.' Aiden wasn't sure where his certainty came from, but the man had carried a presence of evil about him, there was no question about it.

'Maybe the Holy Spirit gave you some insight; you seemed to know what to say to this guy.'

Aiden considered this for a moment. 'Well I suppose so – good timing, eh?'

Alex was silent for a moment, then she turned to look at him. 'Something like this has happened before.'

She explained the incident with Lench. This was the same kind of thing. Aiden could sense the fear in her voice. Alex was scared now, and having seen this man in her café, Aiden knew that she had good reason to be.

Aiden looked at Alex and he saw the concern on her face, the resolute determination battling against the sheer sense of fear that he could see in her eyes. He had to seize this opportunity, and he could almost feel John standing at his side encouraging him.

'Alex, you'll be shutting soon, let me help you clear up and then why don't you come and have some dinner with me tonight. We can order something to be delivered.'

'Thank you, Aiden. Yes I will.'

Aiden smiled; John would have been proud of him.

* * *

Aiden's flat was a mixture of the new and familiar for her. She had been here a couple of times before for home group, but the fact that she was here alone with him now encouraged her to look around, to see things which she might not have noticed on previous visits.

Aiden gestured to Alex to sit down and she sunk into an expansive sofa – the kind that are almost impossible to get out of. It was easy for Alex to close her eyes and relax her muscles. She had not really stopped all day and now she felt incredibly tired. With great effort, she opened her eyes and smiled at Aiden.

'Make yourself comfortable, Alex. I'll get you a coffee, and we can order in some Chinese, okay?'

'Sounds fine. I'd like the crispy duck please.'

He called to her from the kitchen, 'I always get the crispy duck – delicious!'

She smiled to herself and then looked at the colours in Aiden's flat. There was a rich dark feel to this place that probably suited the colder weather rather than the summer. There were autumnal colours: dark reds and oranges, with shades of purple and gold. But despite that, the place was cool and, considering its proximity to the high street, very quiet.

She could hear music: he was playing something that might have been Mozart. For Alex, the delicacy of the notes was juxtaposed with the brutality and rush of the day and she almost cried. She thought about Alice again, safe back with her family, and she had to reach for a tissue from her bag.

Soon the smell of coffee reached her. She had taken her shoes off and turned herself round to get comfortable. It felt like an expression of vulnerability, but she did not care. She just relaxed on this man's sofa and it did not seem to matter. She felt safe, safe with him; and there was something else there, an intimacy and a desire for protection and comfort. It might have reminded her of when she was a little girl, but it was not quite the same; she was a woman now, and her needs were different.

The sound of Aiden's voice next to her made her jump.

'Are you planning to fall asleep on my sofa, Alex?'

'No, I hope not!' With a struggle, she sat herself up and looked at him. She was aware of the fact that her hair was now all over the place. She began to feel that sense of dislocation that she had felt a couple of times with John and she sipped some of the coffee he had brought in to try to regain her bearings.

'Who do you think that guy was?' she asked.

'I don't know, Alex, I really don't. But I have a feeling you won't see him again.'

'And God just told you that the scar on his face had been delivered by a woman.'

'Yes, I don't know why I knew. But it wasn't just knowing that he had received that wound from the hand of a woman. It was as if I knew that if I went up to him and said that to him that he wouldn't just leave, he would be . . .' Aiden paused, searching for the right word, 'defeated.'

'"Defeated?" You make it sound like some sort of battle.' Alex didn't particularly like the idea of battles going on in her café. But she knew what he said was true.

'It was a battle, Alex, I think you know that. Anyway, it's over now, and I don't think you need to dwell on it any more. You should try to have sweet dreams.'

She smiled at him, but she knew that she couldn't really afford to be too dreamy here, both the subject matter and her presence with Aiden precluded that. She remembered again that the last time they had spent time together she had wanted to find out more about him; but again, he seemed to be the one asking the questions.

'I hope this doesn't make you give up the café, Alex.'

She looked him in the eye, 'I have no intentions of giving up the café!'

Then she struggled out of the sofa and went to the window.

'Look at this, Aiden.' She beckoned him over and he looked through the glass, out onto the street they had just walked along, and the town beyond it. 'The view from this window is quite impressive isn't it. Look down there,' she pointed to the high street. He peered through the dusk of the summer evening, and under the street lights, he could just make out the little groups of young people walking to and from the pub, full of pointless banter.

'And over there, Aiden, look at that,' she pointed now almost directly across from the flat. In front of them there was a row of houses, ordinary semis by most standards. In the bedroom of one of them, someone was listening to some music. His head nodded rhythmically to the beat of whatever he was listening to.

'You know my vision, Aiden, you know what I am about. I believe God wants to take back some of the ground that the church has lost in the arts. That includes music, literature, painting, sculpture, dance and poetry – the whole spectrum of human expression. So much of it has been stolen from us, and I want it back.

'Now that I have left SLaM I can spend my time focusing on the things that are important to me. Look at the people God has put around me: Conner is a gifted musician; Daisy may one day figure in it all, she has a gift for fashion and design; and then there's my old friend Mr Wicks, a valuable legal advisor. Now I have some money as well. You see, Aiden, God is giving me the resources I need. I have to take this chance while I can.'

'And the café is just a part of it?' he mused. 'Most people think it's your big achievement, but you see it as just a small aspect of the plan, don't you Alex?'

'It's important, but it's just a start. We have given the young people in this town a place to go and some music to listen to, and there will be more. In God's time there will be more. Whether it's more cafés, a fashion label, or some other arts project, I don't know, I will see what God has to say. But I am convinced that someone somewhere has to do this, for the sake of Alice, and thousands like her.'

Aiden remembered Alice, the girl who had disappeared. Here was the driving force behind what Alex was doing. They both fell silent, staring out into the tableau of a suburban town settling itself down for the night.

Alex turned and went back to the sofa. She took a sip of coffee and watched Aiden come back to sit opposite her and he closed his eyes. This was a rare moment, she could sense it. It was a time to be bold.

'And you, Aiden . . .' she said, 'you have come into my life as well, and I need to work out where you fit in.'

He had felt quite safe when the discussion had covered over their ambitions, but this was dangerous territory. Of course, he had wanted this all along, but he still couldn't bring himself to say everything, to reach in to the depths of himself. Maybe that time would come.

'I don't know, Alex. I don't know where I fit in. There are some things I haven't worked out for myself yet.'

She got up again and walked over to the window, as if outside, somewhere in the metropolis, she might find the fulfilment of all of her great ambitions.

'What do you want, Aiden?' She spoke very quietly now, and before he could answer, she turned completely to the window so that she could not see him. The only evidence of the day that she could perceive now was a reflection in orange and purple against the clouds on the horizon. Behind her, she heard him get up and walk towards her. She considered it an act of trust that she did not turn around, but she was happy to give him that trust, to let him touch her or leave her as he saw fit.

There was silence for just a moment, and then she felt his hand gently touch her side, easing round to her stomach, while his other hand rested on her shoulder.

She could feel the whole of him at her back now so that she could relax slightly against him.

'What I want,' he said, pausing to let the words register, 'is to find the person who fits with me.'

Still with his arm on her shoulder, he moved away from her slightly and she turned to face him.

For some obscure reason, at that moment, she saw an image of herself in her mind: she was paddling in a small canoe, moving along under the influence of a strong current. Ahead was the rim of a vast waterfall. If she kissed this man now it would mean the start of something completely new for both of them. New and dangerous. But then, so many of the things she had done recently were dangerous. So much of what had happened had exposed her, driven her away from the safety and tedium of an excessively ordered life. Well, she did want that risk, she decided in the end. He had sensed the slight resistance in her and had had the grace to just wait, neither to pull her or to walk away. So she hung in the balance for a moment, considering all these things, and she remembered those times she had lain in bed thinking about the way she wanted one person in her life, one person with whom she would eventually build such a strong bond that the ghosts of the cruel separation from her parents would be exorcised at last.

Was Aiden the man? Well, he might be, but she just couldn't do it, not yet. She moved away from him slightly, and smiled. 'I'm hungry, let's get that food shall we?'

'Okay, Alex, that's fine.' He ordered some food and they ate and they laughed, and they compared their lives, as friends do.

And then he took her home and, for the first time in a long, long time, Alex climbed into her bed with something like joy in her heart; with a sense of hope for her own life as well as those around her who she loved.

Twenty-Two

Lewis knew the end was coming when two of his contract staff didn't turn up on Monday morning. He subsequently discovered that they had both been in over the weekend and had cleared out all of their personal effects. On his desk were notes from each of them expressing their regret at having to leave and asking for their fees to be calculated and paid. It was unfortunate to lose one contractor, but downright careless to lose two.

Lewis spent the first hour of the day on the phone to his bankers and legal advisor. He gave orders that he was not to be disturbed by anyone. Then, with very mixed feelings he called Martin in. There was none of the confrontational atmosphere of last week's encounter. This felt more like a wake than a business meeting.

Martin came into the office, and this morning he looked very tired. Maybe he had also reached the point where he realised that things could not go on. He slumped into the chair and looked up at his boss. He reminded Lewis of a Labrador looking up at his master from the vet's table just prior to the last injection.

'It's about SEEKA isn't it? Have you had enough then Lewis?' There was no trace of sarcasm in Martin's tone.

'I've had enough, Martin, yes.'

'Do you want my resignation?'

Lewis paused, 'No, I don't think so. I have lost enough people today already. If you feel you want to go then that's up to you, but if you decide to stay I will need you to help me plan the withdrawal of SEEKA from the market.'

There were footsteps outside Lewis's door, and they both looked up to see Dave Somerville shuffle past. He seemed to be caught up in the sombre mood as well. Martin frowned as the old anger flared inside him again. The suspicion that Dave was behind all this had long since taken root in Martin's mind. He had no proof, of course, but the resentment was there – mutual resentment. It was lurking under the current mood, waiting for another chance to manifest itself.

But the pain was not so great, the passion faltered, and Martin realised that although he had once cherished the SEEKA project, he was now almost pleased to see it die. Had he started to want this? When the pressure had built up, when both Lewis and Lench had been leaning on him, had he subconsciously wanted to see the thing finished? Maybe. Maybe the whole thing was costing him too much. He had looked in the mirror at himself that morning, and he had not liked what he had seen. In a way, it didn't matter now. SEEKA was finished. He had worked hard on the project, and had had a massive influence on its development, but he did not feel the sense of bereavement or loss that he had been expecting. His achievement was to see SEEKA launched, but its success in the future would have meant commercial return for Lewis and some sort of evil dividend for Lench. He did not feel obligated to work for either of them. He wanted to do something else now, something of his own and for which he could take all of the credit. There would be nobody standing over him the next time.

Martin brought a phone into Lewis's room and plugged it into a spare socket and the two of them made a series of phone calls, terminating arrangements with various suppliers and cancelling deals that were being negotiated. In some instances, there were contracts that obliged them to allow SEEKA to be used for a fixed period of time: Lewis decided to honour them. The result was that SEEKA would wither away rather than disappear rapidly. There would soon be no more T-shirts, no more club mixes, no more posters and no more mineral water. The whole process might take a couple of months. SEEKA would, in effect, become the event of the summer rather than the event of the year.

Martin needed to make one other call, in private, to kill off an unofficial aspect of the project. He needed to tell Lench that SEEKA was finished.

After he had made some calls with Lewis, he returned to his own office and shut the door. He would use his own mobile for this call. When he came to tap in the numbers, there wasn't the sense of fear and trepidation in his heart that he usually felt. Somehow, there had been a subtle change in his loyalties. He wondered now whether Lench's hold over him would continue or diminish to nothing. He had lost interest in Lench's Group anyway: he could trace that back to the moment when he realised that Lench was going to have Bridget murdered. It had been a significant moment for Martin, prompting him to vomit into the upholstery of his car. But on a more profound level, he had also been angry with that decision. He knew Bridget wouldn't have blown things for them and as it turned out, she had not been the source of the trouble after all. Lench had made a mistake and it had cost Bridget her life.

It was true enough that Martin was happy to see the back of her. She had become quite a nuisance with her demands for sexual antics on the boardroom table, but still he would not have wished her dead. He dialled the number and waited for the voice.

'Hello, this is Lench.' That same clipped English accent.

'Hello, it's me, Martin.'

'Ah, Martin, how are you?'

He never ceased to be amazed at Lench's observance of manners on the phone. Here was a man who had done things that he would not speak of, a man committed to evil, deliberately promoting it for its own sake, and yet his manners were impeccable.

'I'm very well, thank you. Look, I have some bad news. Lewis has seen a picture in the paper.'

'I have seen it as well, Martin.'

'He thinks it's me.'

'It is you Martin, in what one might call an unguarded moment. So, what has he done?'

'He is decommissioning the SEEKA project; SEEKA is finished.'

There was silence. Usually that was Martin's cue to start worrying, but today he didn't care. He almost dared Lench to be angry with him now.

'Martin, I am disappointed to hear this, but I can't say I am surprised. Are you at work at the moment?'

'Yes, I'm helping Lewis to shut down the SEEKA project.'

'Well I'm glad you phoned anyway, Martin, because I wanted to give you a little warning. A friend of mine tells me that the police want to have a very through look at SLaM, and the SEEKA project in particular. My advice is this: go through all of the files and other material that you have and remove anything to do with SEEKA. I suggest that whatever you were going to do this afternoon you rearrange so that you can wipe SLaM clean of SEEKA. Oh, and one more thing: we won't be meeting in the same place next week. I will let you know what we are doing, but in the meantime I advise you to expunge your office of anything to do with SEEKA.'

The phone went dead. There was still something in Lench's tone which made Martin feel uneasy. There was finality. Beneath that refined English eloquence, the real Lench had come to the surface. The importance of staying on the right side of Lench, or at least not getting in his way, seemed to impress itself upon his mind. This was the man who had arranged for the death of his lover, the man who deployed a weapon that could kill him as well – he had no illusions about that.

The word 'lover' hovered in his mind. He pictured Bridget as he had often seen her, standing at the window of the SLaM boardroom, looking out onto a city that she wanted to dominate. He had often seen her from behind, observing the tension in her shoulders, a hallmark of her restlessness. There she was in his mind's eye, standing in one of her short dresses. He remembered the way the material stretched across her.

Closing his eyes, he imagined it all again for a moment now: the way he would come to her while her back faced him and she always knew that he was there. She seemed to have this ability to sense his presence. In the seconds of privacy that they had, he would explore her like a hungry man. He only felt satisfied on those occasions when he sensed that her composure had been replaced with a shiver of expectation.

Now here she was again, in his fantasy, standing with her back to him, the familiar lines of her body silhouetted against the backdrop of the city view that they had from the boardroom. In his mind, he saw himself approach her, eager for her attention. He put his hand on her shoulder and started to move closer to her, feeling her with his fingers, and she turned to him–

'No!'

He opened his eyes in horror and could not suppress a guttural scream. The fantasy had turned to nightmare as he found himself staring into the face of the assassin, wearing her clothes, with her hair and devoid of life. The head inclined slightly, the completely lifeless eyes holding his gaze, gripping him like a vice. A scar snaked like an adventure across his cheek. Looking at his eyes was like staring into the point of your own death.

It must have been the last thing Bridget had seen.

* * *

'Good afternoon, my friend, I have a little employment for you.'

'Who do you want on the slab?'

Lench smiled, 'So quick to jump to conclusions! A little patience, please.' He always found the assassin's blunt approach to things amusing, so refreshing, so entertaining: at heart, the man was such an animal.

'I want you to visit Massey's flat, and I want you to remove everything that incriminates us. Specifically, there is a book I lent him and I would like that back now. And . . .'

'It's done.'

'. . . try not to make a mess. I do not want the place ransacked. This needs to be executed with the minimum of fuss. Is that clear.'

'Yes, boss.' The line went dead.

The assassin would do a good job. Lench knew that. He was a man of many talents, not just killing, and he would want to make amends for the fiasco with the woman from Martin's firm. He hoped that Martin would take the hint, and keep away – stay away. As far as the Group was concerned, he was finished, and as long as he kept quiet, that would be the end of it.

Whilst Lench's mind turned to other matters, the assassin donned his coat and went out into the heat of the day. He didn't like Martin, and he would rather have just killed him, but he was under orders and just at the moment he needed to behave himself. Things had been awkward for the assassin just recently. It wasn't just the blunders involved in killing the woman, it was also his ill-advised trip to the café this other girl had opened. Sometimes Lench thought of him as a brute, a blunt instrument, but he was still aware of the realities of the spiritual battle. He was as used to power and domination as the others in the Group. He was a man under authority like all others, even Lench.

He parked the car and approached the flats where Martin lived. The old disguise was judged to be still worthwhile, and nobody questioned him as he went about his work. In a rare moment of levity, he decided that if he ever had to give up killing people he would make a passable window cleaner.

At the right moment, he placed the bucket and sponge behind a bush and put on the surgical gloves. The lock on the door to Martin's flat was a simple affair, and he was soon in. An alarm chimed out an irregular tune until he deactivated it. He knew he wouldn't have long, but he did not rush. He spent perhaps thirty seconds examining the layout of the flat, and then another two minutes looking at the contents and design of each room.

Once he started, he operated with clinical efficiency, checking all the books, looking through piles of correspondence, checking under the furniture, in the drawers, in the cupboards. It took him just over two hours to cover every inch of the flat and in the course of that search he had found a book about the Group which Lench had given Martin (rather remiss of Lench to have loaned that) and an address book with Lench's phone number in it. He removed a thin metal blade from a small box in his pocket and cut out the page with the number on it.

Nothing was broken, nothing was damaged, nothing was stolen beyond the items that were required for the purpose of the job. It was clean and efficient, and there was now nothing in the flat that might implicate the Group. It wasn't like a kill, but still, he could take some satisfaction from a job well done. He left the flat with the alarm on and the door locked, exactly as he found it, and then placed the gloves back in his pocket.

* * *

The assassin could have taken longer because Martin wasn't going home early that evening. He pretended to leave at about 6.30 p.m. but he would be back at about 10 p.m. when he hoped that even Lewis would have gone home. In a way, his purpose was not so very different from that of the assassin.

He had driven out to a café on the edge of town. It was a dark place, full of anonymous people. He had ordered a large dinner and picked at it, revolted by the piles of meat and gravy set in front of him. Outside, the sky cycled through ever darker shades of grey and blue. Martin unscrewed the newspaper again, but he had read everything that he wanted to read in it. He was alone, bored and scared. And, unbeknown to Martin, a killer was roaming round his house, looking through his personal property.

As 10 p.m. arrived, Martin left the café. He was struggling to remember why he had to go back to the office, such was the state of his disorientation. As he drove back, he remembered his mission.

He searched around his office, and then the other offices looking for any trace of the sales report, or anything else that might incriminate SLaM in general and him in particular. It was a futile exercise, there had only ever been two copies of the report in the office and Lewis had taken them and destroyed them.

He was just about to leave when something in his mind forced him to go back. On his PC, buried in one of the directories, there was a saved copy of the report. He dumped it in the recycle bin and then deleted it permanently from his disk; then he ran a program to delete any temporary material.

It was about 12.30 when he left. He had originally planned to go on to a club, but he suddenly felt so weary that it was as much as he could do to drive home and collapse into his bed.

Twenty-Three

At 9.30 the next morning, they arrived. Like an invading army, the team moved in and took over the office. Given that they were on two floors, and one of those had only a couple of rooms, it didn't take very long. There were warrants of course: it had all been done properly. Martin looked at the reactions of his colleagues. They stood around the coffee machine like a group of refugees whilst the police went through all of their work. Some of them were already on their mobiles, talking to a legal acquaintance, calling home, or even making arrangements for their next assignment. Lewis was looking pale. His face betrayed something that was either confusion or utter resignation. There wasn't any resistance in him; he hadn't even bothered to check the warrants.

Martin watched the police continue with their search. He felt quite calm about it all: the police were way behind the other players in this game. They could pin nothing onto SLaM and, more importantly, they could pin nothing onto him. He saw Dave Somerville leaning against the wall watching it all go on around him. The smug look on Dave's face seemed to say it all; it was as if he had planned it from the start.

Martin felt the anger rising in him. The intensity that Bridget had often seen in him was back again. He thought back to the trouble that had occurred, all because someone had leaned on Lewis and someone had tipped the police off. Someone like Dave Somerville perhaps? He couldn't help it, he just went over to where Dave was standing.

'Are you happy now?' he hissed.

Dave was genuinely startled.

'What are you on about? Do you think I asked this lot to come in? You're even more of a fool than I thought you were. Just remember it's your SEEKA project that they are investigating.' He tried to keep himself to a whisper.

A policeman brushed past them, the fact that they kept their voices down injected more venom into what they were saying.

'My project! You weren't saying that when the first bonus got paid! You had your snout in the trough with everyone else, and it would have succeeded if you hadn't screwed it up with your jealousy.'

The two men stood facing each other, and a couple of the contract staff had turned to look. From the opposite direction, a policeman eased into view like a confident umpire in a minor league game.

'I will have to ask you gentlemen to accompany me please.' He was looking at Dave and Martin, and he evidently had Lewis in tow already. Lewis was allowed to make some hasty arrangements with the contractors. There was a flurry of cheques and the contractors scattered.

'Are you arresting us?' said Martin.

'No sir, I am not. We just want to ask you a few questions.'

There was an uneasy pause as Martin realised that it would be wise to just go along with this.

The police took away crate-loads of files and documents, some of which they had already looked through. Then they took some computer discs and the machines that were in the office. When they had taken most of the papers that were of interest to them the senior officer handed Lewis a receipt and escorted them all down to the station. Lewis, Martin and Dave filed out last and Lewis switched off the lights and locked the door. There was finality about it: he felt as though this was the last time that he was going to shut up the shop at Sound, Light and Music.

But he was wrong.

The trip to the station was completed in silence. Lewis very wisely placed himself between Dave and Martin. The three of them had actually talked about how to deal with a situation like this earlier in the year. Bridget had been there as well. At the station they all asked to speak to the company solicitor and they all said nothing until they had seen him.

It soon became clear that the police had nothing to go on except a photocopy of a document the blackmailer had sent them. Crucially, they had not been able to find a copy of that document at SLaM. The solicitor was looking relaxed and eventually asked that his clients be charged or released.

Martin was still angry. Sitting in an interview at the police station, he was more convinced than ever that Dave had put them up to this. He was probably sharing a joke with the sergeant right now. He didn't want to think about Lench's reaction, and he decided there and then not to tell him. In fact, it was probably none of his business. It looked like his time with the Group was at an end. Clearly, he had more to worry about than Somerville. As for their present predicament, they would be out soon enough, and then, if they stuck to the plan, they would meet together somewhere and discuss the next move.

Meanwhile, Lewis had just finished another session with his over-enthusiastic solicitor who told him that the police had no evidence, and that there was no case, and that the whole thing would be over by the end of the day. Lewis thanked him but found no comfort in what he heard. This had all gone beyond the issue of law now. He had never expected it would come to this: he felt as if a part of him had just died, and now he needed to arrange the funeral.

Staring at the blank wall of the interview room he decided that he had had enough of the business he was in. He had enough money – plenty of it in fact – and he was feeling tired these days. He hadn't realised it at first, but Bridget's death had hurt him in a way he couldn't easily define. The ache inside him told him that he still grieved for her. Maybe he still loved her. It was difficult to tell with all the emotional upheaval of the last few months. Maybe he was even missing Alex. There had been plenty of times when he had wanted to make their relationship more than just professional. She would never have allowed that, of course, and with hindsight he was glad that they had only ever been colleagues and friends, he longed for that kind of companionship now.

His thoughts were disturbed as the door opened and he saw the duty sergeant and his legal advisor standing in the corridor.

'You can go now, Mr Ashbury. We will be in touch.'

His counsel beamed with satisfaction and started to explain the situation. Lewis interrupted him: 'Save it so that you can tell us all together.'

He waited at the front of the station. Martin and Dave joined him soon afterwards and he asked the solicitor to join them for a debriefing. They would be going to a hotel to talk things through. Lewis was going to have his wake.

* * *

In a small conference room at the hotel Lewis asked his counsel to give them a review of the situation.

'Basically, you are in the clear so far. I believe that the police acted on information passed to them about the motivation behind this project of yours.'

'SEEKA,' said Lewis.

'Yes, apparently there was some document that they were looking for, as well as any other memos, letters and so on that might have implicated any of you. I know they have had an initial glance through the papers they took and couldn't find anything. They have also taken your computers and these will be examined in the next day or so.' The solicitor stopped and drew breath.

'It's my view that unless they find something really damning in the next twenty-four hours they won't have anything to hit you with.'

'So we should be able to get back to work soon,' said Dave.

'I think you can reasonably expect the police to return all your files and computer equipment in the next few days. After that you can get back to business as usual.'

'Good, I still have a magazine to produce.' He looked pointedly at Martin. 'At least we still have some reason to be in business.'

'What do you mean by that?'

'I mean that if we had just relied on your SEEKA thing we'd all be out of a job now, wouldn't we?'

Lewis's solicitor started to look uncomfortable. He wasn't paid to witness any unpleasantness between the clients.

'Yes and we know why this has happened! Because you sold us out!' Martin stared at Dave intently. 'You were the one who had the police run their eye over us; you were the one who sent the blackmail threats; you tipped off the cops. IT'S YOUR FAULT!' Now Martin was shouting, and the solicitor looked as if he wanted to slide under the table until this episode was finished.

Dave, though, was unmoved. It was clear that Martin didn't have a clue about what had happened. He was happy to deny it all, and give some back.

'It's all crap, Martin. Everything you say is crap. Okay, so I never much liked SEEKA – a view that I think is well justified now – but I would never have blabbed to the police. Look somewhere else for your blackmailer's identity. Maybe if you hadn't aligned the thing so much with the drug culture this wouldn't have happened. Don't blame me for your own mistakes and stupidity.'

Before the debate could get any more heated, Lewis cut in. He had let this run for a while to see if Dave had been the blackmailer, but nothing he had seen in Dave's reaction led him to believe that he was behind the attempts to destroy SEEKA.

'Enough! Now listen – SLaM is finished! I am making both of you redundant and winding up the business.'

Martin and Dave looked like two boxers caught in mid-blow. Their mouths dropped open and they looked at their boss.

'I am giving you three months' notice on full pay. I would be grateful if you could collect your personal effects from the office in the next week, because after that SLaM will be shutting up shop. We may meet again if the legal circumstances require it, and the company will pay all costs relating to any defence you have to make in this matter.'

He wrote another two cheques, for Martin and Dave, and passed them over. The room had become unnaturally quiet. Lewis stood up. He looked like a man who had been finally released from a great burden.

'Gentlemen, as far as you are concerned this is the end of SLaM. Goodbye, and good luck to both of you.'

With that, he beckoned his counsel to come with him, and left the room.

Martin and Dave looked at each other.

'Well that's that then,' Dave got up. He didn't want to be alone in this room with Martin and so with as much haste as seemed reasonable he headed for the door.

Martin took a little satisfaction from seeing Dave run like a frightened rabbit. But his earlier analysis was correct: he did have more things to worry about than Dave Somerville. He picked up his mobile and dialled Lench's number. It was better to get this over and done with quickly.

He waited for the tone but there was nothing. Then a sanitised voice told him that the number was not available. Fear started to creep up his spine to the back of his neck and he thought about the assassin. He needed to be careful now, very careful.

* * *

Later that day Dave related the events of the morning to his friend Sean. It was a great follow-up story to the 'rural rave' angle they had taken a few days ago. They might even use the picture of Martin looking stunned in the back of the car from a few weeks ago.

'So who was this blackmailer then?'

'Don't know,' Dave confessed quite truthfully, 'maybe one of Bridget's mates, she was probably getting her own back from the grave, if you know what I mean.'

'Well there's no anger like that of a spurned lover,' said Sean. 'She must have arranged it.'

'It certainly wasn't me, I'd have asked for money,' said Dave, and they both laughed, and Dave drained his glass and counted his blessings. The cheque he had received from Lewis included bonus payments and would cover him till he found something else, and that wouldn't take long. All in all things had turned out quite well.

* * *

Lewis had gone back to the office. There was a forlorn silence about the place that contrasted sharply with the activity of previous weeks. SLaM had always been about bustle and energy and life, and now there was a sad, eerie silence, like a church where nobody came any more.

He sat at his desk and got out his address book. He had always considered this call to be his fall-back option. It was a crazy idea, but then SLaM had thrived on crazy ideas. He dialled the number and waited for an answer. This was one occasion when he hoped he wouldn't get an answer machine.

There was no answer to the ringing tone.

* * *

Martin returned home and sat in a chair in his lounge, trying to decide what to do next. He looked at the address book he kept by the phone. He wanted to check the number he had for Lench, but the page was missing. He knew he hadn't taken the address book out of the flat. Fear began to creep slowly round his neck and reach into his heart.

He immediately started to search the flat, looking for anything that might suggest that someone had been there. After about ten minutes, he found the clue that confirmed it. The book Lench had lent him, hidden away under some papers and novels, was gone.

This was it. He had been kicked out of the Group. The two organisations that he'd had the most to do with had expelled him within the space of about six hours. The fear inside him now reached down into his gut and he headed for the bathroom.

Now that he knew that someone had been in his flat, he could see little signs that he had not noticed before. In the cupboard in the bathroom everything looked almost exactly as it had before, except at the back, an old tin of shaving foam had been moved and not replaced exactly where it had been before. He could just see the faint outline of a circular mark on the shelf of the cupboard.

Martin felt himself slide into panic.

'*I must be calm,*' he was talking to himself now, wiping his hands on a towel. As the elements of his self-confidence started to fall away, he tried to think. It was not easy – his mind was distracted by the threat of panic. He didn't want to think about the fact that someone, probably the assassin, had been through his flat, through his personal effects.

He needed to have a holiday – that was it – he needed to get away for a while. He almost ran into the lounge and started to pull up the corner of the carpet. On an impulse, he stopped and closed all the curtains against the summer evening outside. Then he started at the carpet again. When the floor was bare, he removed one of the floorboards to reveal a small metal box.

With some excitement now he opened the box and took out some Euro notes, some American dollars, and his passport. It was time for him to get away from it all, take to the air, and enjoy the sun.

Sitting on the floor, he found his diary and searched amongst the various scraps of paper he kept in there. It was a mess. Cursing, he scattered the papers across the wooden floor. There amongst the calling cards and receipts was a crumpled piece of paper with a number written on it.

His hands were shaking as he picked up the phone and dialled the number. It rang about fifteen times before a distant voice answered. Even over the distance, he knew his brother's voice.

'George . . . it's Martin!' He bellowed down the line. 'Look, I'm taking up your offer; I'm coming over to see you for a few days.'

There was a pause. 'Marvellous, Martin, be great to see you. I think you have the address don't you?'

Martin reassured his brother that he had the address, and then he had to listen as George told him about how much fun they would have out there by the sunny Aegean. Then they were into the final act. It was, as ever, the appeal for funds.

'Look, old chap, don't think me funny or anything.'

Martin knew what his brother was going to say and for the first time ever he really didn't mind. Lending George some money was the least of his worries.

'Hello? Are you still there, Martin?'

'Yes, George, what were you going to say?'

'Oh yes, look don't think me funny or anything but make sure you bring a bit of pocket money with you. To tell you the truth, old boy, I could do with a bob or two, you know, after all the capital outlay here.' Martin smiled and pretended complete incomprehension.

'Hello George?' He shouted, 'I didn't catch that last bit, what did you say?' Then, without waiting for a response, he put the phone down and smiled to himself. But as the amusement died away, he realised that he was alone. The fear started to creep over him again, pushing him on, hovering at his back. He went to find a suitcase.

Twenty-Four

Daisy returned to college with a new sense of purpose. She'd had a good summer; she had been able to keep up the rent on the flat and retain the place for the next year. The job in Alex's café had been the first paid work she had ever had, although of course she hadn't needed the money – not with her inheritance from Alex's father. One way or another, that family had looked after her well.

Then there was Conner. She didn't know how she felt about Conner, except that he was making her review all of the things she believed – and didn't believe. The curious thing was that with other boys she had known the relationship developed to the point where she wanted to sleep with them – it was like a mark of the intimacy they had achieved – but with Conner, it was different. She had shared with him such personal things, and she felt so close to him, yet she knew that he would not sleep with her. He wouldn't even consider himself in a relationship with her and that changed the nature of what they had together.

At college, she attacked the early assignments of the term with a purpose and vigour that surprised both her peers and her tutors. Many of the people around her saw the transformation in her work and attributed it to some experience she had had over the summer. They looked at her designs: the bold contours, the harsh uncompromising use of colour and line, the passion and energy. Her latest assignments stood in stark contrast to the insipid material she had generated in the previous year. Now her work showed courage, and a conviction that had been absent in her first year. Some people, perhaps one or two of her friends, and one of the academic staff, looked more closely at the bold sweep of her new approach to design. They agreed that she had indeed improved – there was no doubt about it. But these people looked beyond that improvement. They realised that, of itself, improvement told them only part of the story. For those who could discern it, a close examination of Daisy's new designs was an uneasy, disturbing experience.

The style of every line she drew, the harsh contours of the drawings, the stark use of colour and contrast all pointed to a fury deep in her heart. She was angry. The anger drove her to produce her best work ever, but it also consumed her – she became more driven and less communicative, spending more time on her own. This passion was making her work shine brightly, but it was also burning up the fabric of her personality.

She was all too aware of the dynamics at work within her. The destructive energy that drove her work had its source in her own personal pain. She was familiar with that pain, of course. She knew that it was born out of fear and rejection. These feelings were the spur for her creativity now. She believed that essentially Conner had rejected her. Yet she knew that his resistance was not based on a rejection of her as a person, rather it was founded on his moral objection to sleeping with her. Aside from that, she believed that he actually loved her. His attitude to her was a paradox that she couldn't understand. To reject her and love her at the same time defied all the categories she had ever used to assess the relationships that she'd had. Her incomprehension had only served to fuel the flames that drove her now.

Since the start of term, she had refused to speak to him. She had not called him and his letters had remained unanswered. He was the focus of her anger; she felt every shade of passion for him, a desire which hungered for his warmth against her, and an anger that might have prompted her to violence. She felt like a powder keg that was ready to explode.

Eventually, she resolved to try and expel the pain in the only way she knew how. She booked a Saturday off from the café, where she still did some part-time work, so that she could go out on the town and have a good time. Conner had actually asked her if she wanted to come out with him that evening. He was going out with the others in the band and some of their mates, although they hadn't decided where they were going yet. She didn't want that; she didn't want to be surrounded by Christians again, she wanted to go somewhere where she wouldn't be judged, somewhere where she could let things go a bit.

Inside herself, she was angry – very angry. Angry with Conner and Alex and God and herself. Most of all, she directed her anger at Conner, because he was the one who both accepted and rejected her, and he was also the person she was closest to at the moment. She just wanted to get out and rave, and meet people, and lose herself.

She couldn't forget about her experiences over the summer. The strength of the people she had met, the morality of their faith, and the 'magic bit', as she called it – the part of the faith where Jesus rises from the dead and people are healed and the blind see, and all that. She was quite impressed with the idea of a moral code – not that she wanted to adopt one herself. It seemed like a good way to live, a bit boring but pretty safe. It was what she called the 'magic bit' that gave her a problem. She could believe in every kind of pick-'n'-mix New Age technique, exotic and undemanding as they were, like a garment you could wear or discard. But the Christian story was not like that: a saviour who lived and died and lived again might start to make demands; might start to impact on her life.

Daisy realised that if she started to believe in miracles, then she would not be so far from believing in a Jesus who was raised from the dead. 'Who moved the stone?' as Conner would say, and if you believed that Jesus was raised from the dead, well you were all but there; in the Christian camp; one of them. It was all very interesting and it made for a good debate, but she wanted to keep it all in the rational part of her mind, the part that assessed and evaluated, the part that was easier for her to control.

It was Saturday evening, and she put on her club gear and went into the city. She wanted to spend some money, get drunk and have a good time, but even as she left the house and made her way up to the bus stop she could feel something inside her warning her, whispering to her about the futility of the exercise. She pushed it aside and walked on.

Daisy stood at the bus stop trying not to feel too self-conscious. Her dress was short, very short, and she would have to take great care about how she sat or everyone would see too much of her legs. The thought amused her and embarrassed her. It made her more determined to go out, but also it made her want to go home and put her jogging bottoms on and relax in front of the TV . . . and call Conner.

'Damn Conner!' she whispered under her breath.

She got on the bus and headed into town, glaring at a couple of boys as she sat down. Without her quite realising it, her old enemies were busy inflaming the feelings in her: fear, self-pity, and a deep indefinable sense of being unloved. The spirits were able to emerge from their hiding places, sniffing out the opportunities to hurt her again.

She started to feel the old anger, the old sense of injustice rise in her. She hadn't felt it for a long time. Everyone had a claim on her it seemed: the Christians, the boys leering at her, the landlord, the college. She wanted to be herself, and she was going to be herself tonight. The boys were still glancing at her as she sat with her legs tightly crossed.

She decided, then, that she would take a taxi home.

It was about ten as she got off the bus right in the heart of clubland. The streets were busy with the bustle of night life: the sounds of people in the amusement arcades, the smell of cooked food on the street corner, and apprehension was beginning to weave itself into the threads of her soul. Nobody here knew her, and nobody cared. She was alone and she felt unsure. She had been up to town plenty of times, but always with others: it didn't seem so good when you were on your own.

She headed for a nightclub and paid her fee. One of the bouncers tried to chat her up and in an act of defiance against her feelings, she kissed him, hard. His breath stank and she recoiled at the taste of him. As she went into the club, she could hear the bouncers laughing at something one of them had said about her.

Inside there was the familiar disorientating noise and heat. What she wanted was here: the opportunity to fall in with a senseless mass of people, none of whom would judge her. It was not so much immoral as amoral. She wanted to convince herself that she'd had enough of morality. As she felt her senses slip from their moorings and go with the tide of the music and the atmosphere, she longed for a lifestyle that would let her enjoy the alcohol and the music. This was a lifestyle that rejected the things which her parents stood for – a false respectability, climbing up the career ladder, compromising on everything to succeed – some life that was.

She recalled her conversation with Conner. She had the uncomfortable feeling that she was definitely existing at the moment, rather than enjoying the kind of life he described. She remembered seeing a film where one of the characters had talked about consciously deciding for this sort of lifestyle. Was it that bad? More to the point, was the alternative any better? She wondered if they sold drugs here – probably not. She wouldn't actually have touched them anyway, not after what happened to Will. That was one self-imposed rule that she wanted to stick to.

She bought a drink and drained it immediately, then she went into the toilets to look at herself, to hitch up her dress and redo her make-up. At the door of the toilets, she looked out into the heaving mass of life. She felt as if she were about to dive into a very deep pool, maybe even lose herself in it. So be it, that was what she was here for, that was what she wanted.

She went out into the heat and the light and joined the masses.

* * *

Caleb Wicks sat up in bed. He would have sat bolt upright, but age and aching joints prevented any sudden movement these days.

'What are you up to now, Daisy?' he whispered. Next to him, his wife turned over and settled again. Caleb eased his way out of bed and got his dressing gown. This special gift for prayer that he had seemed to ask an awful lot of him. He had felt privileged to be given a gift of prayer for particular people when they where in special need, and he knew that it worked, but with Daisy it always seemed to be after he had gone to bed. He was beginning to wish she would consider staying in a bit more.

In the study, he sat down in the chair. He knew that if he wasn't careful he would fall asleep again. As he settled down and started to talk to the Lord about Daisy, something like a voice in his mind spoke to him. It was really very clear: *'Conner will call you.'*

'Oh no,' he said to himself, *'it's going to be a long night.'* He got up slowly and went to put the kettle on; he needed to have a cup of tea. He would do the same thing later as well; if he didn't have a good strong cup of tea ready when he woke his wife there would be no end of trouble.

* * *

Daisy had been at the club for about an hour. She didn't think it was longer than that, but she couldn't be sure. No one had taken much notice of her, that was certain. She went to the bar and bought herself another drink – the fourth of the evening.

'Hello Daisy.'

She turned round to see who had just shouted at her over the noise of the music. The voice had seemed familiar, a bit like Will's, but she often heard a voice and thought of Will. It was just a trick her circumstances played on her.

In the half-light she saw Conner. Her brain registered it was him, but because she was seeing him completely out of context she couldn't bring herself to believe it.

'Conner?'

'Yes. Well, fancy meeting you here – you should have come with us after all.'

She didn't face him. In fact, she tried to hide behind the glass in her hand.

'What are you doing here?'

Conner couldn't help but notice the hostility in her tone. 'I'm having a night out with my mates. How about you, are you here with anyone?'

'No.'

'Well then, you can come and meet some of the guys from the band.' His voice contained just a hint of steel, as if he were giving her a command, or perhaps reacting to her own coldness with him.

She faced him for the first time. As she stared into his face, she recognised who she had been so far that evening, the sad girl on her own in a club who had drunk too much. She seemed to have lost some of the dignity that she had fought so hard to acquire over the summer.

They threaded their way back to a group sitting at a table in the corner.

As she sat down next to Conner in a group of about ten people, she realised that she hadn't really enjoyed being on her own. She had done it to prove a point and she couldn't remember very clearly now what that point was. One of the other girls in the party was studying fashion and design and she struck up a conversation with Daisy. They managed to exchange a few words over the noise of the music.

Later they all danced together and Daisy felt a strange kind of bond with this group. They accepted her. They did not attack her about what she wore, or what she said, or the cigarettes she smoked. And they wanted to have her with them. She had learnt an important lesson about herself recently: she enjoyed belonging. The evening helped to further shatter her illusions about Christians. She assumed that most or all of the people she was with were Christians, and yet they were right there in the thick of it, dancing and laughing – enjoying themselves.

Later, the music mellowed out and, if anything, she had an even stronger desire to stay with these people, to be with them – especially with Conner.

Daisy had found out that he was staying with the drummer in the band, a guy called Mark. She asked if he wanted to come back with her to her flat.

'I don't think so, Daisy.'

'Please Conner, I need to talk to you . . .'

He looked at her. He knew that he would say yes to almost anything she asked, and he said yes now. He made his apologies to his friend.

'I'm going to be leaving with Daisy. I'll see you tomorrow.' He tried to say it in the most matter-of-fact way that he could.

'Oh really, Conner! Well, you behave yourself now,' said Mark.

'Don't worry, I will.' As Conner turned, Mark placed a hand on his arm. They looked at each other and there was a half-smile on Mark's face.

'No, really,' said Conner, 'I will behave, don't worry.' They embraced and Conner led the way out of the club. They found the taxi Daisy had promised herself, and headed back to her place.

The taxi took them through the darkness of the early hours. They both sat at the back and she had put a hand out and taken his. This should have felt good, it should have been a moment of enjoyment, excitement, even passion. Instead, there was something inside her, something that made her feel restless, uncomfortable. The adrenaline was flowing all right but for all the wrong reasons. There was apprehension in her heart.

How did she feel? What was happening to her? She asked herself the questions, and the answers came whispering back to her: she was afraid, she was full of self pity, she felt unloved. She didn't even know where the words came from, except that they had always existed, deep in her heart, woven into her being, part of the warped fabric of Daisy Masters.

The taxi pulled up outside her flat and they got out. She thought that maybe being in her own flat would put her more at ease, but it didn't work. She wanted Conner there and she wanted him gone. She didn't want to believe that he had identified something that was causing her so much pain. She did not want to believe in possession, and she had sat on her bed every night since the time he had suggested it and cursed him and denied it. Still, there was that small voice in her head that told her it might be true, and if it was rubbish why was she feeling so down? And now, as she came into her flat, she realised that she was facing this crazy unbelievable truth, the truth that there might be something inside her that needed to be pulled out, expelled, exorcised. Wasn't it the stuff of movies; hadn't she watched it with her mates and laughed it off? Well, she couldn't laugh this off.

'Conner.' There was a weight in her voice that made him almost panic.

'Yes?'

'I think I might be possessed.'

He stood staring at her for a few moments, searching for the right response.

'What makes you think that, Daisy?'

'It's just what you said when you were round here that evening, and I have spent days trying to tell myself that it was rubbish, and I did think it was rubbish, but there is something in me that is restless and is causing me . . . pain. I can only describe it as pain.'

Her voice was beginning to quake as she continued to speak. Conner could see that she was quite pale now. He was almost paralyzed. He had been thinking about the business of resolutely resisting the temptations that would undoubtedly present themselves – and now this! He felt considerably out of his depth. In his mind he whispered, 'Lord . . . help!'

Then in his mind, he saw an image of old Mr Wicks, who had been a regular visitor to their house after Alex had arrived. The whole family had become close to him, and Alex and he had often talked about him. Taking out his mobile, he phoned directory enquiries. He hoped they would have his number; he didn't want to bother Alex.

Directory enquiries gave him the number.

'Thank you God!'

He looked at Daisy. She stood pale and withdrawn. The little dress she was wearing seemed so inappropriate now. He put the phone down and went to her, but as he hugged her, she flinched and so he pulled away.

'Just do what you need to do, Conner.' Her voice was just a whisper. Now he was scared.

He dialled the number and heard it ring. He looked up at the clock: it was 2.10 a.m. As the ring continued, he almost cringed. He felt like he was deliberately shattering something fragile.

'Hello.' Mr Wicks answered, and he almost sounded as if he was expecting the call. Conner tried to explain the situation, but before he had gone on for too long, Mr Wicks stopped him.

'Yes, I know, Conner. To tell you the truth, I have been expecting your call.'

'You have?'

'Oh yes. Now don't worry. Where are you?'

Conner gave the address.

'Okay, now stay there with her. Mrs Wicks and I . . .'

'Mrs Wicks?' Conner was amazed.

'Of course. I would always want to have someone else present, and where we are dealing with a female I would always want to have another female present. Now just stay there and keep her there. We will be with you in about forty minutes.' The phone clicked off.

Daisy watched it all, and the pressure inside her was beginning to tell. She could feel it deep within herself, and she suspected that 'it' was 'them', and for the first time she was so frightened that, while Conner wasn't looking, she whispered a word for the first time in a new way.

'Jesus.'

There was no blasphemy – this was a prayer.

Deep within her the spirits struggled: they had felt the time of danger coming hours before she had. In some ways, they knew her better than she knew herself. They knew what might be coming.

Conner sat at the kitchen table watching the second hand make its steady progress round the clock face. Daisy went into her room and got changed. She put her T-shirt and jogging pants on, and then she sat on the bed and tucked her knees under her chin. Something was inside her, she knew it. Something was there: whatever it was, it was there in her. She thought back over the last few months, and the circumstances that had brought her to this point. It was as if the whole 'Jesus-thing', so distant and far away before had suddenly rolled into her life, had come crashing in and now it was all over her, good guys and bad guys, angels and demons. She felt as if she was starting to go mad.

Conner got up, took his hands out of his pockets, and looked at her, hunched on her bed like a frightened child. He looked out of the kitchen window and she studied the frown on his face, trying to forget about the extremities of her own situation. There was something in Daisy – actually inside her – telling her that Conner hated her; how he was in it for something else. But she wasn't convinced. If it was the demon whispering in her ear, he wasn't doing a very good job because she didn't believe it. Conner hadn't hurt her, and it wasn't Jesus that was causing her problems. She had brought them along with her; they were her baggage.

The clock showed 2.35 a.m. Daisy fidgeted, restless. She could feel herself sweating although there was a cool night breeze blowing in through the kitchen window. She wanted to disappear somewhere, behind her bed, or out of the door – anywhere. She couldn't wait much longer; she felt as if her soul was being pulled apart. At least once, she thought she was going to vomit.

'Hold me, Conner.'

He came over to her and she gripped him as if he were the only thing between her and oblivion.

Her grip tightened on him and she held him so hard that he thought he was going to have a selection of bruises to show off in the next few days. The nail of one of the fingers in her left hand dug into his bare right arm and he could feel her desperation. The pain was constant but he was getting used to it. It was only when the doorbell rang, and they both jumped that he looked down and noticed that she had drawn blood from his arm.

He went to the door. As he turned, Daisy felt the nausea rise again. Whatever it was that was in her was starting to writhe, screaming at her to run away. She closed her eyes and whispered again the name of a saviour that she did not believe in.

Mr and Mrs Wicks came in like a calm breeze across the battlefield. They looked as unhurried as they ever did. Mrs Wicks had brought a small carton of milk that she placed on the table next to Daisy's design work. She smiled at them, 'We shall have a drink when this is over.'

They had evidently been in bed asleep until Conner had called them. Mr Wicks was still in his pyjama top with an overcoat and trilby hat, and Mrs Wicks had a coat over her quilted dressing gown. Conner thought they looked like a mad couple from some kind of sitcom, and he almost laughed, despite the situation. It really was quite surreal.

But when the spirits saw them, they went berserk. Daisy started to shake visibly and a low growl came from her. She couldn't believe that she had made the noise she could hear coming from her throat.

'Come here, Conner.' Mr Wicks's voice made him jump. He felt a bit like a junior doctor helping out in some surgical procedure, and now he was frightened. Mr Wicks took off his trilby and Mrs Wicks put down her bag, and they both looked at Daisy.

Caleb Wicks spoke. 'In Jesus' name, be quiet!'

There was silence.

'Now, Daisy, listen to me. I am going to try to find out whether there are any demons in you, and then I am going to tell them to go in the power of Jesus. Do you understand that?'

She nodded.

'Good. And do I have your co-operation for this?'

She nodded again. She really did not understand all this, but she had gone too far now, she needed to see it through. She was scared and she felt sick and she was sweating profusely, but if this had any meaning and relevance then it needed to go the whole way.

One might have expected a Hollywood-style deliverance scene, with special effects, lots of growling and the poor clergyman pinned to the wall by some supernatural force, clutching his Bible in an act of self-defence. But in the end, there was very little fuss. One by one, Caleb Wicks told each demon to name themselves, and since he was acting in the power of Jesus, they had to do just that. One by one, he told them to go in the name of Jesus, and so they did: unravelled from her, unweaved from the person she was, allowing the very core of her to rest again.

Then came the peace. To Conner it felt as if the removal of these spirits had allowed silence into this room for the first time, ever. Daisy sat with her back to the wall, her T-shirt damp with the sweat of a fear now passed.

Mrs Wicks put the kettle on. The room was so quiet that the only sound they could hear was the gentle whine of the heating element as the kettle warmed the water.

Conner made some tea for the Wicks's and coffee for himself and Daisy. He sat next to her and held onto her hand; he could not begin to guess at the sense of freedom that she was feeling for the first time in her life. He wondered what Alex would make of it all.

Mr Wicks was humming to himself as he rinsed the cups, and Mrs Wicks suggested that both Daisy and Conner come back with them. Daisy could go in the spare room and Conner could sleep on the sofa. Daisy certainly was so tired now that she simply nodded when she thought it was expected of her. Mrs Wicks helped her collect some clothes, her toothbrush and her house keys.

Conner wandered into the kitchen where Caleb Wicks was drying the cups they had used with a rather tatty old tea towel. He smiled at Conner.

'Well, what an evening, Conner! I expect we shall all sleep soundly tonight.'

Conner looked at him, wide-eyed. 'I want to be able to do that,' he said.

Caleb Wicks feigned surprise, 'What, dry cups? Don't they teach you young people anything these days?'

'No!' hissed Conner. 'You know what I am talking about. The deliverance thing – I want to be able to do that.'

'Really,' said Caleb, placing the last mug on the kitchen table. 'So am I to understand that God called you to this?' He looked over his glasses at Conner, the expression on his face was intense, even threatening.

'Well, I don't know,' said Conner, 'but I'd like to be able to do it.'

'Tell me, Conner,' said Caleb, running his hand over greying wisps of hair, 'have you learnt to read the Bible as if God were sitting next to you, whispering every word to you?'

Before Conner could answer, Caleb went on: 'Have you learnt to pray so that your very tears fall to the ground? Or have you loved the poor and the weak so much that you have given of yourself beyond your own endurance? Have you done any of these things?'

Conner stared at the older man, uncertain how to respond.

'My dear Conner,' said Caleb, reaching out and placing his hand on the boy's shoulder, 'do the simple things first. Love the Lord, and those around you. Then we shall see what God has in store for you after that.'

'Yeah, okay,' said Conner, again unsure how to respond and feeling slightly foolish.

'And let's start,' said Caleb Wicks, 'by loving Daisy and looking after her, shall we?'

Mrs Wicks appeared with Daisy at her side.

'Are you ready to go dear?'

'I think so,' said Caleb. 'Come on then Conner, let's be going now?'

Mr Wicks picked up his trilby and they went out into the chill of the early morning.

In the car, Daisy curled up on the back seat next to Conner. She had never felt so free, so liberated. She felt as if she had come to the end of a long journey, and she felt clean and normal and loved.

Daisy sensed that this was how a child should feel with their parents: secure and loved. She had never felt it before: the sense of belonging overwhelmed her, like an orphan coming home.

Twenty-Five

Martin Massey was in an almost hysterical state as he packed to go to the airport. Every five minutes he had to stop what he was doing and calm himself, reassuring himself that the assassin was not hiding behind the curtain or about to burst through the door. When he eventually finished, he sat on the side of his bed and surveyed the room. The answering machine light caught his attention. He had received eight calls, but he did not listen to any of them.

The assassin had been there. The assassin had thumbed through all his belongings, all of his possessions: they had all been touched, defiled. He could not have felt more violated if someone had come in and ransacked the place.

He let out a long sigh and checked that he had the code for his alarm, and that the gas and water were turned off, then he checked the alarm code again. It was definitely time to leave, time to put this place behind him. But now that the time had come, now that he was running away from his own flat, he found himself hesitating, dithering. He felt as if something precious was slipping away. Perhaps it was his sanity, or his will to live.

'Rational, I have to be rational,' he whispered, without realising that he was doing so.

He picked up his bag and went out into the hallway. The adrenaline from his fear was enough to get him out to the car park. He packed the bag in the boot and then, for no firm reason, went back to the flat for one final check. Something in his mind told him that it was a foolish thing to do. It was time to go, and at this rate, he might even miss his plane.

Looking in his flat one last time, Martin felt as if he were looking into a stranger's home. He checked the kitchen: everything was switched off. He looked in the drawers of his desk: he had left nothing of value. Finally, he pulled back the curtain and looked down onto the road below. It was meant to be the completion of the ritual.

But something went wrong. His heart stalled as he saw a figure, a man standing outside on the pavement. It didn't look like the assassin but he couldn't be sure. Suddenly, he felt the moisture on his hands, the breathlessness: he was afraid.

He finished locking the flat and then, instead of walking out of the front door, he climbed out of one of the windows in the ground floor lobby letting slip a muffled curse as he banged his shin on the window sill, but at least he was out. His car was parked a short distance away, and about thirty yards further on he saw the figure. He could see more clearly now. It wasn't the assassin, but someone was looking up at the window of his flat.

Martin wished he had gone to the bathroom again before he left. Bending low, he scampered across the communal garden and on towards his car. He decided not to use the remote locking device, as the noise would attract attention.

He made it to the car, unlocked it and climbed in. Hunched in the driver's seat, he fumbled the ignition key into the starter and the car sprang to life. He watched as the man turned round: Martin got a clear sight of the man's face as he looked straight at him. The figure turned and started to walk away from him, ignoring him completely.

Martin considered for a moment the possibility that he had clambered over the gardens and banged his shin to avoid someone who had no interest in him at all. He took a deep breath, trying to rid himself of the useless energy the adrenaline had created. His hands shook on the steering wheel as if the whole car was vibrating. At least now he was on his way. He pulled out and started to accelerate down the road. In a moment he would be past the figure and away. He glanced at the dashboard clock and made a mental calculation, it was 7.52. The plane took off at 10.40. If he wanted to give himself an hour to check in this was going to have to be a fast journey.

His thought processes suddenly froze as his vision was enveloped in white light. He hit the brakes and swerved. The car jolted onto the pavement and stopped. Optic nerves continued to fire as he saw floating shapes form on the dash and in the windscreen. Then his ears told him that there were footsteps running away from him and it reminded him of the evening at the rave. Was this another reporter? Would his face be in the papers again?

There were tears in his eyes now. He turned round and in the visual chaos, he could just see the figure disappearing away from him. He couldn't go after him, not now. He was on the run. Damn the press! This wasn't the assassin, or someone from the Group, this was another mugshot for the tabloids. His vision clearing, Martin forced the car back into gear. Now he was determined to get away. He knew that in a few days he was going to open an English newspaper and see his face caught again behind a windscreen, frozen somewhere between comedy and horror. He bumped the car down from the pavement and sped off towards the main road.

He parked in an anonymous residential street near a station on the Piccadilly line. His fear had, once again, hardened to resentment and frustration. He had been reduced to a fugitive, hounded by the press, fleeing the country. His internal anger was pointless and he tried not to encourage it. He had neither the power nor the will to exact vengeance against any of them. Lewis, Lench, Dave Somerville – they had all beaten him. He wondered now, too late, why he hadn't ordered a taxi and kept his own car in his garage. As it was, it would have to sit here in the street for as long as he was away.

There was too much to think about, too many issues in his mind. He turned them over again and again as he boarded the train and it started to lurch and rattle on the steady journey across Greater London, towards the airport. As the train pulled into Heathrow, he found that he had to wait his turn to get off with everyone else. In just a few days he had become ordinary again.

He had made good time in the end, and there was about half an hour to spare. He was nearly there. He had nearly escaped. Nobody except his brother knew where he was going, not Lewis and not Lench.

He bought some more Euros at the Bureau de Change and sat in the café with a paper and his back to the wall.

He had his mouth full of pastry when his mobile went off. He chewed frantically and then swallowed hard, spitting crumbs as he answered the phone.

'Hello?'

'Hello Martin.' It was Lench, smooth as ever, but sounding somewhat distant. Somewhere near him, the PA announced the final call for a departure to Rome.

'Martin, you sound like you're at an airport. Going anywhere nice?'

He had to resist the temptation to just switch the phone off. 'I thought I would get away for a few days, you know.'

'What an excellent idea. Well, I will come to the point because I don't want you to miss your plane. The end of SEEKA means the end of you as far as the Group is concerned, although I think you probably guessed that. I have had to make some arrangements to ensure that there is no evidence of any connection between you and either the Group or myself. It has all been a disappointment to me, Martin . . . are you still there?'

Martin was silent, with the phone pressed to his ear. He felt like a small boy being told off by the headmaster, but something in his mind was resisting this, something told him not to be talked to like this.

'Yes, I'm here,' he said.

'Good. Look, as far as I am concerned, Martin, our association is over, finished. The fact that you are running away tells me you know this, and you are afraid. That's good. But don't worry, Martin. I won't be sending our friend after you; I won't even come after you when you come back, as you must eventually. In return, of course, I need to be assured of your complete discretion. If I find that you have tried to damage either the Group or me with some foolish accusation I shall be forced to take action. Is that clear?'

He really wanted to bite back. He really wanted to tell Lench what he thought of him; that he was a damn fool to have had Bridget killed; that his stupid assassin had botched it and caused more harm than Martin ever had; that in the end he'd had to do everything himself and all Lench had done had been to make demands on him. He wanted to tell Lench that he was in no position to make threats.

Lench continued, 'Martin, it is unusual for you to be so silent, but perhaps you have a lot on your mind. I think we can safely say that this is the last time we will be speaking. Just remember one thing, Martin: you belonged to the Group once and in a sense, nobody leaves the Group. You are one of us now and you always will be, so be careful. Do you understand? . . . Martin, are you there?'

He didn't care now – he'd had enough. His plane was leaving in eight minutes.

'Just be careful yourself, Lench. You are the one who has made the mistakes – you still might have to pay for them.' He switched off his phone before Lench could answer. It was a sweet moment amongst all the bitterness.

The 22.40 flight for Athens left on time. Martin tried to look forward to the life that he might be able to lead out there. Perhaps it was a good idea to be heading out into the sun as the autumn approached, and he did like Greek food, and then there were the girls. Perhaps it wouldn't be all bad. But he hadn't wholly convinced himself. Behind it all there were other deeper issues. He had joined the Group; he had involved himself in the rites; he had degraded himself with the others and thought nothing of it. So where did that leave him now? For the first time in months, he felt ashamed of what he had done.

* * *

Lench sighed and looked across the table. This fool, this insolent pup, Martin Massey, had managed to have the last word. In other circumstances, his anger would have driven him to extreme measures: he did not tolerate any attitude from those he considered beneath him.

The assassin sat opposite him and the pair of them thought through all of the implications of what had happened. It was probably more accurate to say that he had led the assassin by the nose, metaphorically speaking, through the implications of the whole sorry business. It had become such a mess that he had decided that he would need to tell the other members of the Group what had happened. The shame of it all nagged at him, a constant reminder of his foolishness, his weakness. Now he needed to work out the limits of his liabilities before he tried to close off this whole sorry affair.

Of course, the sum of the whole thing was failure. And the consequences of failure were ignominy and punishment. In the last few months they had both failed a number of times in some critical situations. The assassin had been punished for his performance with the murder of Bridget. Lench's turn would come soon, and when that time came his civility and refined tone would count for nothing, he would wallow in his own fear and self-loathing, as well as the derision of the others.

The imperative now was to see all of the liabilities dealt with. First, there was the issue of this woman, Alex Masters. Perhaps something could be done with her to compensate for what had happened. Recently he had started to think very seriously about having her murdered. It was a dangerous proposition and he had the feeling that there was something he was overlooking, but she was deadly. She represented a danger to him and all he stood for because she was a hungry Christian, a Christian with a purpose and some integrity. She had too many qualities to be placed in the little boxes he and others like him had prepared over the years. She was too passionate to be ground down into going through the motions of her faith, too strong to be passed off as a weak and feeble invalid, too full of compassion to be castigated as one of the 'religious types'. She led the normal Christian life, and demonstrated that such a life was credible. To Lench she was poison.

Then he thought about the girl that had been with Alex Masters during their fateful encounter, a feisty young thing she had been. He only wished he had encountered her in different circumstances, perhaps more intimate circumstances.

He certainly didn't want to encounter that traffic warden again: an aggressive and domineering woman. The fact that he had gone back to his car and moved it hadn't stopped her giving him a ticket, damn her.

He thought about the ticket for a moment, and then something like a lump of cold and bitter fear dropped into the pit of his stomach.

The ticket.

The ticket could prove he had been there, outside that flat where Alex lived. The traffic warden might recognise him again. And he had hit Alex Masters, he had hit her in front of two witnesses, and one of those was independent of Masters. The more he thought about it, the more a vast black hole opened up beneath him. What if they had gone to the police? What if Masters was killed and the police eventually came calling, especially if the other girl mentioned their little meeting.

Then there was the assassin. The man who had gone into Alex Masters' café and caused a disturbance, the man who had allowed a variety of people to see his scared face. A man now implicated just as much as Lench.

In that moment, Lench realised that he could not risk another attack on Alex Masters. In fact, the situation was more absolute than that because there was a spiritual sense in which he could never harm her again. The assassin and one or two of his other friends might scoff at that idea, but Lench knew too well the power of spiritual forces working for and against their purposes.

Finally, there was the issue of Martin and SEEKA. In a way, this was the most straightforward aspect of the whole thing. Martin was gone, and good riddance to him. As long as he kept his mouth shut that was the end of it, and SEEKA was history. If there was any flak from SEEKA it would hit SLaM, and possibly Martin as a senior employee, but it would go no further than that.

It was obvious now that the woman Bridget Larson was the most likely source of the blackmail attempts Martin had talked about. She had probably spent the morning before she was killed gathering the material she needed to strike at Martin. The fool: another of his errors was to let his indifference to her become too obvious. If only the assassin had been able to get to her as soon as she arrived home. It took Lench a moment to remember why the assassin hadn't finished the job as soon as Bridget had arrived home. Someone from the gas company had been there with her. That one coincidence had derailed the whole plan. Lench cursed under his breath.

'What are we going to do?' said the assassin, twitching with agitation. He reminded Lench of a barely-trained animal, straining to revert back to its own base instincts.

'There is nothing we can do now.'

'What do you mean, there's nothing we can do? I will kill the woman, Alex Masters.' He spoke the words as if they were an irresistible statement of fact.

'No!' Lench sat forward matching his will against the assassin's. 'It is too dangerous, for both of us. We have both been fools with her and her friend, and we must pay the price for it.' Then he added, 'She is protected.'

The assassin snorted and removed a long, thin-bladed knife from one of his boots. 'What protection does she have? None.' Lench watched the figure in front of him straining against the imposition of discipline. There were occasions when the assassin needed a firm hand.

'Don't parade your weaponry in front of me,' he growled, 'she is protected.'

He repeated the words again, more quietly this time, but with no less conviction. There was silence except for the tick of the carriage clock. Lench leaned forward across the desk, fixing the assassin with his gaze.

'If she is not protected, why did you run from her presence?'

The assassin started to answer and then fell silent. He had to admit that, yet again, Lench was right. He slide the knife carefully back into its sheath in his boot.

In a moment of insight quite out of keeping with his character, the assassin saw that there was nothing more for him to do, and so he rose from the chair and left Lench to his own thoughts.

Alone in his study Lench surveyed the situation. It had not been a total failure. No doubt SEEKA had been a useful exercise while it lasted. But that was small consolation in the light of the other things that had   happened. It was only now that it was far too late that he realised that whilst SEEKA had been a tactical victory, the other side had been playing the game on an altogether different level. They had managed to put people into the right places. This was strategy, long-term strategy. It might just be that Alex Masters and the others were going to achieve things that would make SEEKA seem paltry and insignificant by comparison. For the first time in perhaps years Lench sat alone and tasted real, nauseating, fear.

Twenty-Six

Daisy spent the rest of the night in deep, peaceful sleep. For the first time in her life she felt neither the condemnation of others, nor the need to fight against that condemnation. She was free.

What exactly had happened? She began to recall the events as if they had happened to someone else, but what did it mean? One thing she did know was this: a burden so profound that it had almost become a part of her was now lifted. Something like an oppression, that had weighed her down for years, had been taken away. The Christians around her had done their thing, and by their definition, she was no longer possessed; by her definition, she was free.

She thought about these things when she first woke up. In fact, the change in her was so profound that she was almost aware of the difference before she was fully conscious. Before today she had been called awake by a subtle voice, challenging her to do something to justify herself that day, condemning her because she knew that the tasks she would set herself were too much. It was a revelation to her now: she had been conscious of failure every day, even before she had got out of bed.

Now, this morning, there was no voice. She felt as if she had been justified, although she didn't know what she had done to deserve it. The fear she had felt before was now a lie. There was in fact nothing to fear. The pain from the lack of love was gone, its power shattered by the actions of the people around her: Mr and Mrs Wicks, who seemed to have no other motive than a concern for her welfare; and Conner, the boy who had treated her with dignity.

She got out of the bed and thought about Conner. His love had driven him to take all sorts of risks with her. She knew that he found her attractive – he was real in that sense – but it was an indication of the strength of his love that he had not taken advantage of her physically, sexually.

Grabbing her dressing gown, she left the bedroom and walked down the stairs. In the silence, she could just make out the sound of snoring coming from the living room. Daisy pushed open the door and looked in.

Conner was lying on the sofa, sprawled across the cushions, his left leg dangling in mid-air. He seemed to bring his own sense of disorganisation to everything that he did, even sleeping. She glanced at the clock on the wall. It was just after 7.30. Quietly, she shut the door again. She needed to talk to Conner, but it could wait until later.

In the kitchen, she could hear someone moving around and the sound of a kettle boiling. Mrs Wicks emerged in her quilted dressing gown.

'Ah Daisy, come and sit in the sun lounge with me dear, and we'll have some tea.'

These people seemed to be in the same league as Miss Goldsworth when it came to making tea.

Daisy nodded and walked through to the little conservatory at the back of the house. She could already feel the warmth of the sun.

This room, even more than the others, seemed to be permeated with a sense of peace. If she believed in holiness, she would say that it dwelt here, a room that looked out onto the back garden of the Wicks's suburban home. The sense of unreality made it more difficult for her to focus on what was happening, and what had happened. All the same, she needed to do some thinking. She didn't know what she felt about last night. She didn't really know what had happened.

Mrs Wicks came in with some tea and placed it on a little table near to where Daisy was sitting. Stacked under the table Daisy could see back copies of a magazine her mother used to read. A brightly-coloured jumper lay half-knitted in amongst some balls of wool on the floor.

'I call this hour of the day my "quiet time",' said Mrs Wicks as she poured some tea and picked up the bundle of knitting by the side of her chair. 'I find that it is a good time to think about things. There's no noise, no distractions. I expect we will be able to sit here for a while before the men disturb us.' Her language reminded Daisy of a rather elderly great-aunt she remembered from when she was a very small child. She had always referred to male company as 'the men', and she had always called her husband by his surname when referring to him in front of others.

Mrs Wicks leaned forward in conspiratorial fashion: 'You see dear, Mr Wicks isn't much of an early riser and an expedition across London at 3 o'clock in the morning is quite reason enough for him to have a lie in until 8.30 at least. And as for young Conner, well I think you have looked in on him already.' The knitting needles started to click erratically.

Quiet descended again, and Daisy tried to think of an adjective to describe how she felt. The sense of release, the lightness of a burden lifted – but she couldn't find the words. The sun continued to shine into the conservatory where they were sitting, giving a gentle warmth. In the garden, she could see the carefully tended roses, and clematis climbing across the wall. Somehow, all of the flowers and shrubs had an air of 'aliveness' about them – a quality of texture, colour and vibrancy that she had never noticed before. She could not think of a better word to describe it.

'How are you feeling today, anyway?'

Daisy thought about the question before answering.

'Relaxed, and confused.'

She wondered if they all expected her to suddenly 'see the light' and get religion. She stopped herself here; she wasn't going to use that phrase anymore. She realised now that it belonged to an earlier phase of her life; these people and their faith had earned some respect. She had seen too much of them to think that they were just plugged in to some quasi-religious set of rules, that somehow in their naïveté they had lost touch with the real world.

The knitting needles continued to click.

'By the way, Mr Wicks and I don't expect you suddenly to become a Christian because of last night.'

'You don't?' Daisy's reply betrayed her surprise. Could this woman read Daisy's mind?

'Oh no! We have done what we were supposed to do. We have helped to release you from something that should never have had a hold on you, and now we will give you some breakfast and send you on your way. It's a small thing really. We're here if you need us.'

The needles continued, as if Mrs Wicks's hands had decided that whatever else happened they were going to get this jumper finished.

'I think Conner will expect something from you now, but you should not worry too much about him. He is still young, isn't he, bless him.'

Daisy looked out of the window again and studied the flowers. She felt as if she wanted to believe something but she wasn't sure that she could. She did believe that there had been something in her – she didn't know what – and she felt in herself that it was gone, they had gone. As she considered the events of the previous night, she felt an urge to go out into the garden. There was something like a voice in her. It spoke with a tone that seemed vaguely familiar. It was as if the voice had been speaking to her since she could remember but there had been so much other noise, so many louder voices shouting at her, that it was only now in the true peace that she could hear it. *'Come into the garden and hear my song.'* Song? All she could hear was the click of the knitting needles.

She got up from the chair and looked out of the window.

The knitting stopped for a moment: 'Would you like to go out into the garden for a few minutes, Daisy?'

'Yes please.' Mrs Wicks unlocked the door and Daisy walked out into the sunlight. She stood amongst the flowers and looked at the scene around her. The colours seemed to have such an intensity that her eyes watered. She shut them and the voice came again.

'This is my song, my song of love to you Daisy, my beloved,
For the winter is past, the rains are over and gone,
Flowers appear on the earth,
The season of singing has come.'

She had a sense of love surrounding her and penetrating her. She felt the focus of an energy, a person. She couldn't tell whether the tears in her eyes were from the brightness of the sharp colours or from the sense of acceptance that she now felt.

Daisy realised that this new sense of perception must be related to what had happened last night. But there was more; she knew now with a certainty and clarity that she was loved. And she believed this fact with such a deep and profound sense of realisation that she knew that she was changed in that moment. This was not a development over months; this was instantaneous. Love was there in that garden with her. Personal and intimate, closer than anything else she had ever experienced, far removed and far more profound than the intimacy she had learned from the variety of sexual engagements that she'd had. In fact, her experience of sex had, until recently, been her primary frame of reference, and yet that comparison was false. It was a different intimacy. If she had been loved in her own home by her parents she might have been better equipped to quantify the experience, but all she could do was marvel at the scale of the love and acceptance that she now felt. The tears continued to flow, falling from her cheeks down onto the soft grass below her.

Mrs Wicks continued with her knitting, glancing up occasionally to see Daisy walking in the garden. She whispered prayers of love and encouragement as the needles continued to click.

The door from the house opened and Conner walked in. He was still half asleep as he wandered into the conservatory, rubbing his eyes.

'Hello Conner.' Mrs Wicks smiled at him. He looked a complete mess.

'Hi. Where's Daisy?'

'Oh, she's out in the garden, dear.'

He looked out and Daisy was standing there on the lawn, perfectly still now. Conner walked up to the glass and looked at her.

'I think you might want to put on some clothes before you go too much further,' said Mrs Wicks. Conner realised that all he had on was a T-shirt and some boxer shorts.

'Oh yeah, sure.' He turned round and wandered back into the house. As he pulled on his trousers, the events of the previous evening played back in his mind. He didn't feel competent enough to assess all the implications right now. Looking at the clock, he realised it was only 7.40 a.m. How was anybody expected to assess anything at 7.40 on a Sunday morning? It wasn't natural – it certainly wasn't natural for Conner.

He thought about Daisy and the profound effect this must be having on her. Surely she would become a Christian now; surely she would fall down on her knees and give in to the Lord and then . . . and then what?

Well, for a start, a major obstacle to his involvement with her was removed. It looked obvious now: they could be together, become an item. Surely that was going to happen. After all, didn't they both want each other? He was human, he was male, he had sensed the energy between them. His faith hadn't lessened his capacity for desire – in many ways, it had sharpened it.

And yet, now that he was at the threshold of having one of his desires fulfilled, he wasn't sure that he wanted it to happen. It was as if his passion had not so much been for Daisy herself as the desire to see her healed. If that had happened, what was left?

There was a knock on the door and Daisy was there, with a cup of tea.

'You look like you could do with this.' He was suddenly embarrassed in her presence. She looked bewildered, and he reminded himself of what she had been through. Whatever he thought, whatever questions he had, Daisy had much more to deal with. She had to deal with her own reactions to last night – she might not even have thought about her relationship with him yet.

'Are you okay, Daisy?'

She nodded, 'Yeah, I'm fine. A bit tired, you know.'

'I'll go and see if Mrs Wicks can do us some breakfast,' suggested Conner.

Mrs Wicks was already busy in the kitchen. 'Mr Wicks and I like to have a bit of toast and bacon on a Sunday morning. I hope you young people will join us.' Then she quickly added, 'You aren't vegetarian are you? I could always do you some beans instead. We always have beans in the cupboard.'

At that moment, Caleb Wicks appeared in an outlandishly checked dressing gown. Mrs Wicks waved some cutlery at him.

'I was just saying to these young people, we like a bit of bacon and toast on a Sunday, but we do have beans if they prefer.'

'Or even bacon and beans, unless one of them is vegetarian of course,' said Caleb.

Whilst Conner looked at them, bemused by this bit of domestic banter, Daisy couldn't help smiling. They really were the most extraordinary pair. She imagined that they must have spent hundreds of years together to get to this stage, where their actions and attitudes were so completely uninhibited. They were like Adam and Eve: they might have been completely naked and they still would have behaved in the same way.

Now all Daisy wanted to do was go home and perhaps spend some time with Conner. There were things that they needed to say to each other – although she wasn't sure she knew what they were.

There wasn't much in the way of conversation, but the scene had a reassuring ordinariness about it. Daisy drew comfort from it all after the strangeness of the previous night. Mr Wicks even contrived to glance through the Sunday paper before his wife corrected him.

'Not when we have guests, Caleb. Have you no manners?'

He sighed and folded the paper, dropping it on the floor. Conner glanced at it and noticed that the sports section was still visible. He spent the next ten minutes trying to pick out the football scores.

* * *

Daisy and Conner walked down to the station together. Going back on the train had been their choice, as Daisy hadn't wanted Mr and Mrs Wicks to miss church. Besides, she wanted to have some time with him.

'Conner, I need to talk to you about last night, and you and me.'

'Umm?'

She took his hand. It was the most affectionate thing that had happened between them. 'The thing is, it's true to say that something has happened to me. I don't know what it is and whilst I have changed and I know that, I can't say that I am a Christian now, because it wouldn't be true.'

They carried on walking, and she longed for some response from him. He was silent, and so she tried to explain herself.

'The truth is, I don't know what I believe. What I do know is that I am loved, and accepted; it's like a huge weight that was on my shoulders has gone.'

He looked at her as if he was trying to understand the ground on which she stood.

'Don't try to understand it all, Conner; goodness knows I have never really understood you,' she teased, smiling at him. She knew that she had something else to say.

'The thing is, I guess I'm not so desperate for attention. I've got a better idea of love now. I do love you, but I don't want to. . . do you know what I mean?' She looked at him helplessly.

And he did understand, he understood it all. And the fact that she was saying this now was a sign of how far she had come. The needs and longings within her had been replaced by self-confidence and a sense of peace that allowed her to relate to people without using them or being frightened by them.

'It's okay, Daisy, it really is okay.'

He couldn't think of anything else to say, and so he took her in his arms and they stood in an embrace together. Standing by the side of the road, with the intermittent Sunday traffic going by, they found out a little more about the love that they now shared together.

There was a sense of resolution for Daisy, even in the uncertainty that she felt. Maybe there was no need to work out everything now. She had got all that she could hope for. The weight had been lifted, she had confronted the change in her relationship with Conner and they had both dealt with the implications. There was no anger in either of them, just an assurance that the peace they felt was bigger than the questions that remained unanswered.

As they continued their walk down to the station, Daisy was again aware of the intensity of the sights and sounds around her, and amid the drone of the Sunday traffic, she could hear something which caught her attention. Surely she would never have noticed it before today. She stopped and focused her senses, and then she caught it again. As faint as a whisper, but unmistakable, she could hear the sound of church bells.

Twenty-Seven

In the late summer of that year, a business deal was finalised. The details, when they emerged, surprised everyone. Alex used some of her own funds to buy the remains of SLaM. Lewis was happy to sell what was left to her, and his mind turned to the possibility of new projects. For Alex, the shell of SLaM would form a new organisation that would be the vehicle for the fulfilment of her ambitions.

It had to be done in a professional way. The material they produced, and the message they communicated had to stand its ground out on the street amongst the noise and chaos, all the sounds and all the light. It was something that SLaM had been very good at doing, but Alex knew that the real assets of the firm had been the brains and the creative talent. There wasn't much of that left now, but in a move which amazed some of her supporters, she set about getting some of that talent back to help her.

Alex knew that she needed some more help. She sat alone in her flat, listening to the wind of a chilly October evening buffeting the windows. Much time had been spent thinking and praying about the next move, the wisdom of it, and the incomprehension she would face from her own supporters. There was a restlessness about the weather that evening, and it infected her as she stood and paced around her lounge again. Finally, she picked up the phone. It was answered within two rings.

'Hello?'

'Hello, Lewis. It's Alex here.'

Lewis sounded almost overjoyed to hear from her. 'Alex! How are you, how is business?'

'It's doing really well, thanks. Listen, Lewis, I have another business proposal for you.'

There was an almost imperceptible pause before she went on. This was the point of no return.

'Lewis, I want you to come and work for me.'

He actually laughed, and made no effort to hide the fact.

'Look, Lewis, I know you're not a Christian. There's no secret in that fact, and I'm not going to ask you to comment on any spiritual direction that I choose to take. But I need your wisdom, your knowledge of the music business, of all the current trends. I want you to act as my advisor on contemporary youth culture.'

Lewis sat back in his chair. It was not often that he was genuinely rendered speechless, but he was now. After what seemed like an eternity, he gathered himself together.

'Alex, you know I don't believe in Jesus like you do. I don't read the Bible, I don't go to church – do you really want me around.'

'Yes, you would be my first employee.'

He promised to call her back once he had considered it. The irony of the situation hadn't escaped Lewis. He had spent the last few months longing to call her to ask her to work for him again, and now she was the one who was calling him, asking him to help her.

It was indeed true that he did know most of what there was to know about the prevailing trends in youth culture. He was the ideal man to help plot a course through the shifting sands of fashion, music and magazines. He spent a day considering Alex's offer. The more he thought about it, the more the idea appealed to him, for both personal and professional reasons. In the end, he repaid her honesty with his own. He would do all he could to fulfil her expectations within the brief that she gave him. He would help her to listen to the sounds, to see the visions, to tap in to what was happening in the hearts and minds of young people across the nation. If she wanted to use that to further her own spiritual objectives, so be it.

Personally, he had never considered religion to be one of the real things in life. Not like money, or power, or music, or sex. Or even love, if that was what you were into. But in the end that didn't matter to him: she knew what she was getting when she took him on. As far as Lewis was concerned, this was a job, something to do. He wasn't especially bothered about the money – he had made his fortune. What really attracted him was the fact that he would be able to keep busy, and that this was going to be different, and therefore a challenge for him. He remembered that moment when he had sat at his desk and looked into the face of despair. He wanted to be busy enough not to have to go to that place again.

So, to the great surprise of some of her supporters, Alex took Lewis on as an advisor, and she made it clear to all her associates that she considered this man to be a valuable member of the team.

Shortly after the acquisition of SLaM, the assets were transferred to a new company. Alex remembered the freshness and optimism of SLaM's sunflower. It had all been lost in the end, but she wanted to recapture some of that idealism and take it into her own organisation. The sunflower became a prominent symbol for the company.

A new set of directors was appointed, and dates set for the board meetings. Initially they would need to meet to discuss the company, and plan future strategy. The board meetings were to take place in the very same room where the ideas behind all of SLaM's projects had been worked out.

On the day of the first board meeting Alex arrived early, as she had done so often when she had worked for SLaM. On the second floor, she went into the boardroom. She was not alone: at her side Mr Wicks, now legal advisor and company secretary, was leafing through some papers.

Alex had considered his inclusion to be even more important than Lewis's, and not just because of his expertise in law. As they prepared for this first meeting, she needed him to do something else for her, something that hinged more on his relationship with God than his legal knowledge.

She regarded the table in the middle of the room with a kind of dread fascination, and noticed again the dull, insistent hum of the air-conditioning. She had come to associate that noise with the kinds of conflict and suppressed hatred that had so often characterised SLaM meetings. She turned to Caleb Wicks, and the look in her eyes stopped him from shuffling his papers for a moment.

'Please can you do something for me?'

'Of course, Alex, what is it?'

'Can you pray over this room? Some bad things have happened in here, some bad decisions were made here. This place needs to be clean.'

'I'll pray over the room,' he said, 'and for you as well, Alex, because it seems that you have been given that most deadly of commodities, power. So, God help you.' And with that he invited the Holy Spirit to come both into the room, and on Alex, and into the company she now ran.

From the corner of the room, Angel watched as a shaft of light descended and spread out to fill the whole of the room. Alex had made it. She had reached this point in her destiny, and it was no small achievement. She'd had to deal with a whole range of difficulties along the way, and both her spiritual and physical life had been under threat. But now she was poised, ready to strike the blow for his God, and hers. She now had the potential to do things that a billion angels could not do: it was time to reclaim some ground.

When Caleb turned back to Alex, she was kneeling on the floor. He gently laid a hand on her shoulder as he prayed for her, and in his mind, he recalled from scripture the moment when Samuel anointed David to be King over Israel. This too was a time of appointment and anointing. Alex Masters: orphan, student of Jesus, and precious child of the Father, was about to meet her destiny.

The real battle was about to begin.